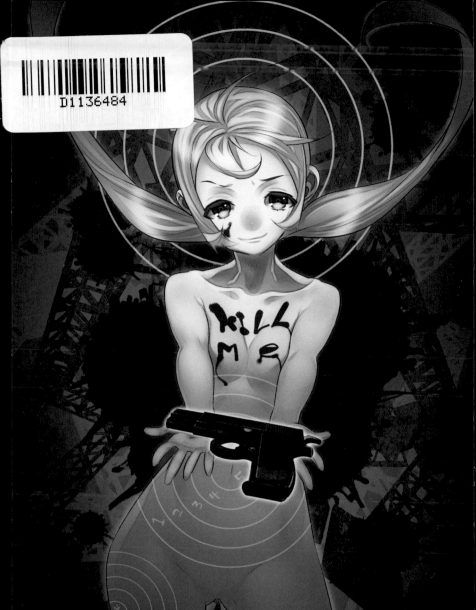

PUELLA MAGI
KAZUMI★MAGICA
The innocent malice
3
ORIGINAL STORY BY MAGICA QUARTET
STORY BY MASAKI HIRAMATSU
ART BY TAKASHI TENSUGI

3

PUELLA MAGI KAZUMI MAGICA
T h e   i n n o c e n t   m a l i c e

Original story by Magica Quartet / Story by Masaki Hiramatsu / Art by Takashi Tensugi

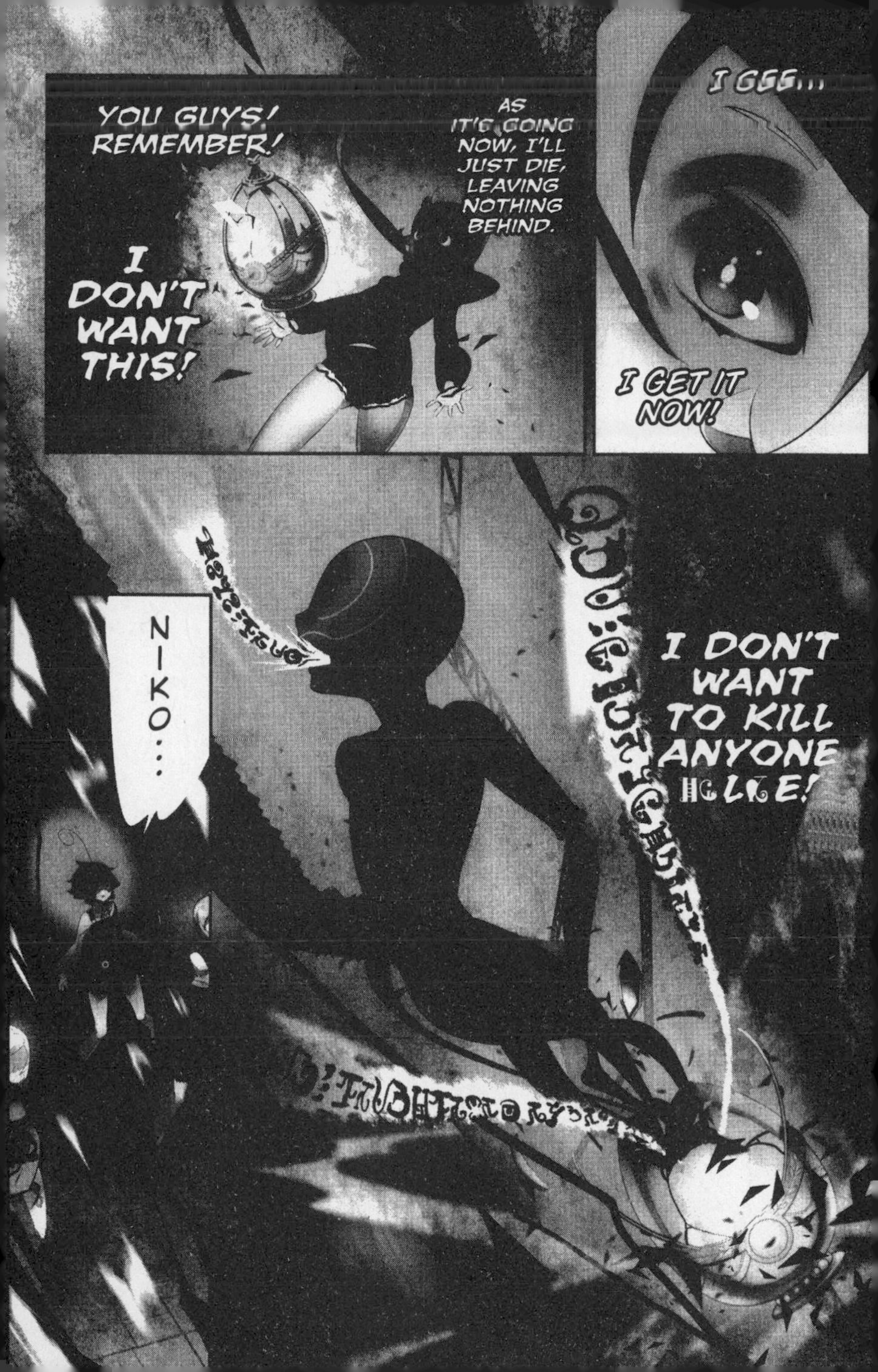
I GGG...
I GET IT NOW!
AS IT'S GOING NOW, I'LL JUST DIE, LEAVING NOTHING BEHIND.
YOU GUYS! REMEMBER!
I DON'T WANT THIS!
I DON'T WANT TO KILL ANYONE ELSE!
NIKO...

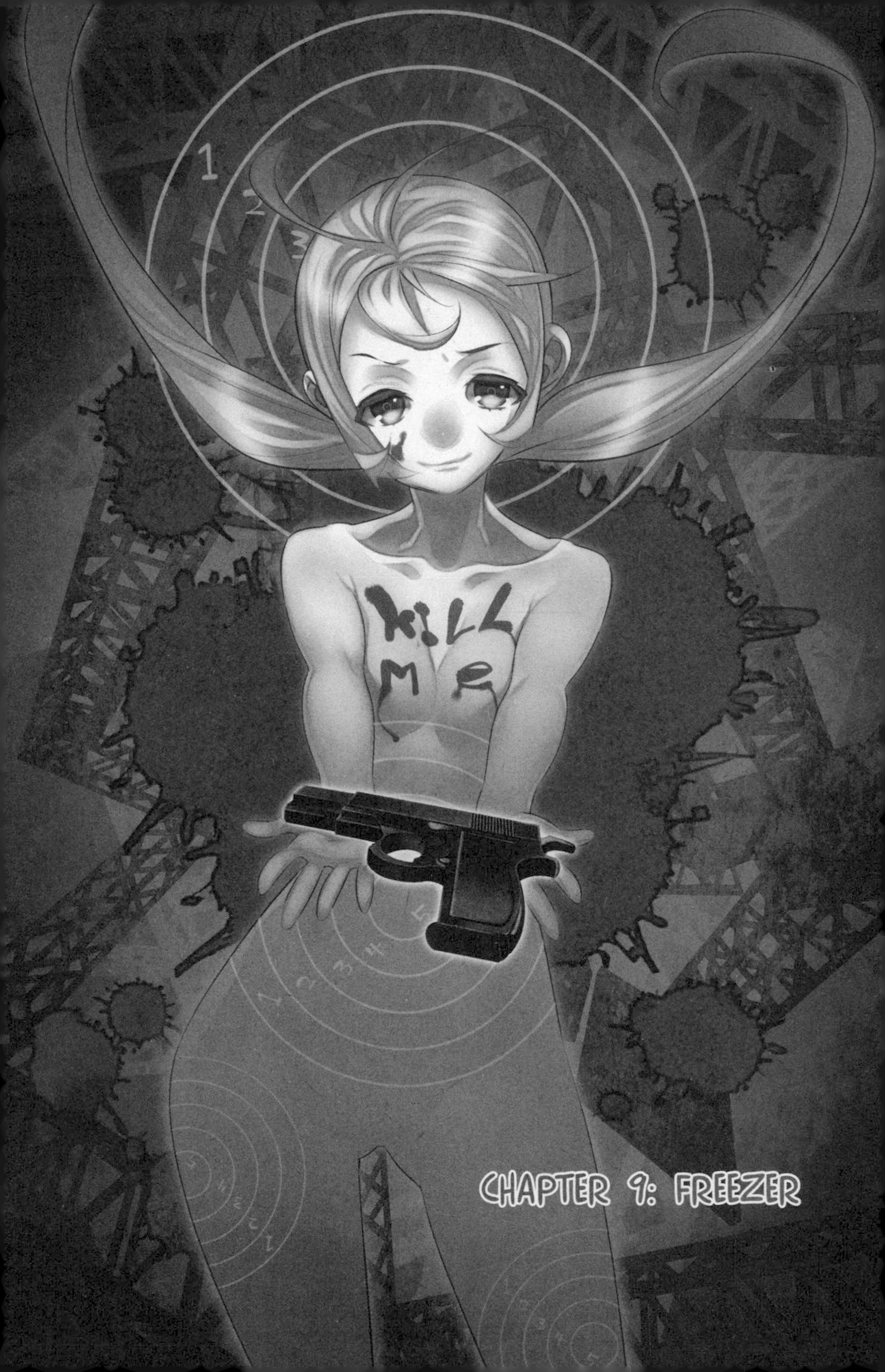
KILL
ME

CHAPTER 9: FREEZER

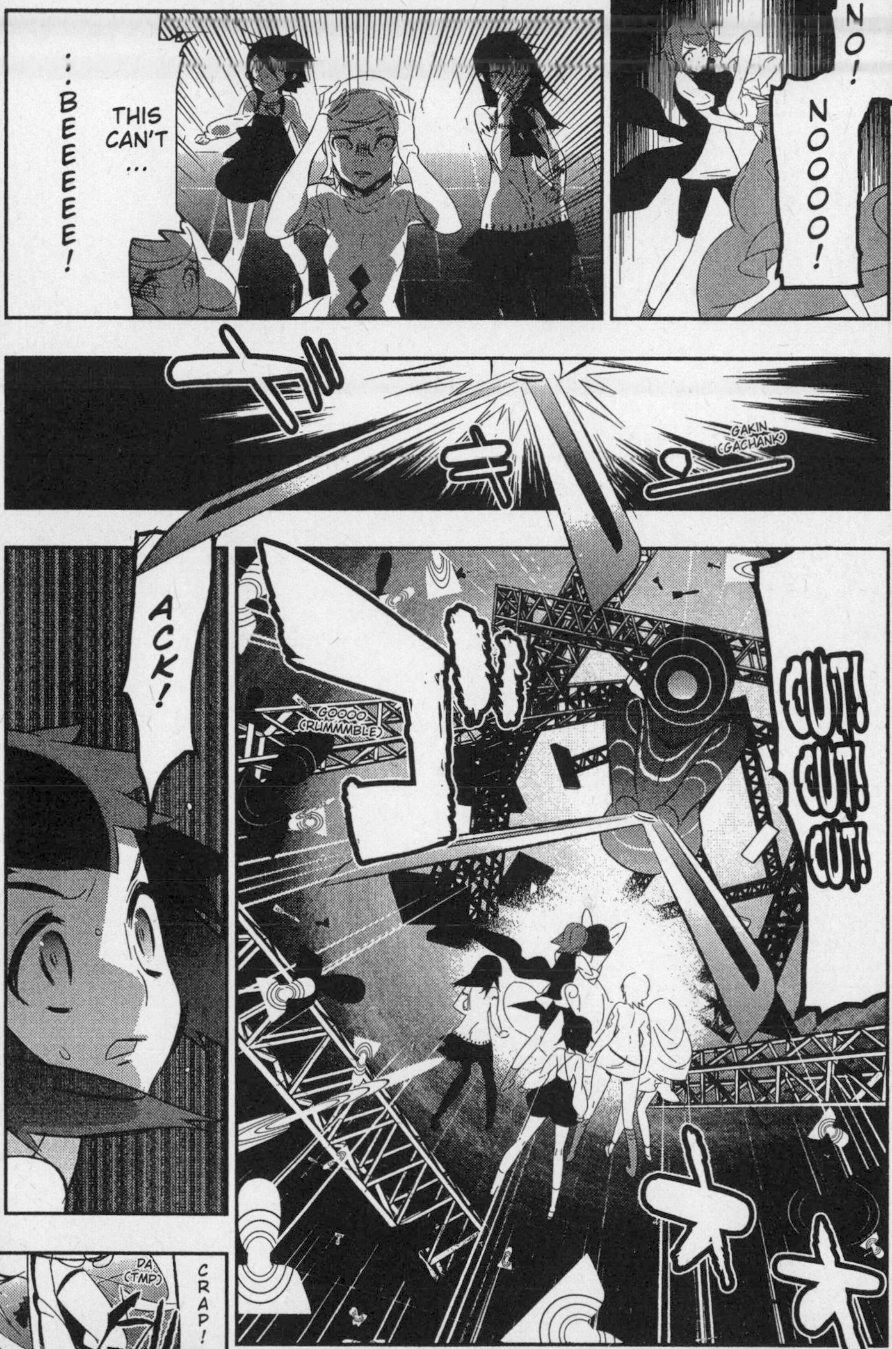
NO! NOOOOO!
THIS CAN'T ...
...BEEEEEE!
GAKIN (GACHANK)
CUT! CUT! CUT!
GOOOO (RUMMMBLE)
ACK!
CRAP!
DA (TMP)

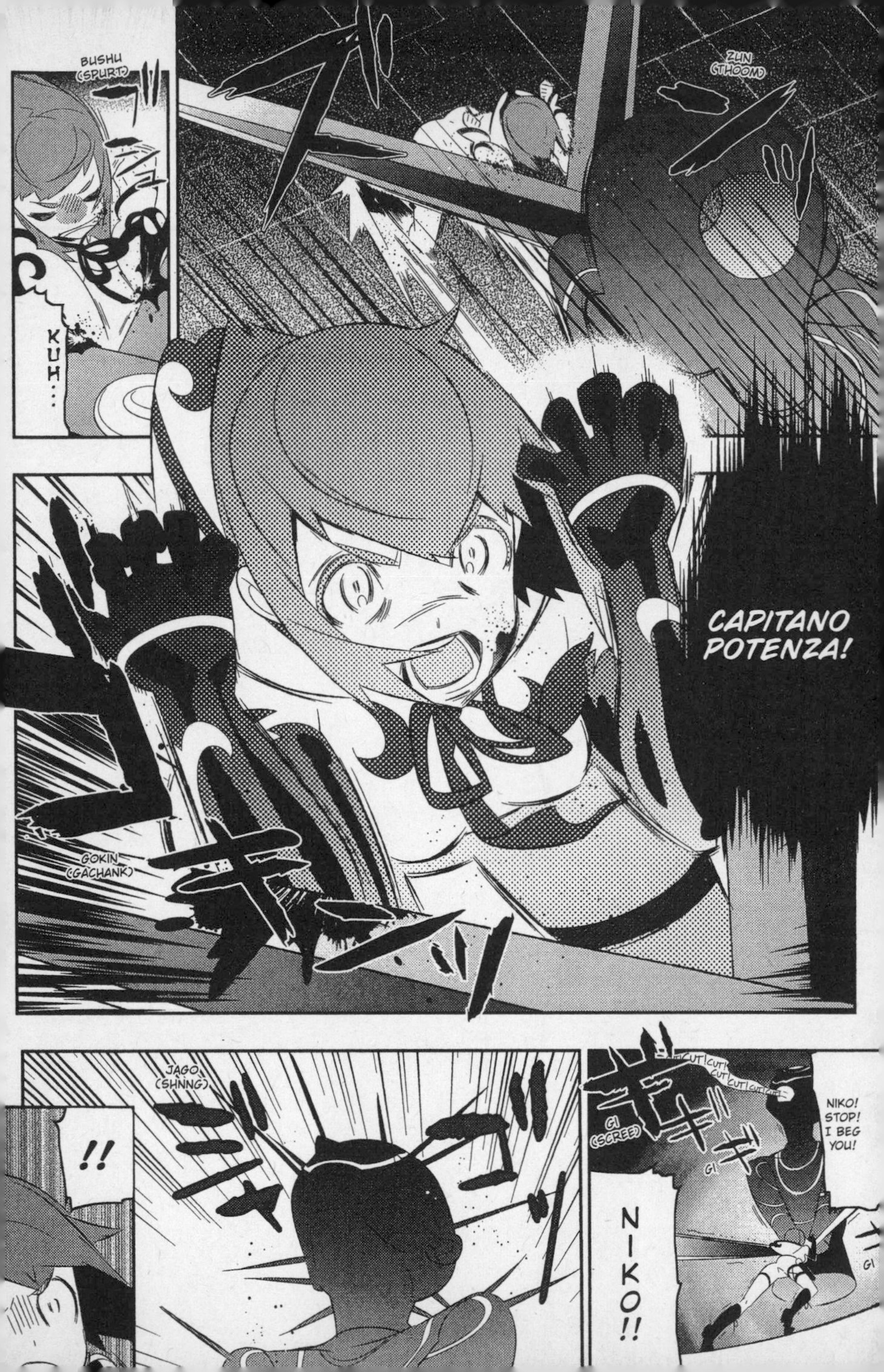
ZUN (THOOM)
CAPITANO POTENZA!
GOKIN (GACHANK)
BUSHU (SPURT)
KUH...
CUT! CUT! CUT! CUT! CUT!
NIKO! STOP! I BEG YOU!
GI (SCREE)
GI
GI
NIKO!!
JAGO (SHNNG)
!!

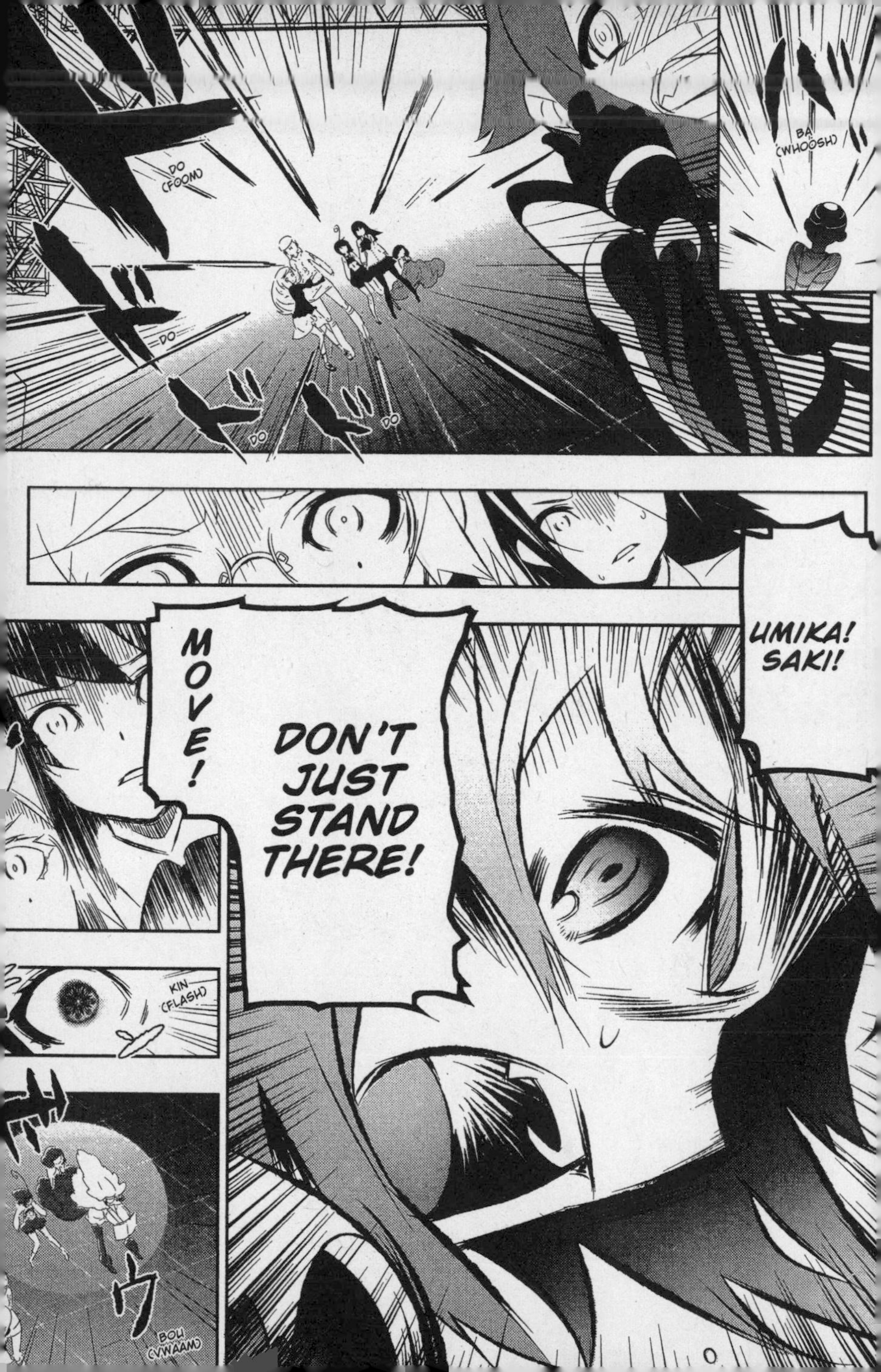
BA (WHOOSH)
DO (FOOM)
DO
DO
DO
UMIKA! SAKI!
MOVE!
DON'T JUST STAND THERE!
KIN (FLASH)
BOU (VWAAM)

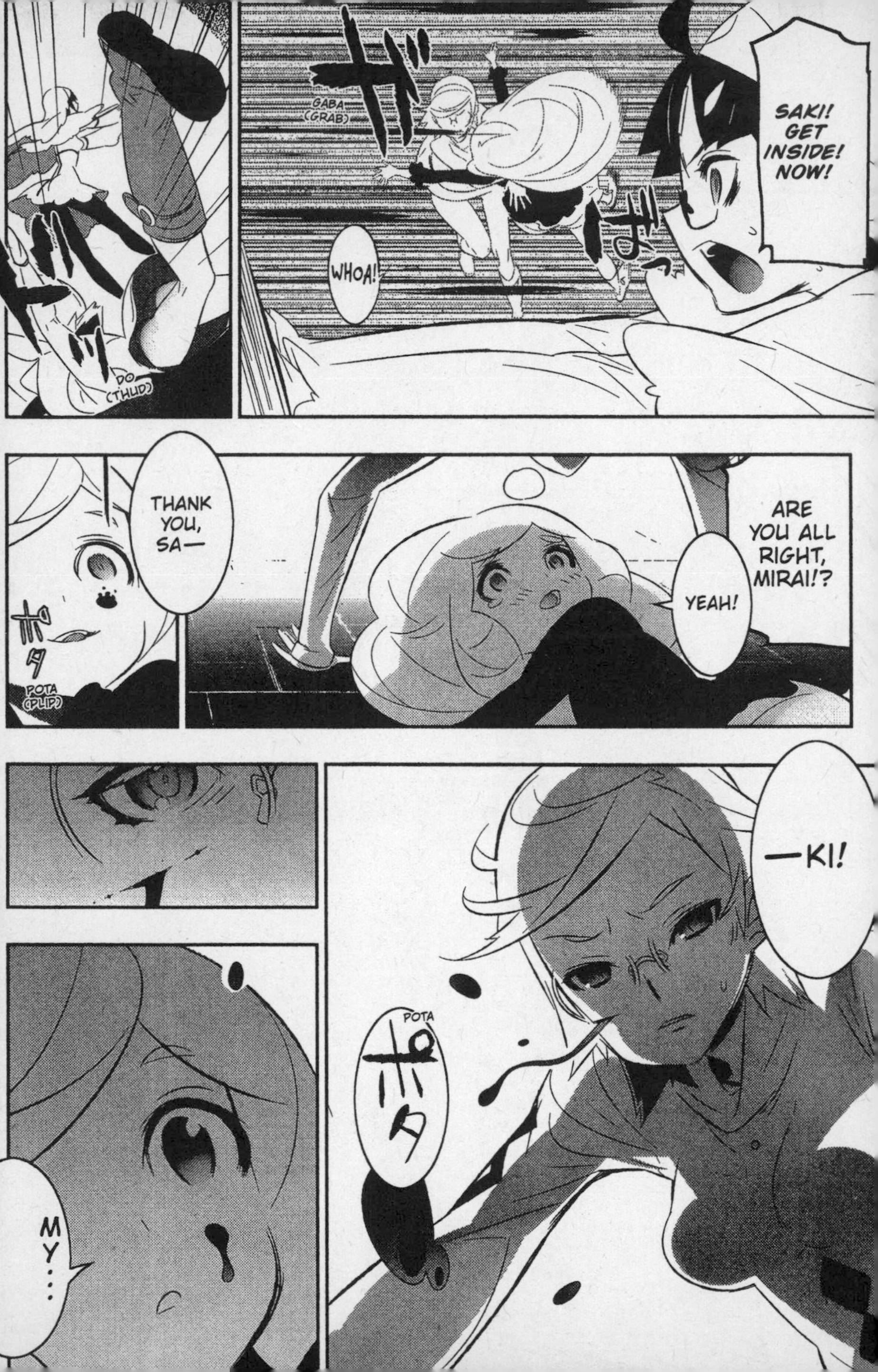
SAKI! GET INSIDE! NOW!
GABA (GRAB)
WHOA!
DO (THUD)
ARE YOU ALL RIGHT, MIRAI!?
YEAH!
THANK YOU, SA—
POTA (PLIP)
—KI!
POTA
MY...

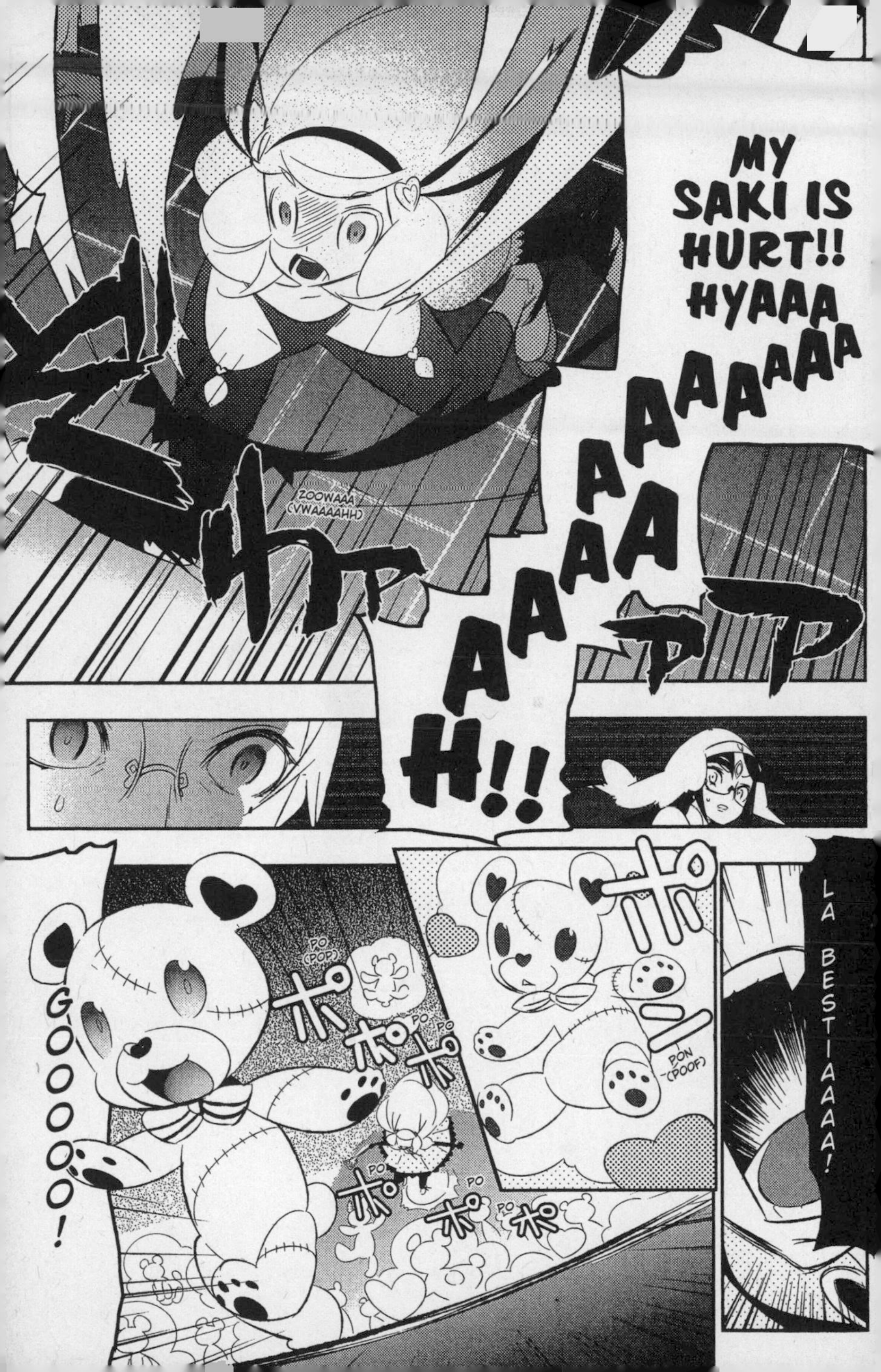
MY SAKI IS HURT!! HYAAAAAAAAAAAAAAAAAH!!
ZOOWAAA (VWAAAAHH)
LA BESTIAAAAAA!
PON (POOF)
GOOOOOOO!
PO (POP)
PO
PO
PO
PO
PO

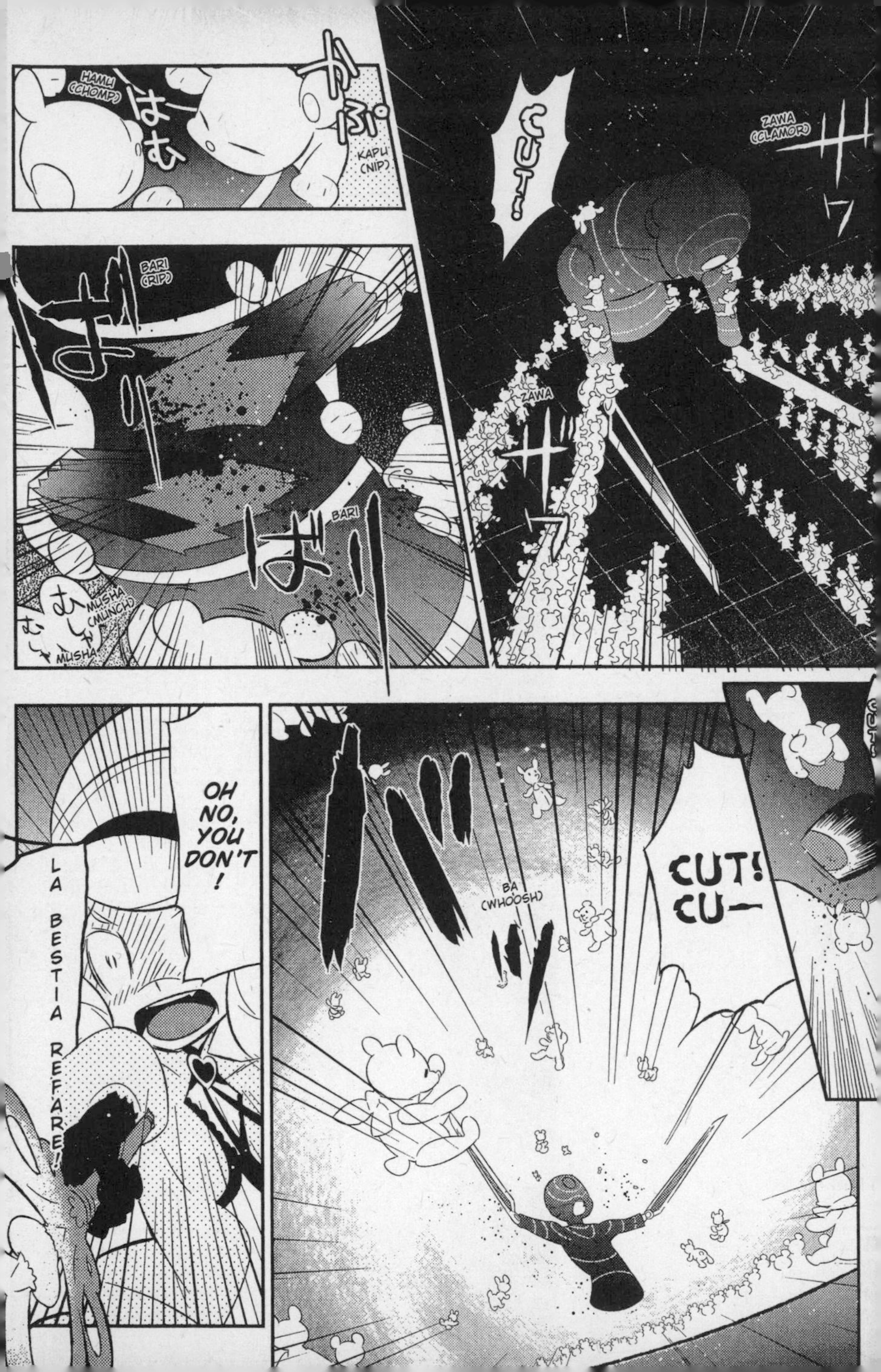
CUT!
ZAWA (CLAMOR)
ZAWA
HAMU (CHOMP)
KAPU (NIP)
BARI (RIP)
BARI
MUSHA (MUNCH)
MUSHA
CUT! CU—
BA (WHOOSH)
OH NO, YOU DON'T!
LA BESTIA REFARE!

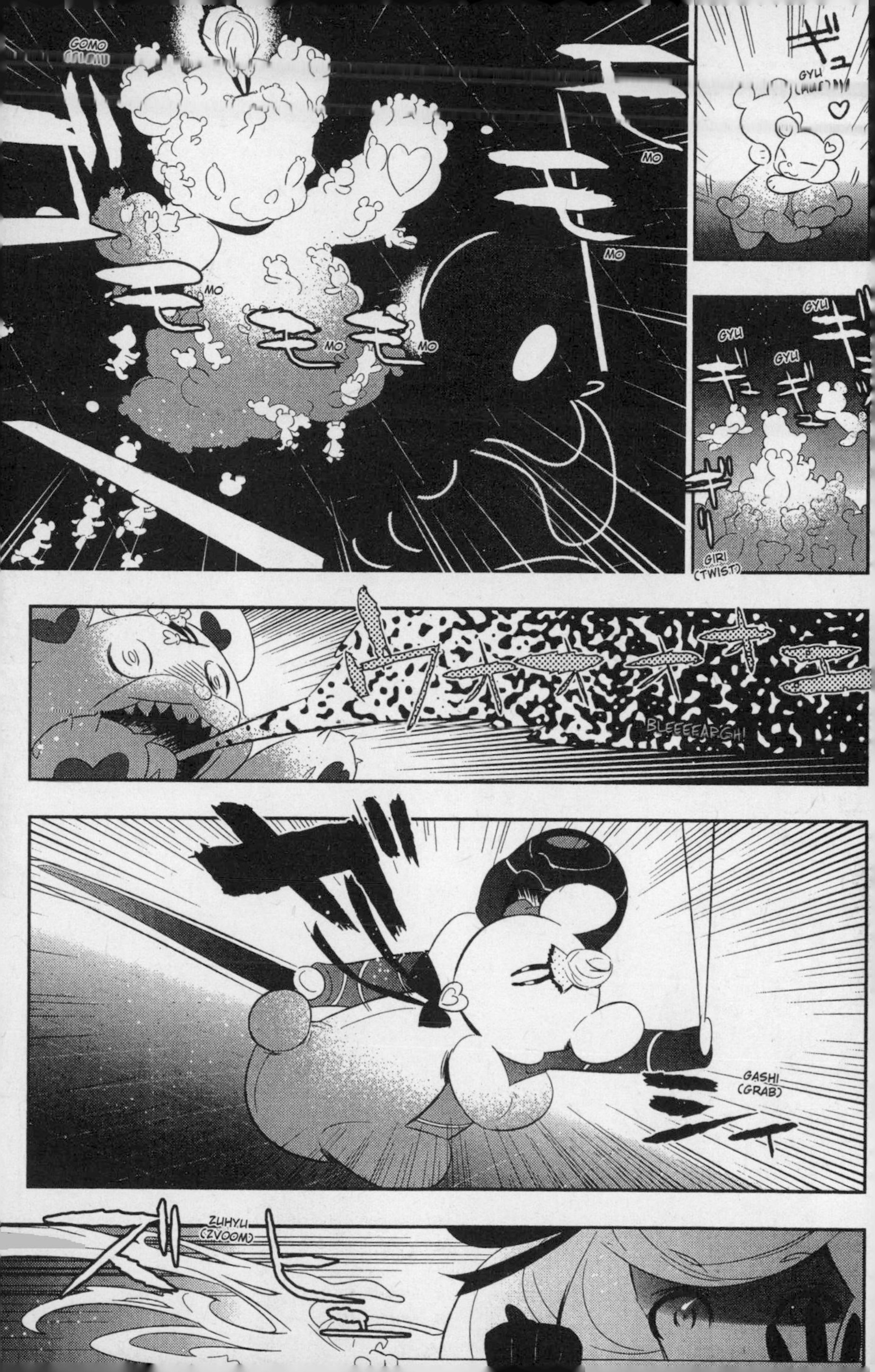
GYU
GYU
GYU
GYU
GIRI (TWIST)
GOMO
MO
MO
MO
MO
MO
BLEEEEAPGH!
GASHI (GRAB)
ZUHYU (ZVOOM)

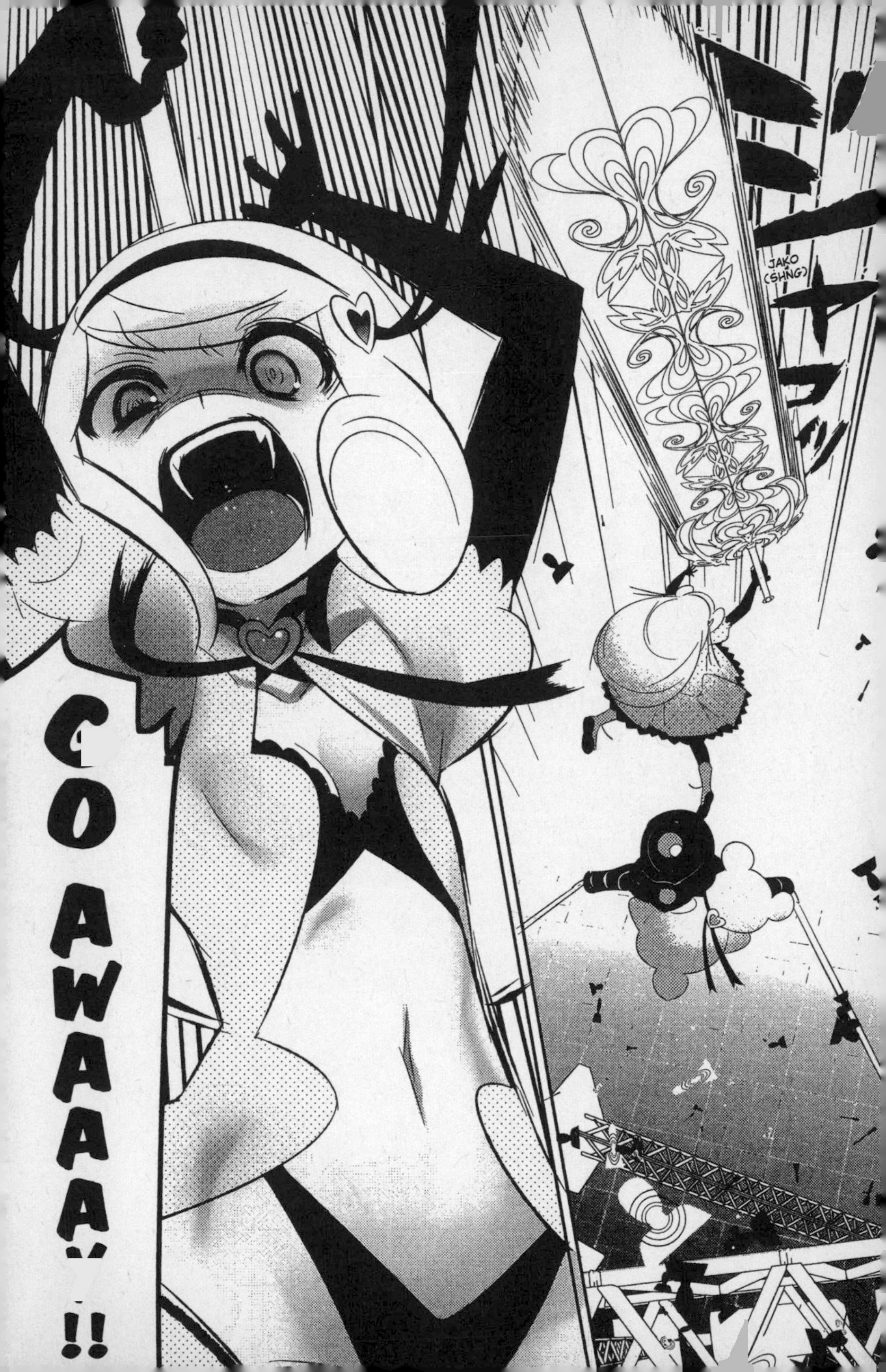
JAKO (SHNG)
GO AWAAAY!!

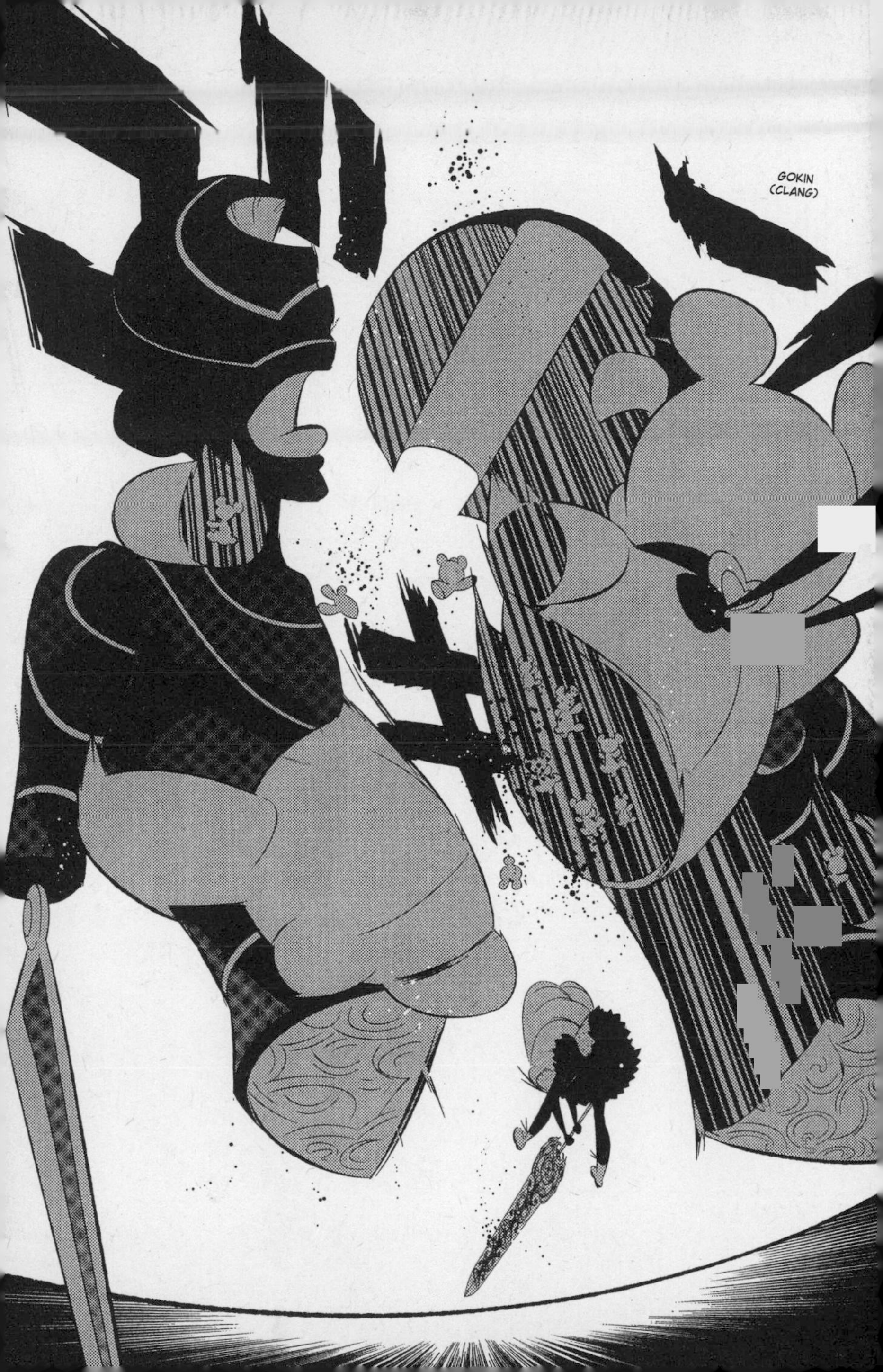
GOKIN
(CLANG)

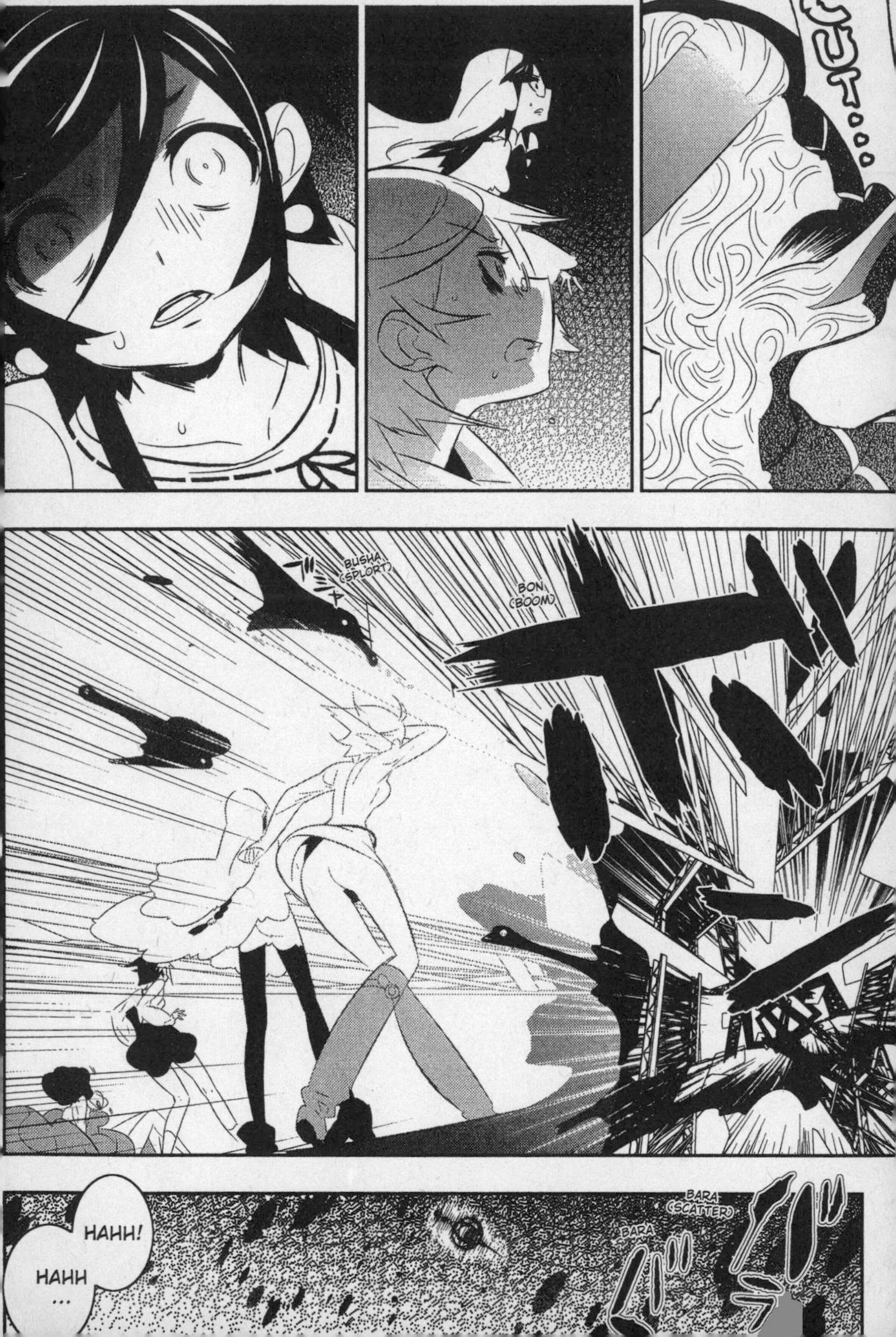
CUT...
BON (BOOM)
BUSHA (SPLORT)
BARA (SCATTER)
BARA
HAHH! HAHH ...

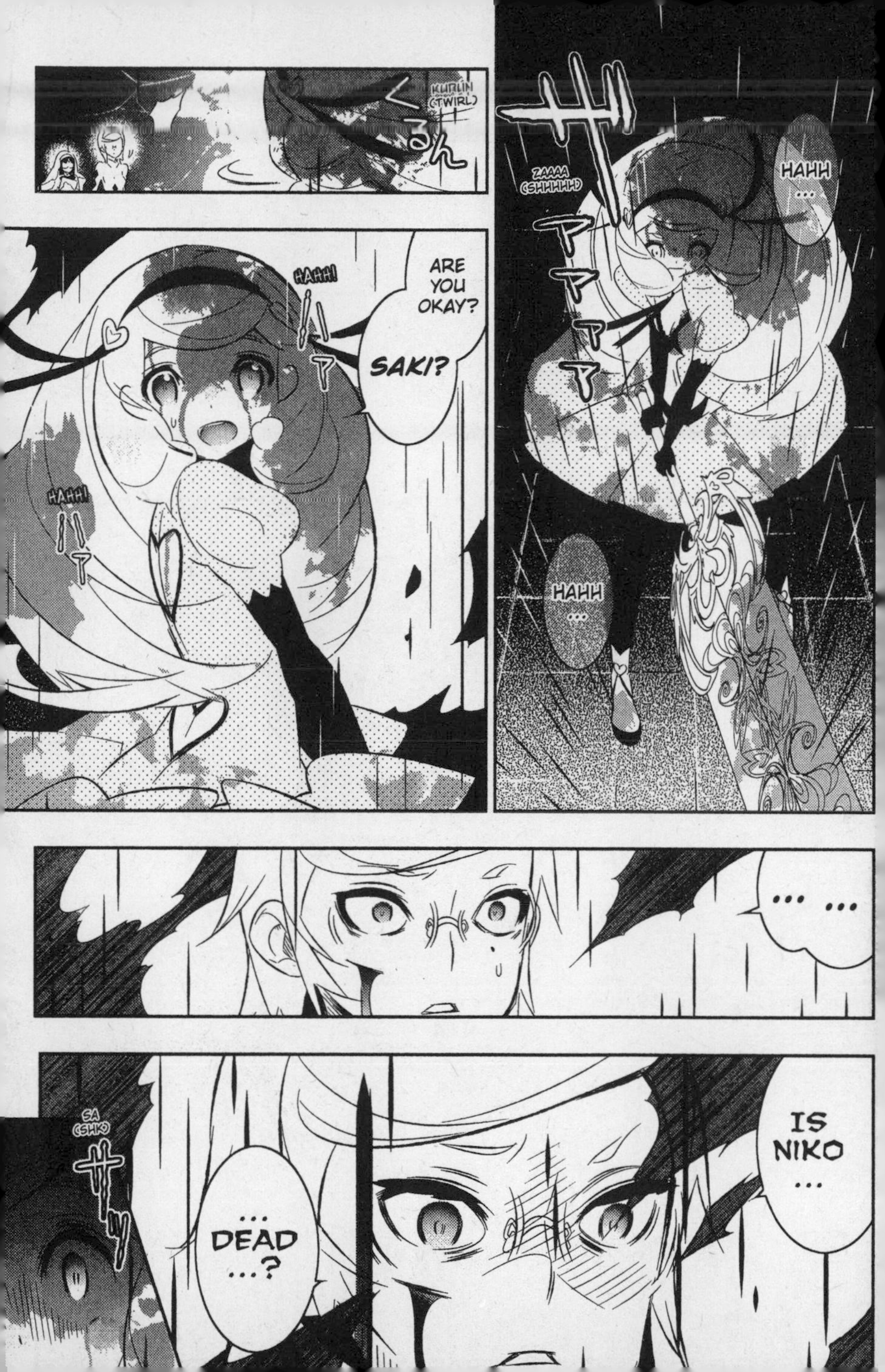
ZAAAA (SHHHHH)
HAHH ...
HAHH ...
KURUN (TWIRL)
ARE YOU OKAY?
SAKI?
HAHH!
HAHH!
... ...
IS NIKO ...
... DEAD ...?
SA (SHK)

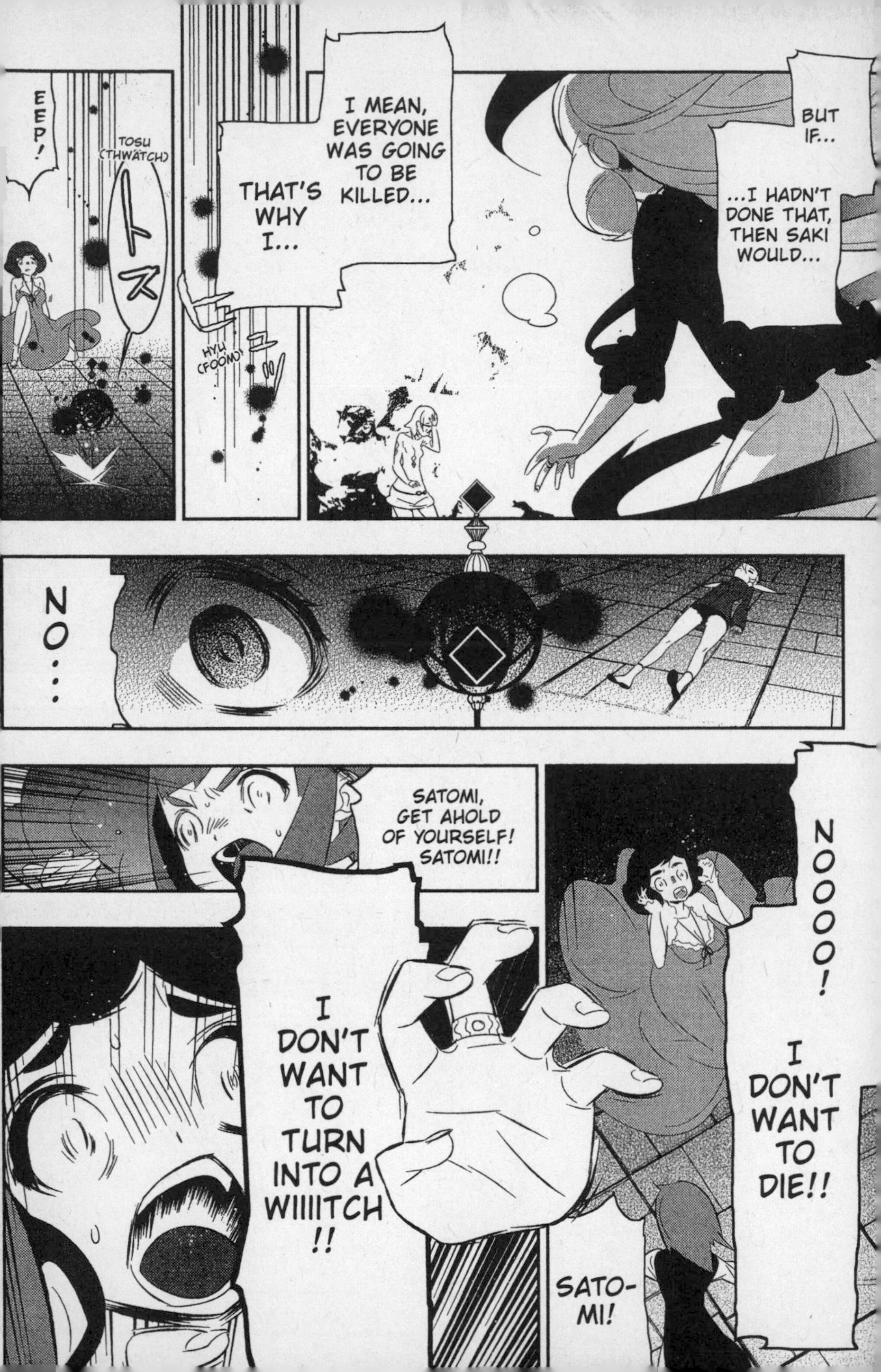
BUT IF...
...I HADN'T DONE THAT, THEN SAKI WOULD...
I MEAN, EVERYONE WAS GOING TO BE KILLED...
THAT'S WHY I...
HYU (FOOM)
TOSU (THWATCH)
EEP!
NO...
NOOOOO!
I DON'T WANT TO DIE!!
SATO-MI!
SATOMI, GET AHOLD OF YOURSELF! SATOMI!!
I DON'T WANT TO TURN INTO A WIIIIITCH!!

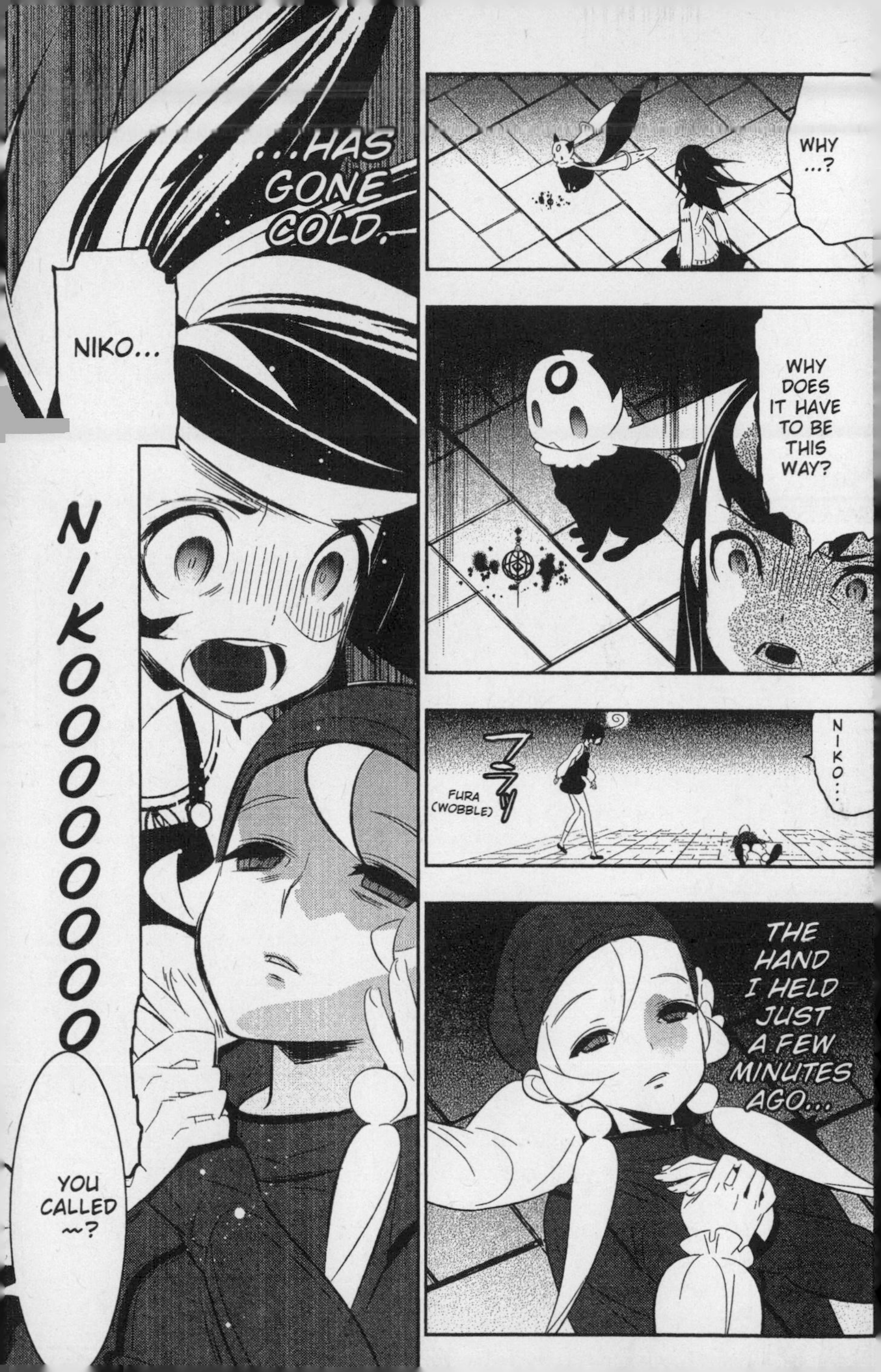
WHY ...?
WHY DOES IT HAVE TO BE THIS WAY?
NIKO...
FURA (WOBBLE)
THE HAND I HELD JUST A FEW MINUTES AGO...
...HAS GONE COLD.
NIKO...
NIKOOOOOOOOO
YOU CALLED ~?

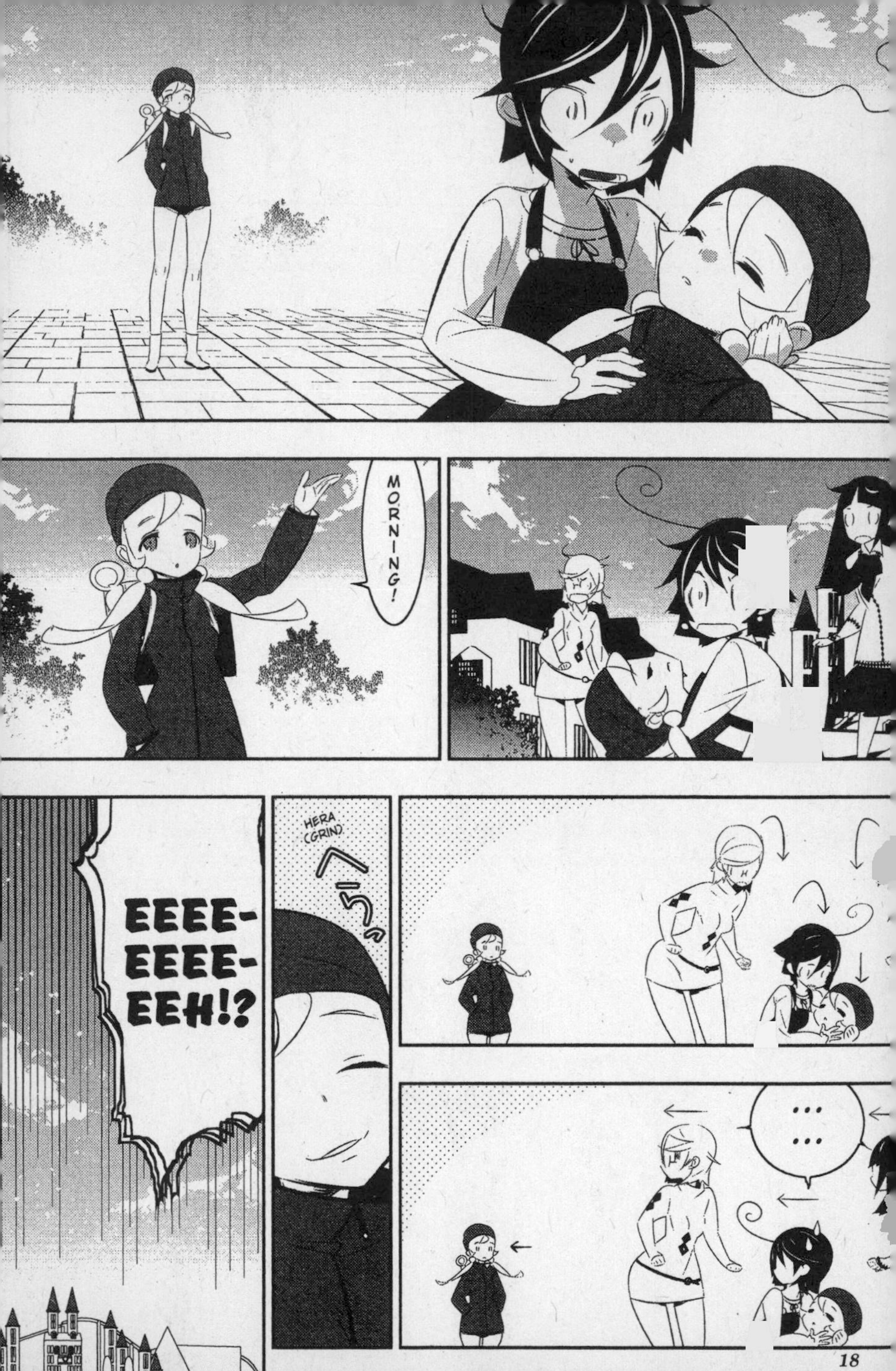
MORNING!
EEEE-EEEE-EEH!?
HERA (GRIN)
へらっ
...
...

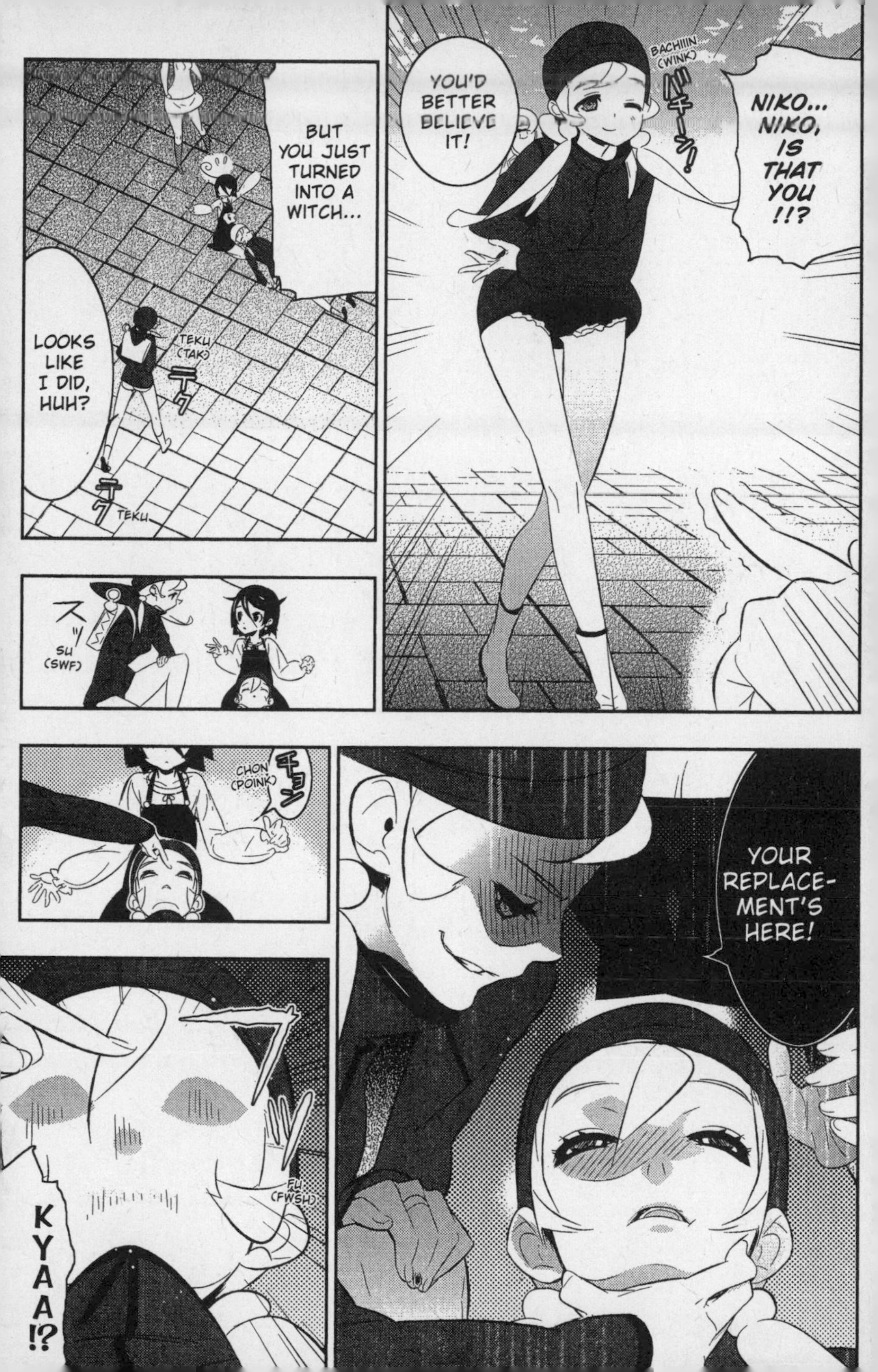

NIKO... NIKO, IS THAT YOU!!?
BACHIIIN (WINK)
YOU'D BETTER BELIEVE IT!
BUT YOU JUST TURNED INTO A WITCH...
LOOKS LIKE I DID, HUH?
TEKU (TAK)
TEKU
SU (SWF)
YOUR REPLACEMENT'S HERE!
CHON (POINK)
FU (FWSH)
KYAA!?

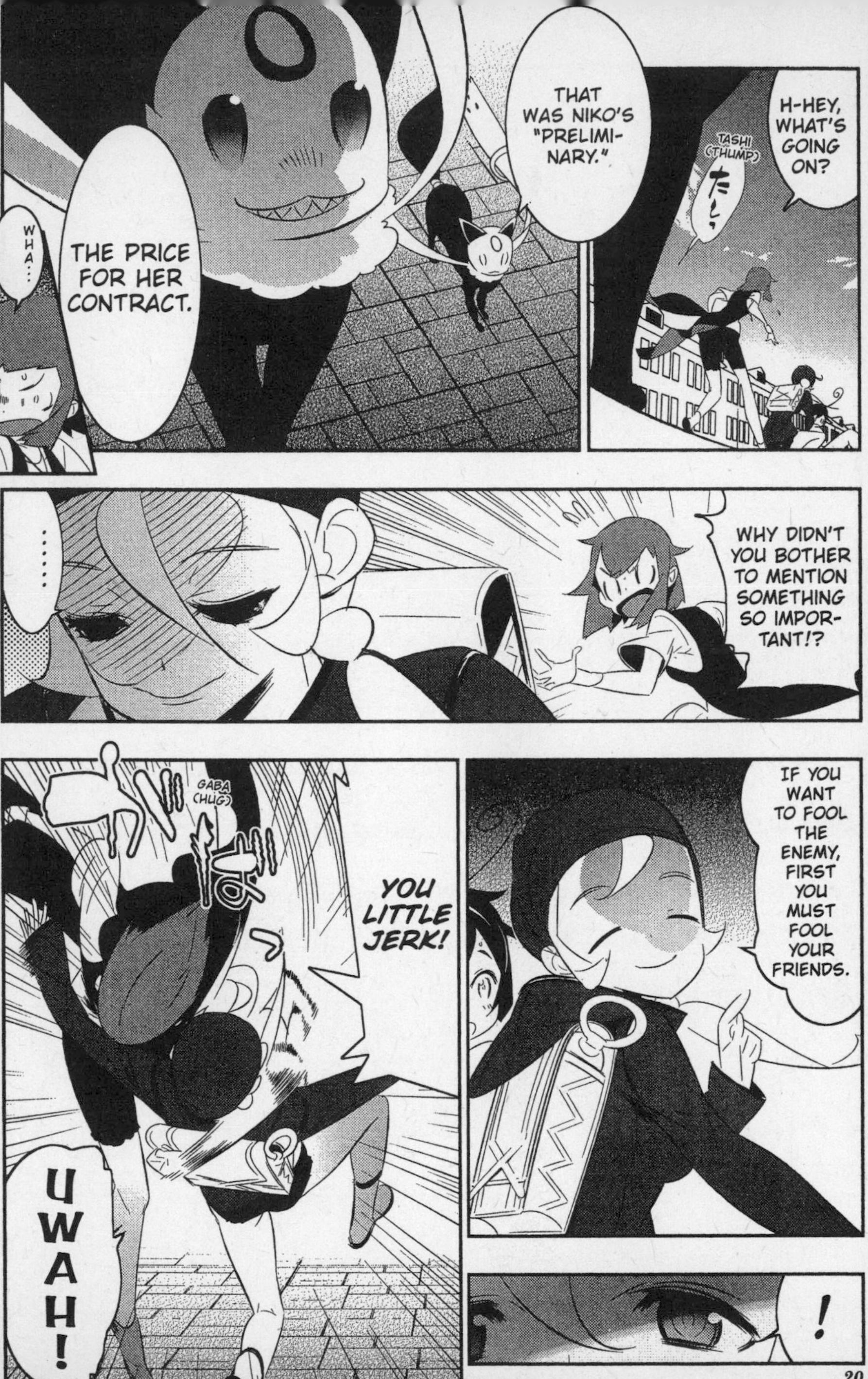
H-HEY, WHAT'S GOING ON?
TASHI (THUMP)
たっ
THAT WAS NIKO'S "PRELIMINARY."
THE PRICE FOR HER CONTRACT.
WHA...
WHY DIDN'T YOU BOTHER TO MENTION SOMETHING SO IMPORTANT!?
......
IF YOU WANT TO FOOL THE ENEMY, FIRST YOU MUST FOOL YOUR FRIENDS.
!
YOU LITTLE JERK!
GABA (HUG)
UWAH!

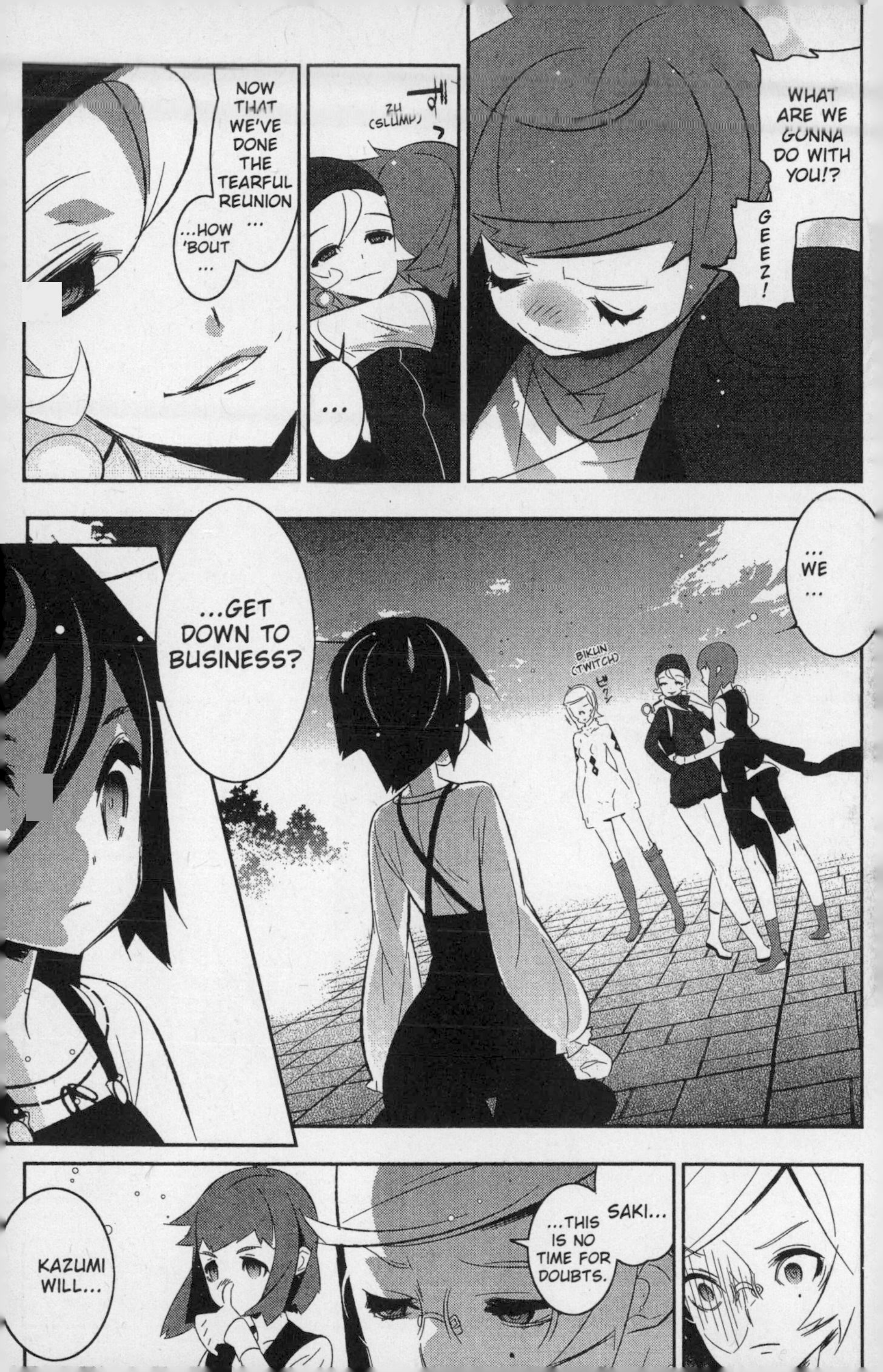
WHAT ARE WE GUNNA DO WITH YOU!?
GEEZ!
ZU (SLUMP)
...
NOW THAT WE'VE DONE THE TEARFUL REUNION...
...HOW 'BOUT...
...WE...
BIKUN (TWITCH)
...GET DOWN TO BUSINESS?
SAKI...
...THIS IS NO TIME FOR DOUBTS.
KAZUMI WILL...

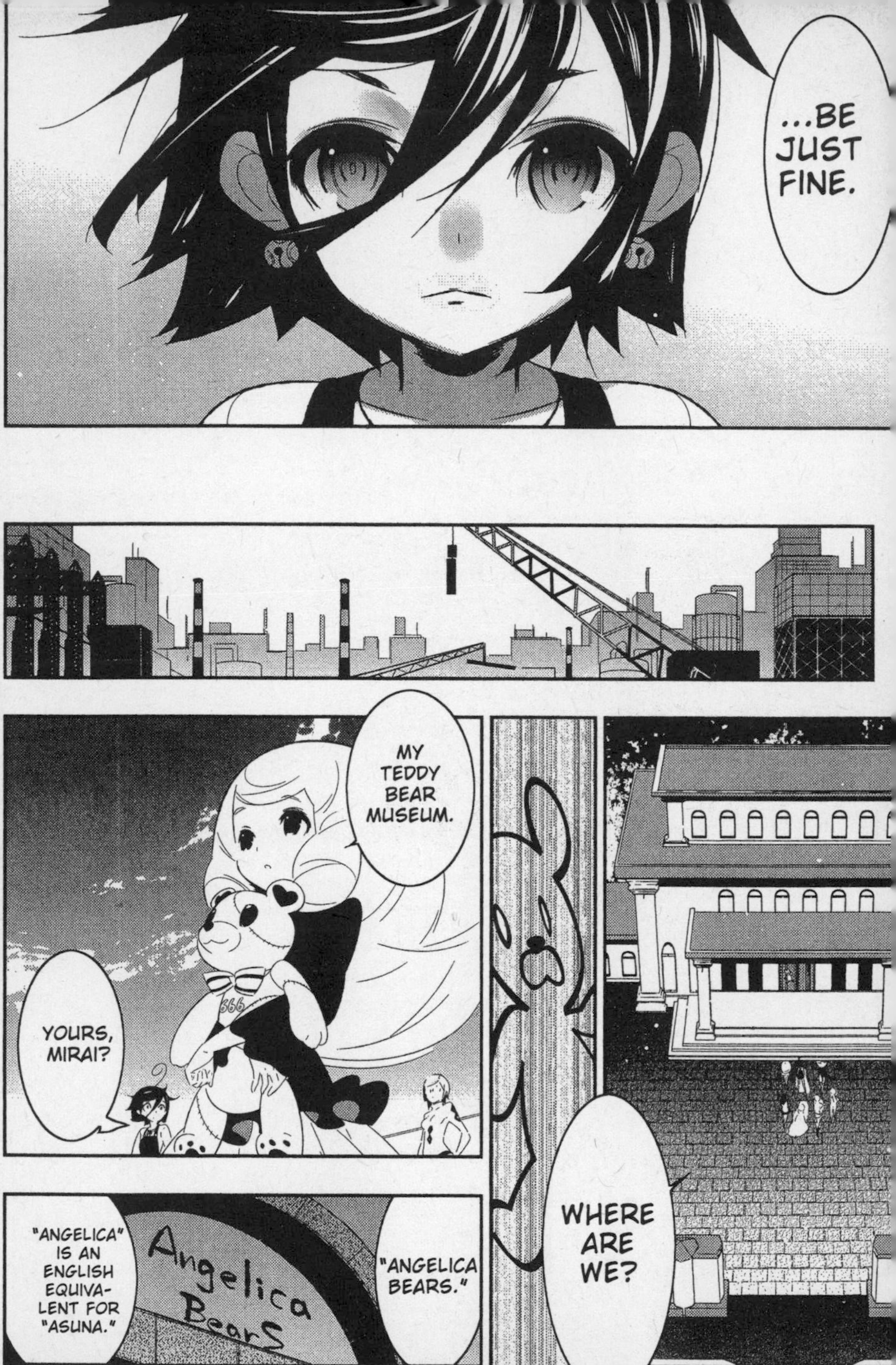
...BE JUST FINE.
WHERE ARE WE?
MY TEDDY BEAR MUSEUM.
YOURS, MIRAI?
"ANGELICA BEARS."
Angelica BearS
"ANGELICA" IS AN ENGLISH EQUIVALENT FOR "ASUNA."

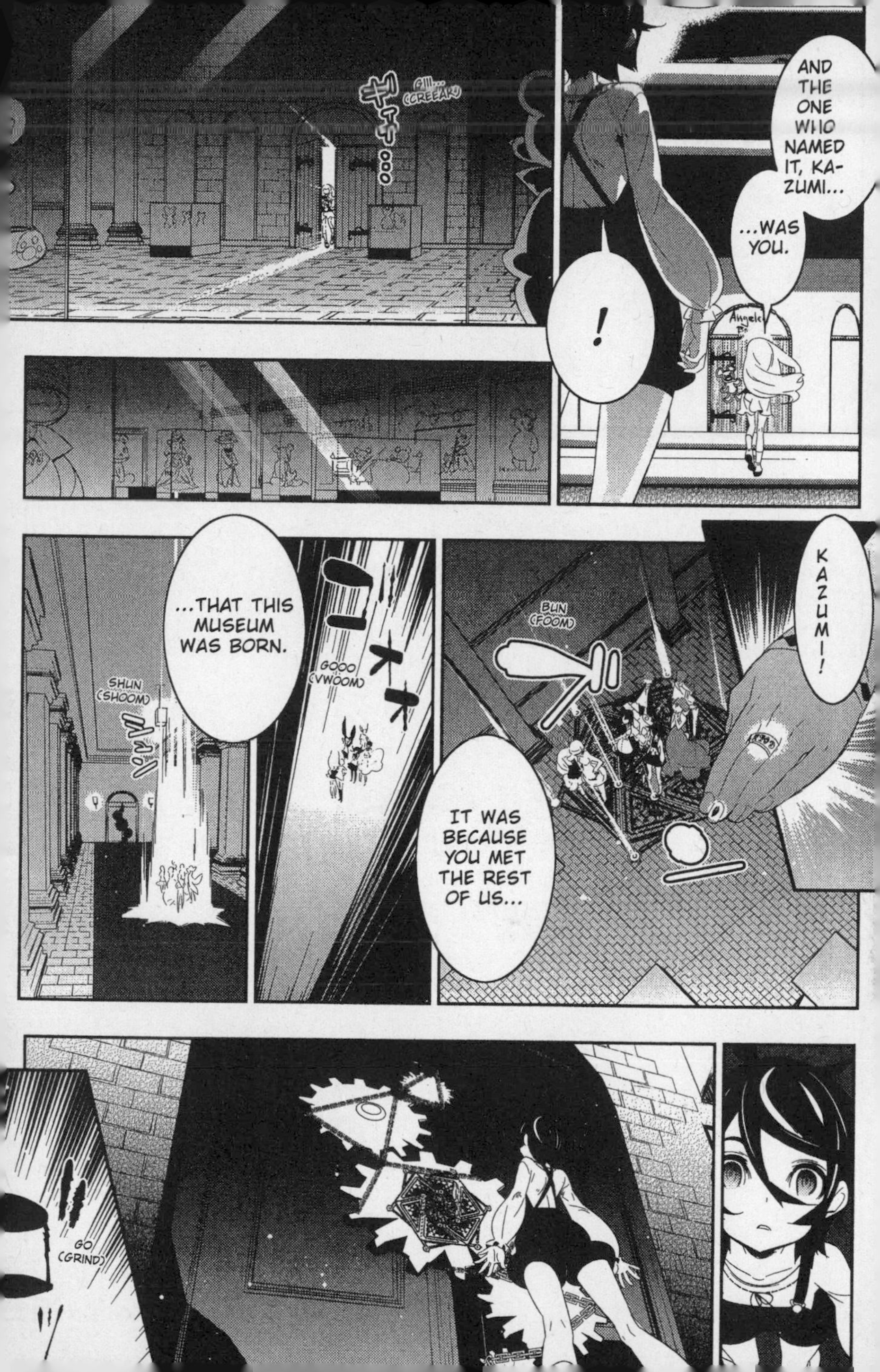
AND THE ONE WHO NAMED IT, KA-ZUMI...
...WAS YOU.
!
GIII... (CREEAK)
KAZUMI!
BUN (FOOM)
IT WAS BECAUSE YOU MET THE REST OF US...
GOOO (VWOOM)
...THAT THIS MUSEUM WAS BORN.
SHUN (SHOOM)
GO (GRIND)

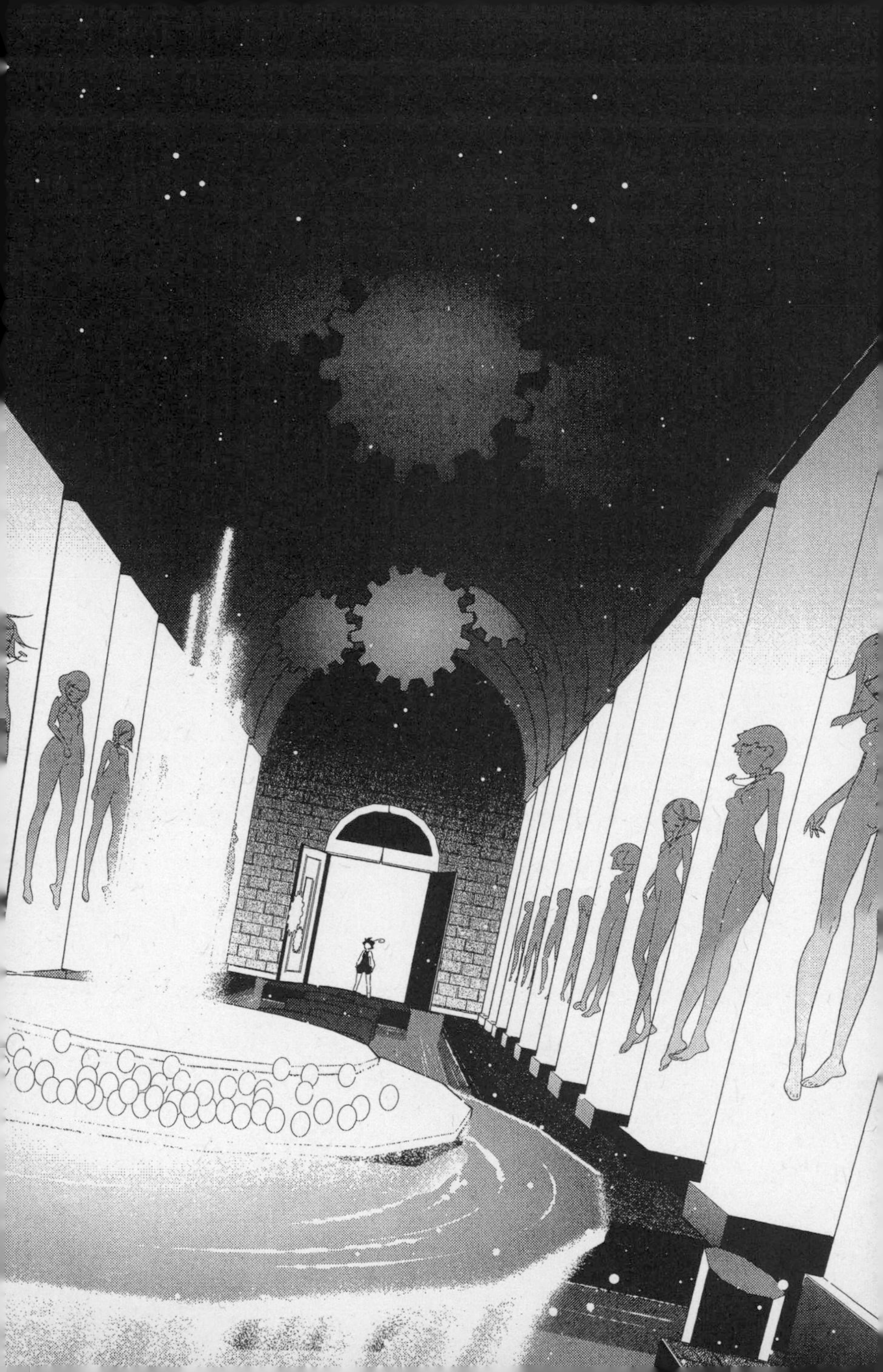

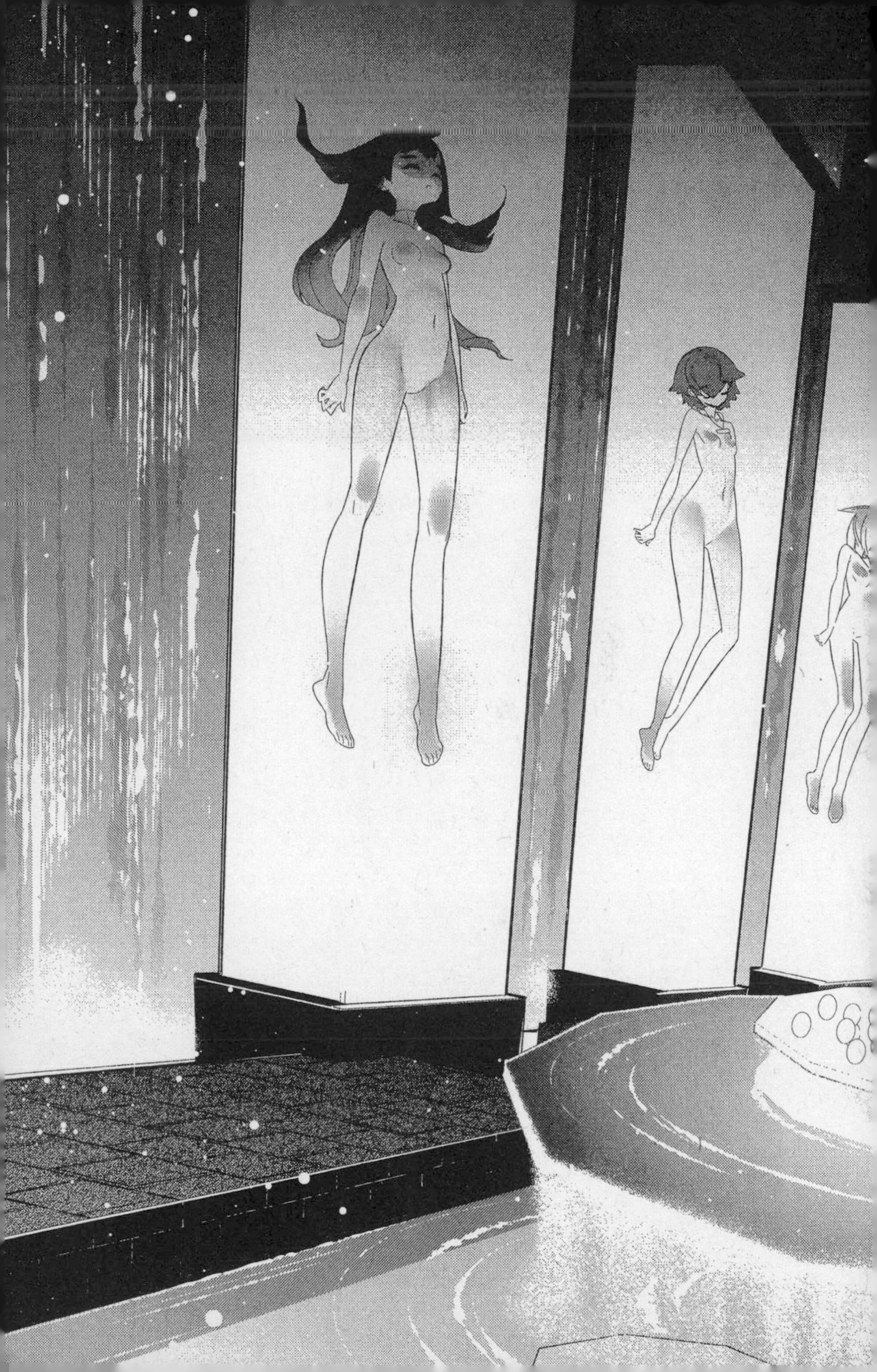

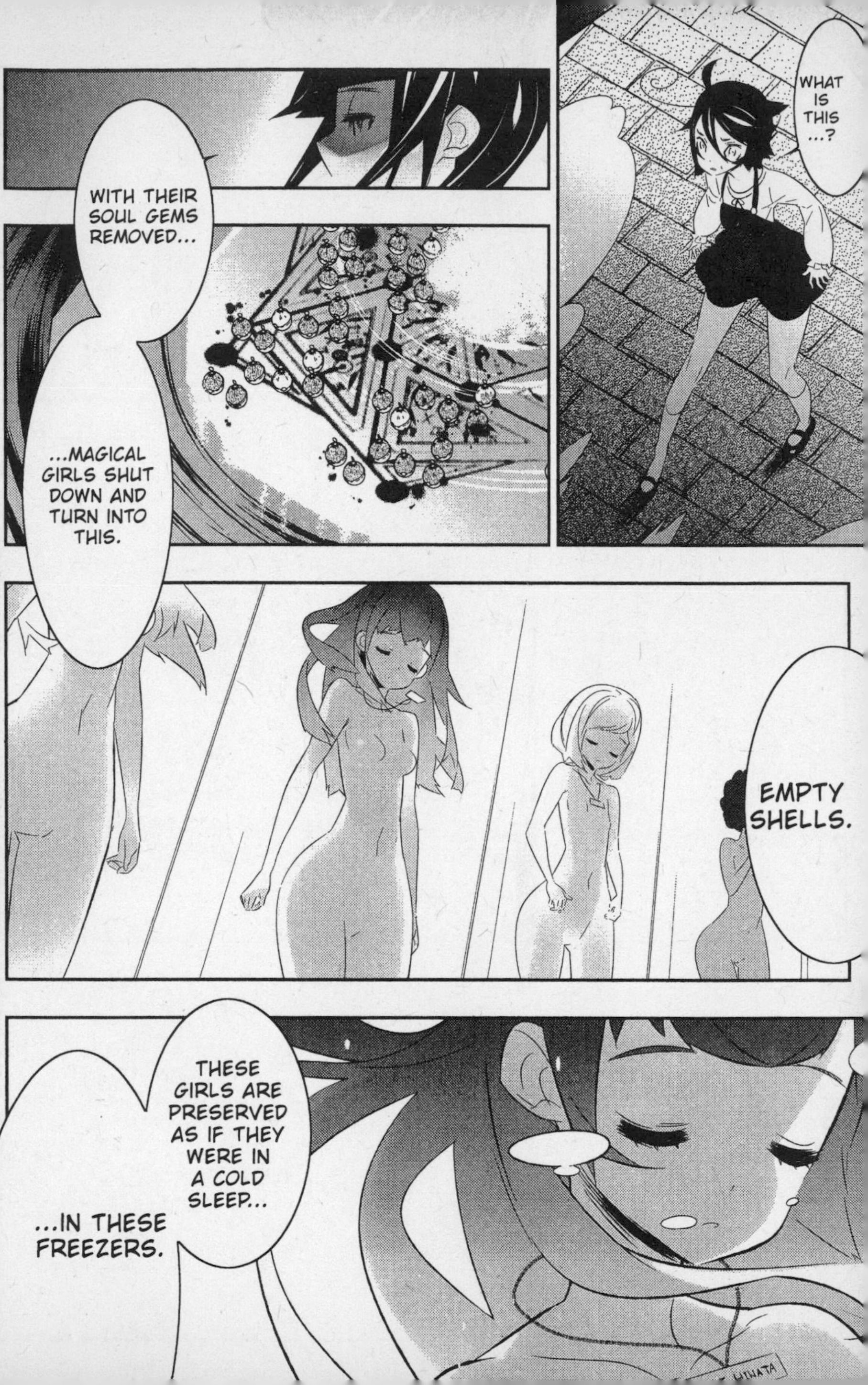
WHAT IS THIS ...?
WITH THEIR SOUL GEMS REMOVED...
...MAGICAL GIRLS SHUT DOWN AND TURN INTO THIS.
EMPTY SHELLS.
THESE GIRLS ARE PRESERVED AS IF THEY WERE IN A COLD SLEEP...
...IN THESE FREEZERS.

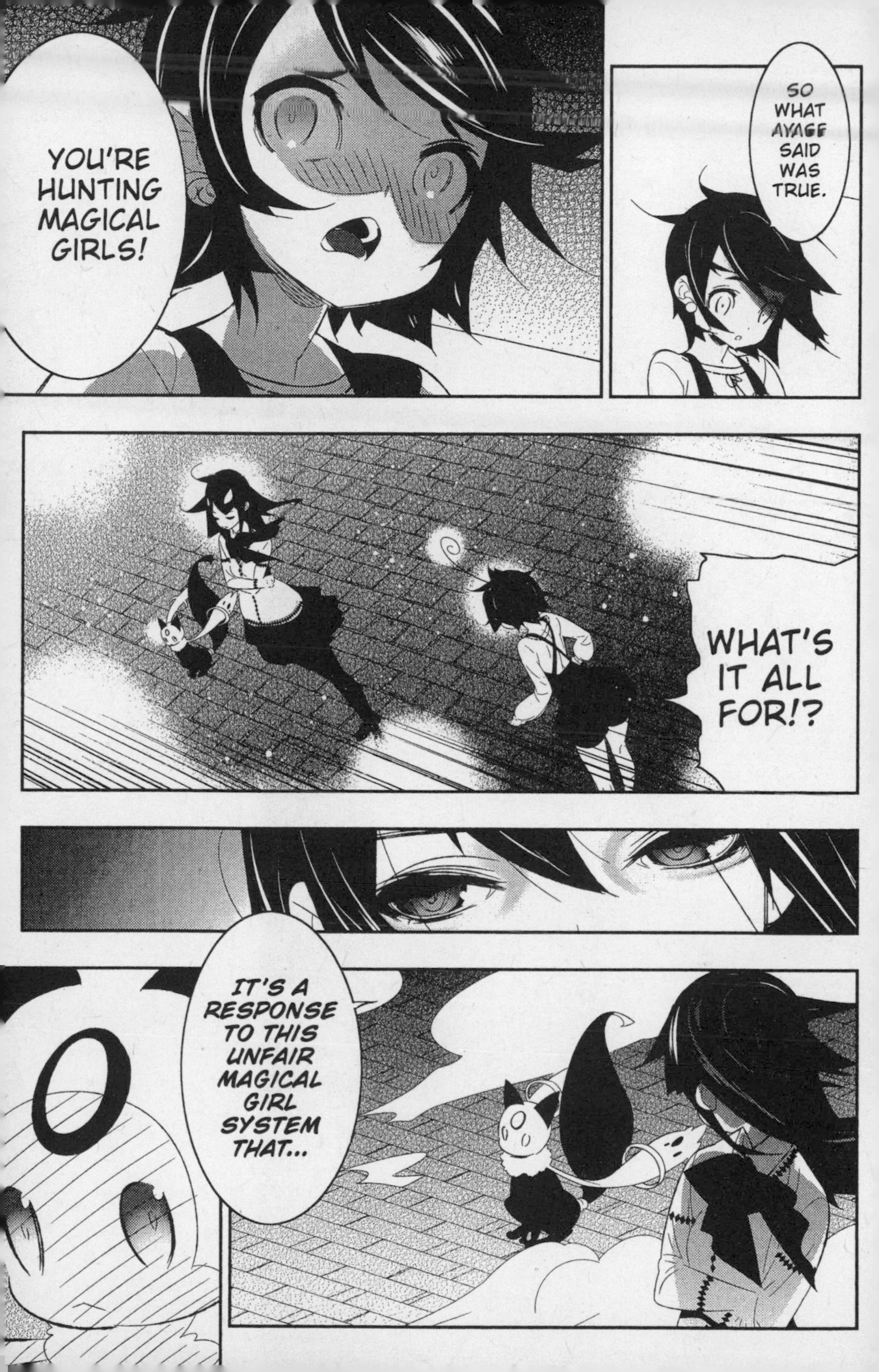
SO WHAT AYAME SAID WAS TRUE.
YOU'RE HUNTING MAGICAL GIRLS!
WHAT'S IT ALL FOR!?
IT'S A RESPONSE TO THIS UNFAIR MAGICAL GIRL SYSTEM THAT...

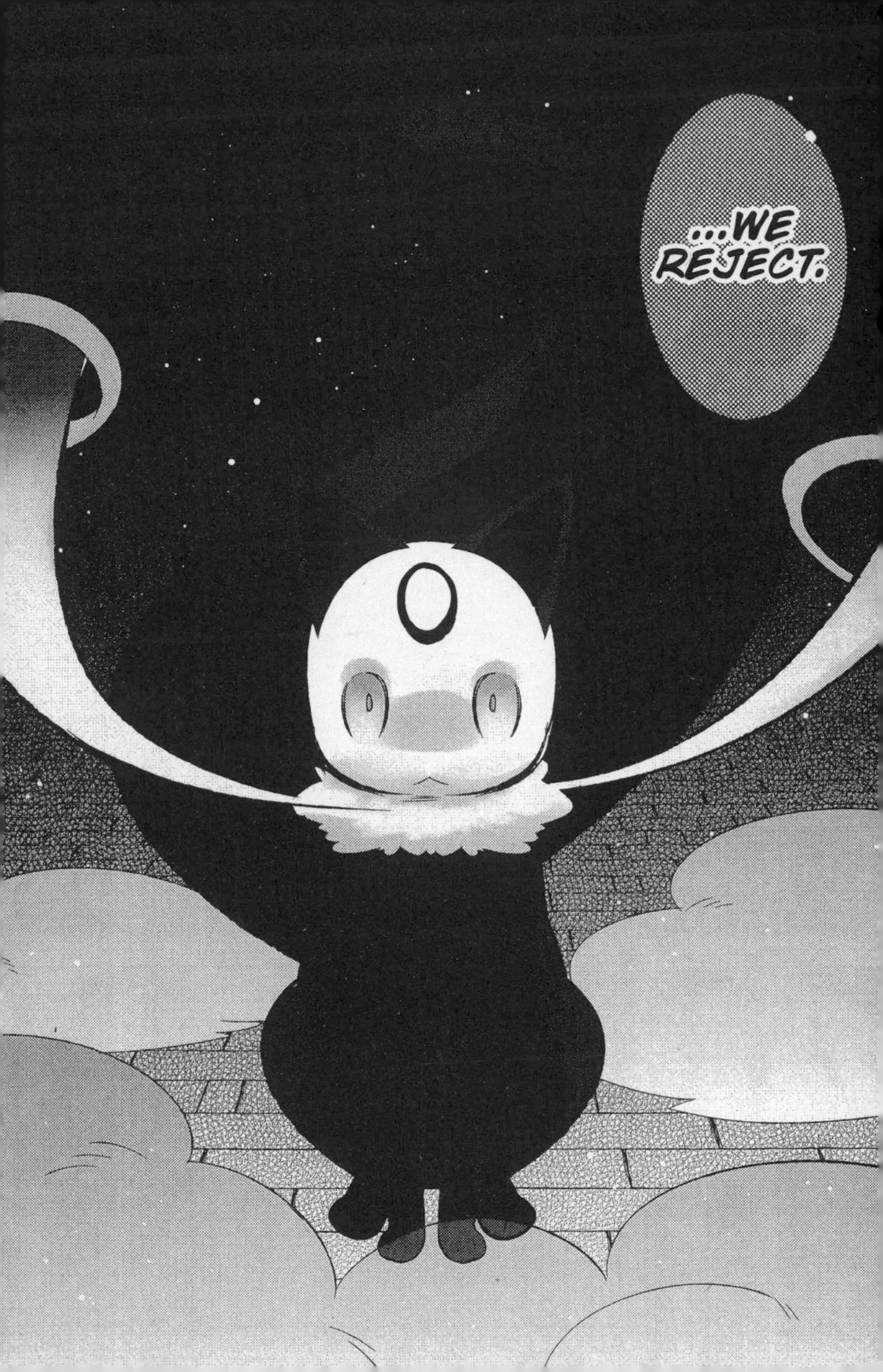
...WE REJECT.

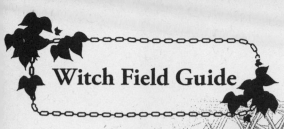

Witch Field Guide

The Bullet Witch

Her main attribute is guilt. Because she always feels like someone is attacking her, any human who enters the wards is quickly wiped out.

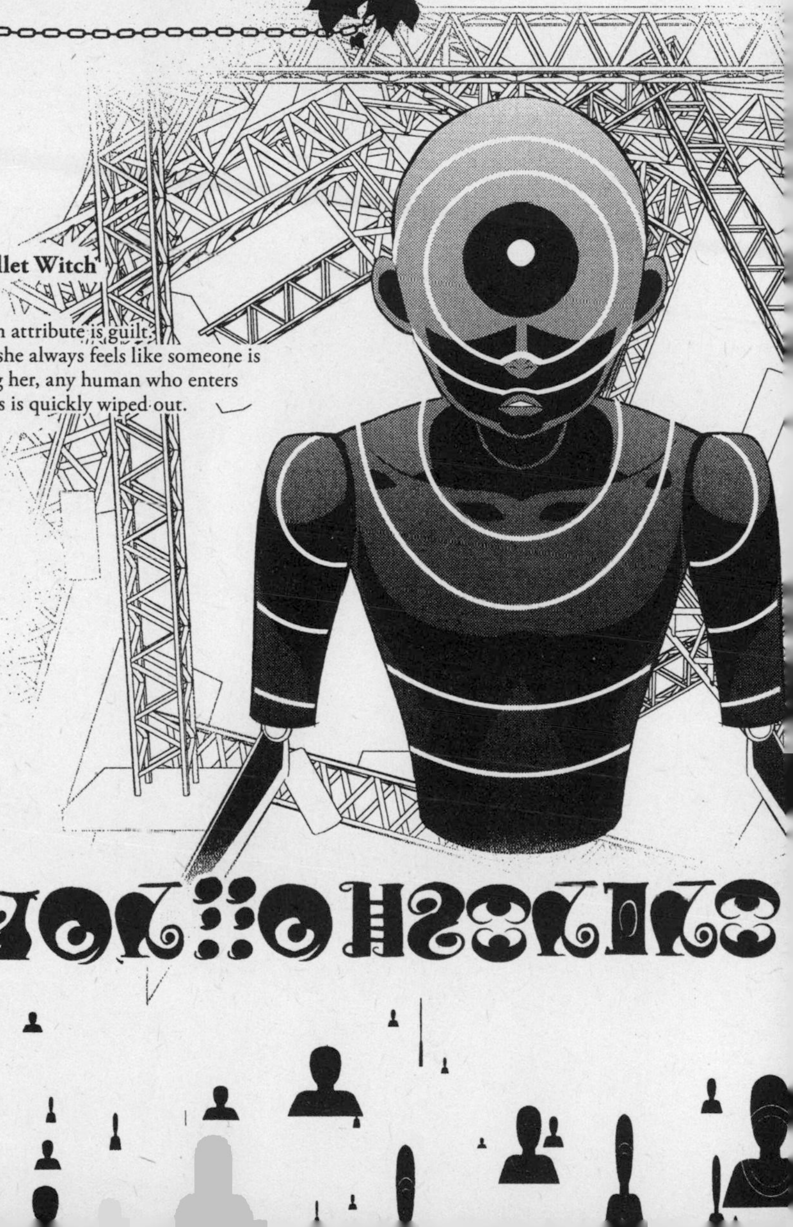

PUELLA MAGI
KAZUMI ★ MAGICA
The innocent malice

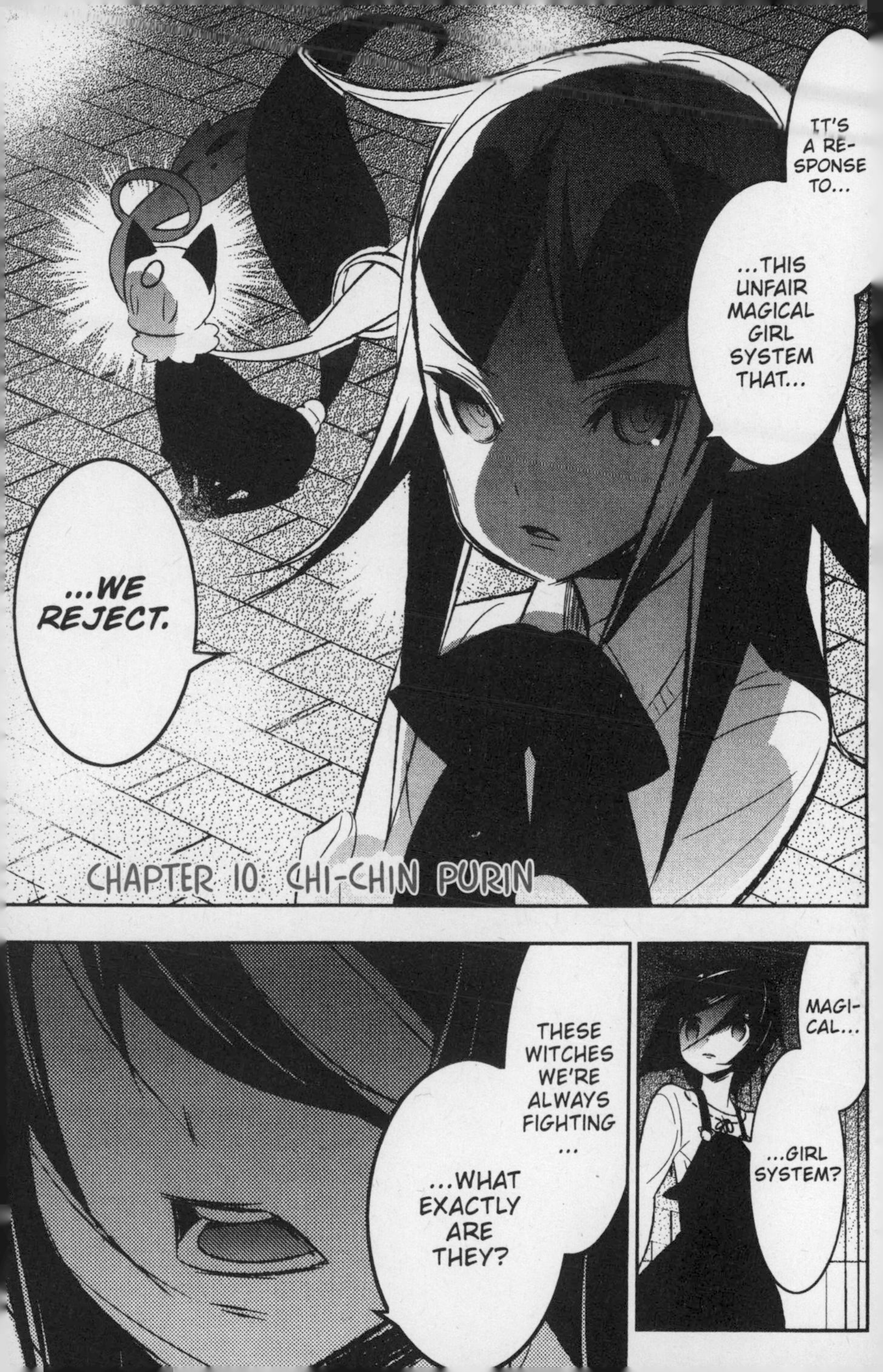
IT'S A RE-SPONSE TO...
...THIS UNFAIR MAGICAL GIRL SYSTEM THAT...
...WE REJECT.
CHAPTER 10: CHI-CHIN PURIN
MAGI-CAL...
...GIRL SYSTEM?
THESE WITCHES WE'RE ALWAYS FIGHTING...
...WHAT EXACTLY ARE THEY?

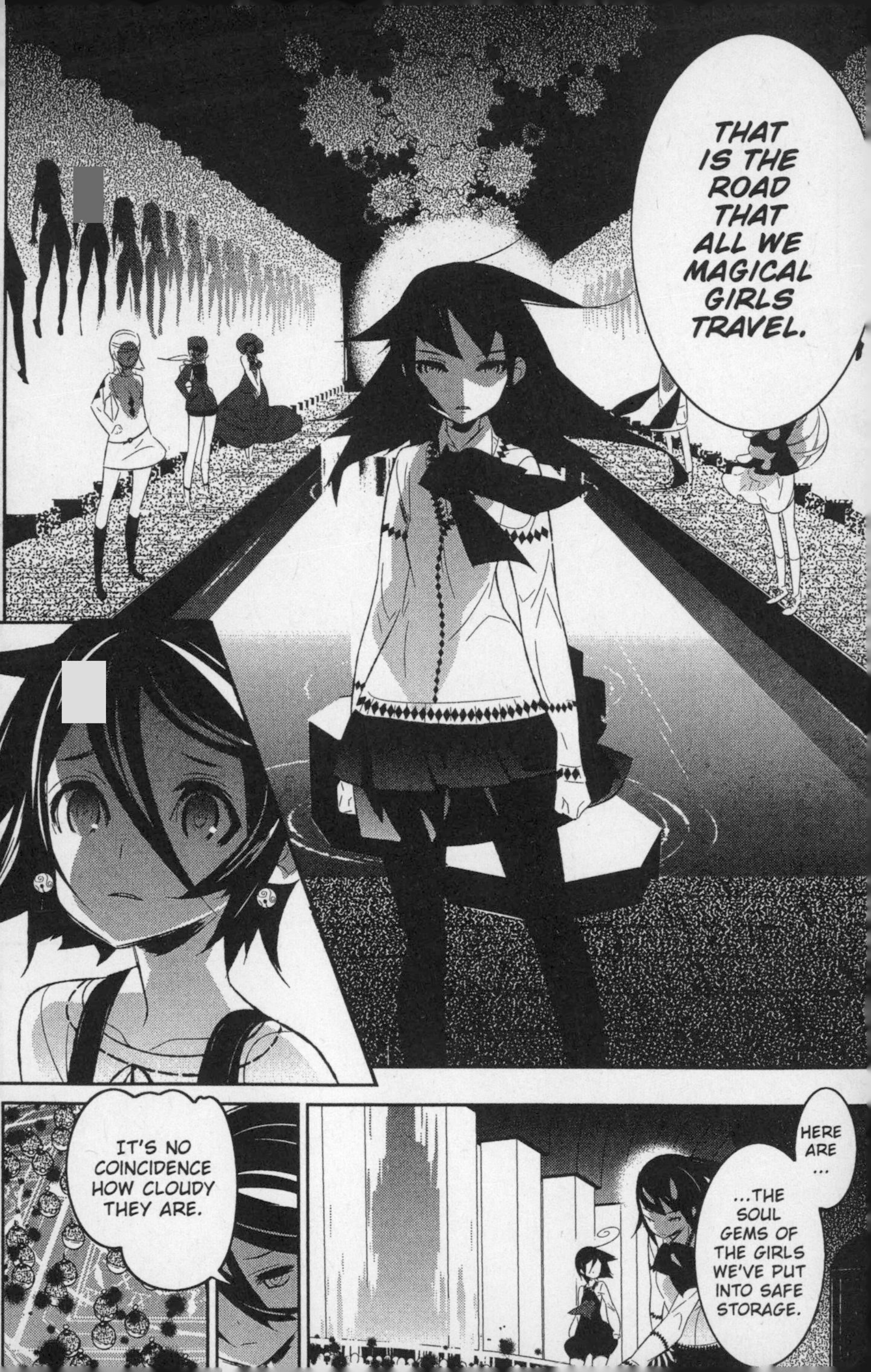
THAT IS THE ROAD THAT ALL WE MAGICAL GIRLS TRAVEL.
HERE ARE ...
...THE SOUL GEMS OF THE GIRLS WE'VE PUT INTO SAFE STORAGE.
IT'S NO COINCIDENCE HOW CLOUDY THEY ARE.

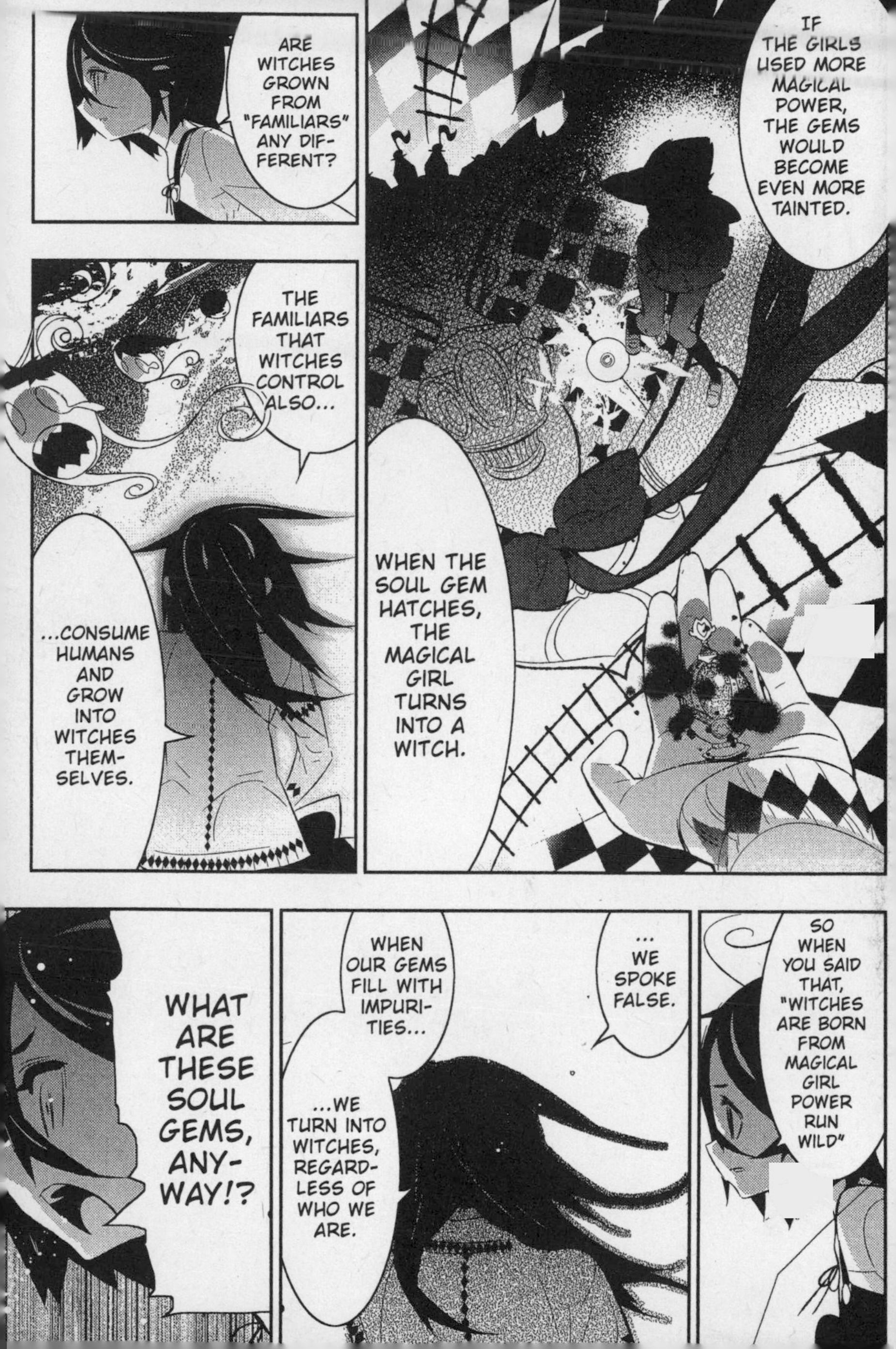
IF THE GIRLS USED MORE MAGICAL POWER, THE GEMS WOULD BECOME EVEN MORE TAINTED.
WHEN THE SOUL GEM HATCHES, THE MAGICAL GIRL TURNS INTO A WITCH.
ARE WITCHES GROWN FROM "FAMILIARS" ANY DIF-FERENT?
THE FAMILIARS THAT WITCHES CONTROL ALSO...
...CONSUME HUMANS AND GROW INTO WITCHES THEM-SELVES.
SO WHEN YOU SAID THAT, "WITCHES ARE BORN FROM MAGICAL GIRL POWER RUN WILD"
... WE SPOKE FALSE.
WHEN OUR GEMS FILL WITH IMPURI-TIES...
...WE TURN INTO WITCHES, REGARD-LESS OF WHO WE ARE.
WHAT ARE THESE SOUL GEMS, ANY-WAY!?

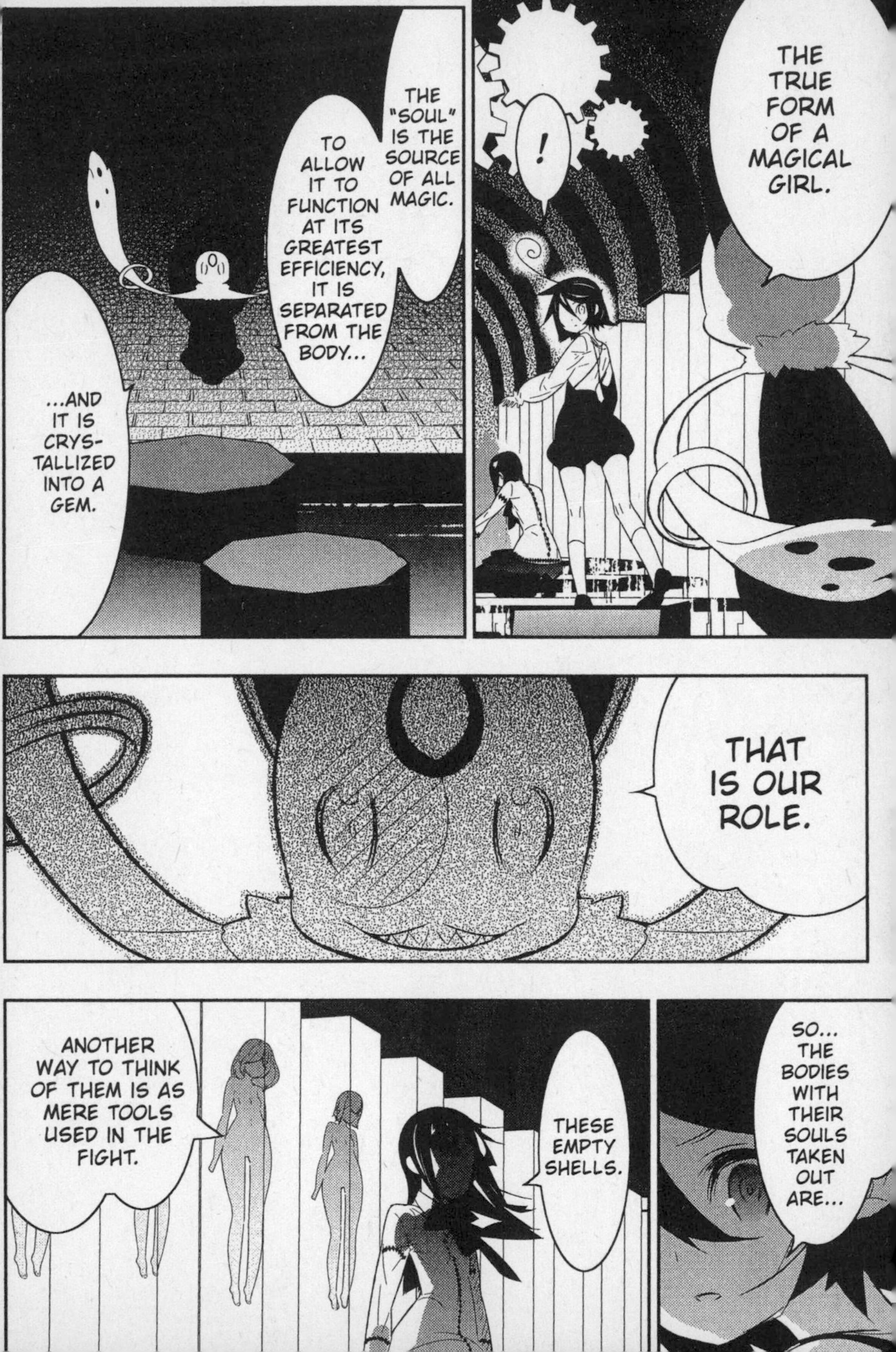
THE TRUE FORM OF A MAGICAL GIRL.
!
THE "SOUL" IS THE SOURCE OF ALL MAGIC.
TO ALLOW IT TO FUNCTION AT ITS GREATEST EFFICIENCY, IT IS SEPARATED FROM THE BODY...
...AND IT IS CRYS-TALLIZED INTO A GEM.
THAT IS OUR ROLE.
SO... THE BODIES WITH THEIR SOULS TAKEN OUT ARE...
THESE EMPTY SHELLS.
ANOTHER WAY TO THINK OF THEM IS AS MERE TOOLS USED IN THE FIGHT.

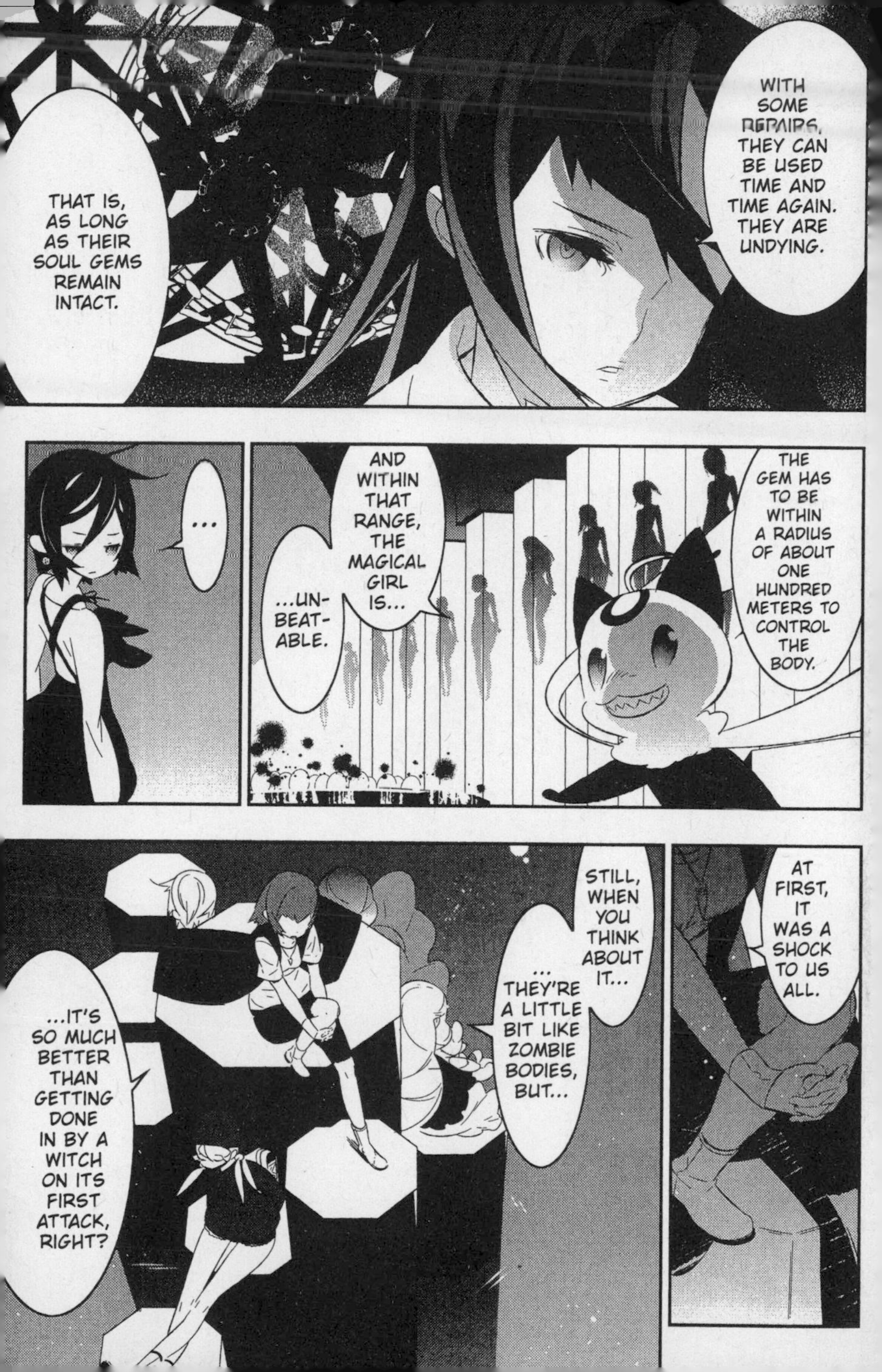
WITH SOME REPAIRS, THEY CAN BE USED TIME AND TIME AGAIN. THEY ARE UNDYING.
THAT IS, AS LONG AS THEIR SOUL GEMS REMAIN INTACT.
THE GEM HAS TO BE WITHIN A RADIUS OF ABOUT ONE HUNDRED METERS TO CONTROL THE BODY.
AND WITHIN THAT RANGE, THE MAGICAL GIRL IS...
...UN-BEAT-ABLE.
...
AT FIRST, IT WAS A SHOCK TO US ALL.
STILL, WHEN YOU THINK ABOUT IT...
... THEY'RE A LITTLE BIT LIKE ZOMBIE BODIES, BUT...
...IT'S SO MUCH BETTER THAN GETTING DONE IN BY A WITCH ON ITS FIRST ATTACK, RIGHT?

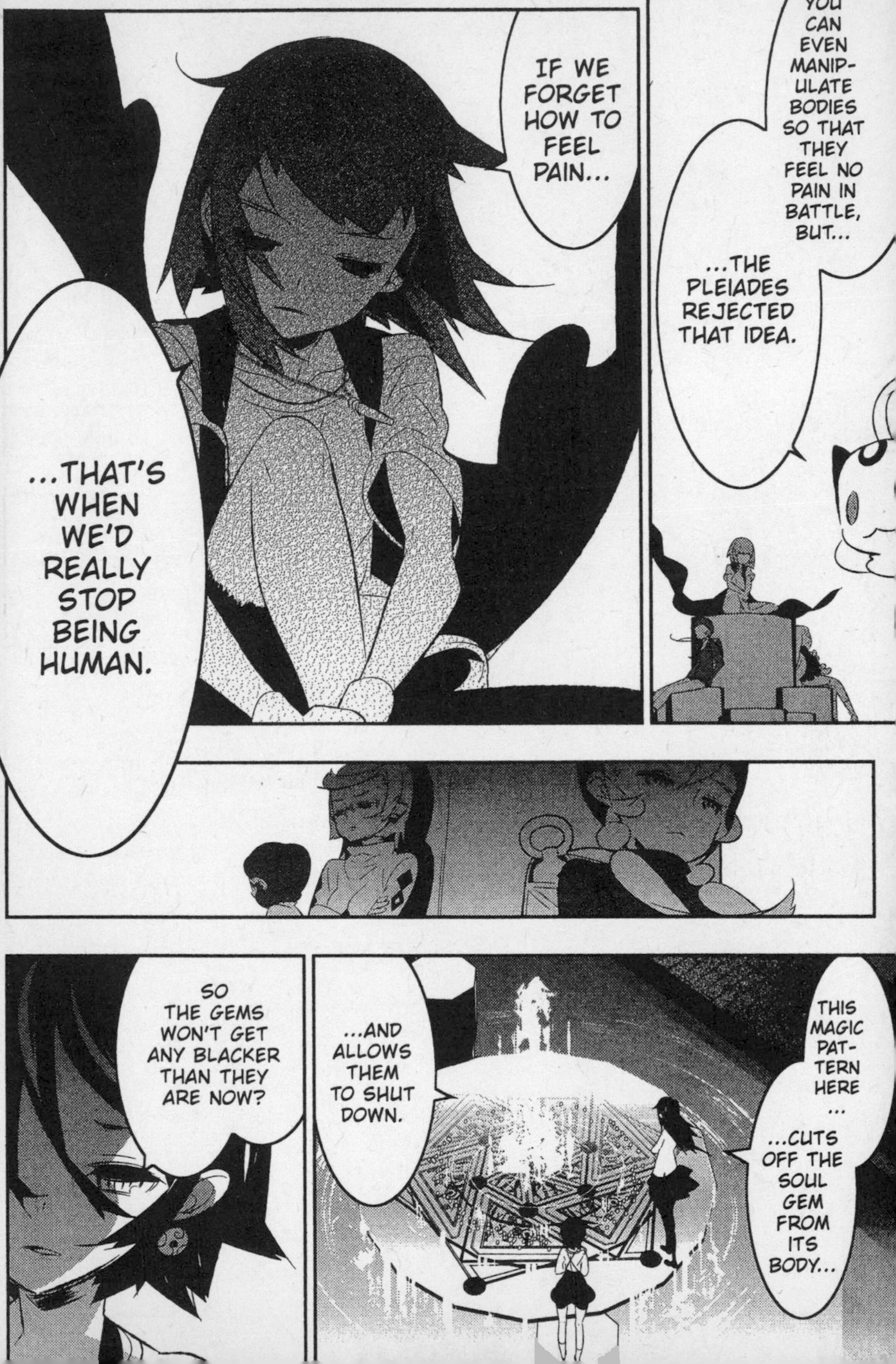
YOU CAN EVEN MANIP-ULATE BODIES SO THAT THEY FEEL NO PAIN IN BATTLE, BUT...
...THE PLEIADES REJECTED THAT IDEA.
IF WE FORGET HOW TO FEEL PAIN...
...THAT'S WHEN WE'D REALLY STOP BEING HUMAN.
THIS MAGIC PAT-TERN HERE...
...CUTS OFF THE SOUL GEM FROM ITS BODY...
...AND ALLOWS THEM TO SHUT DOWN.
SO THE GEMS WON'T GET ANY BLACKER THAN THEY ARE NOW?

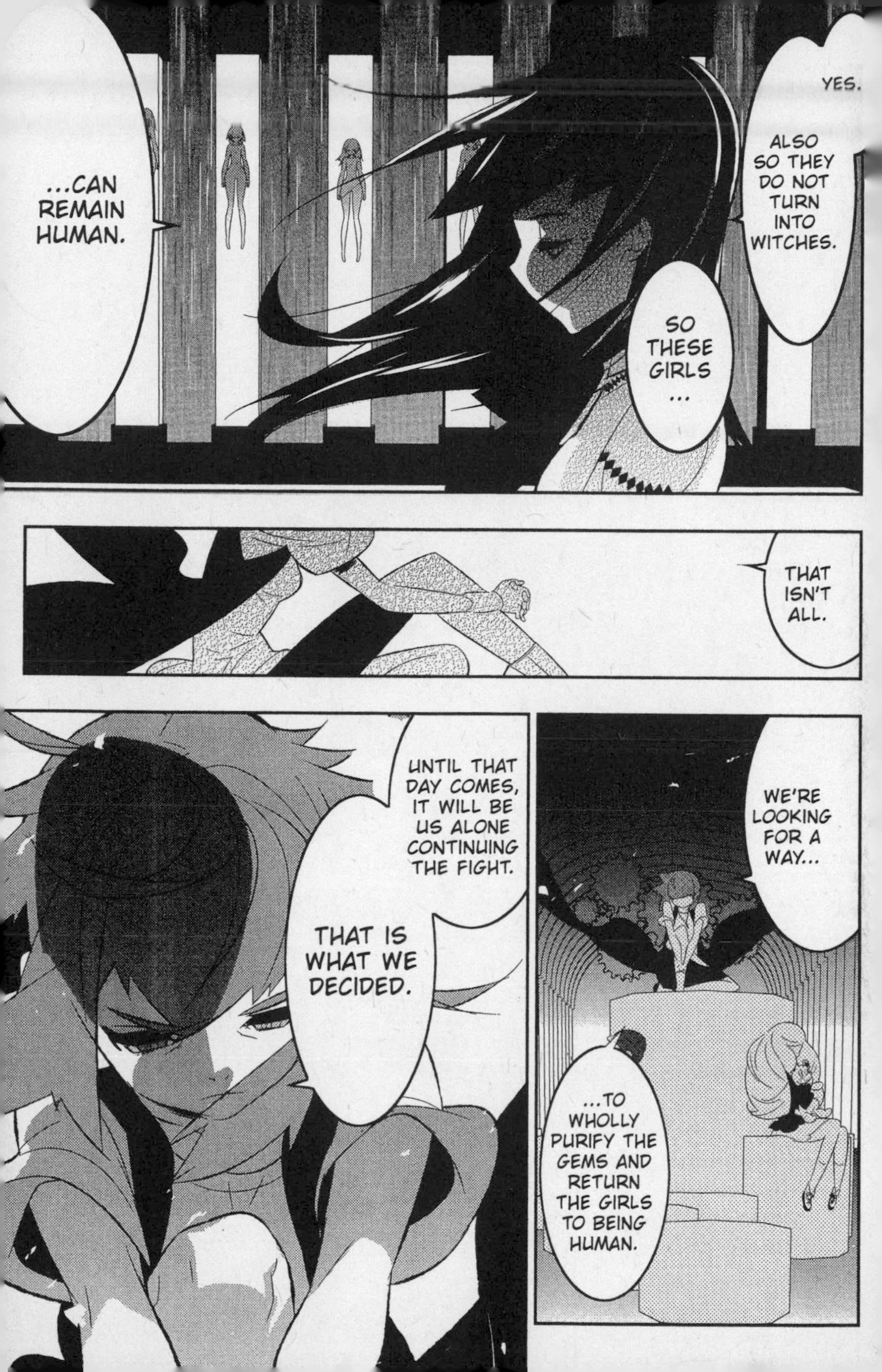
YES.
ALSO SO THEY DO NOT TURN INTO WITCHES.
SO THESE GIRLS ...
...CAN REMAIN HUMAN.
THAT ISN'T ALL.
WE'RE LOOKING FOR A WAY...
...TO WHOLLY PURIFY THE GEMS AND RETURN THE GIRLS TO BEING HUMAN.
UNTIL THAT DAY COMES, IT WILL BE US ALONE CONTINUING THE FIGHT.
THAT IS WHAT WE DECIDED.

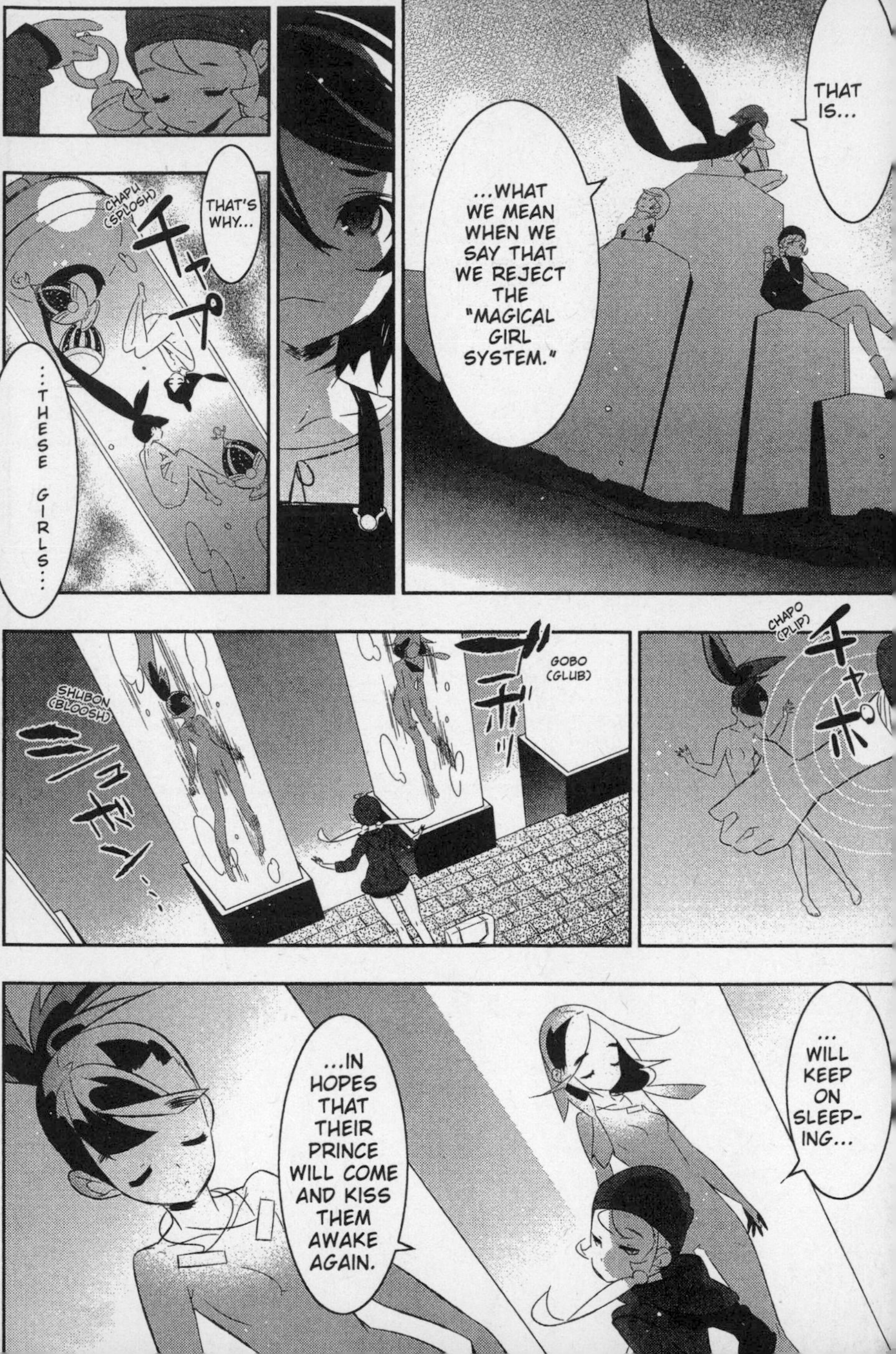
THAT IS...
...WHAT WE MEAN WHEN WE SAY THAT WE REJECT THE "MAGICAL GIRL SYSTEM."
THAT'S WHY...
CHAPU (SPLOSH)
チャプ
...THESE GIRLS...
CHAPO (PLIP)
チャポ
GOBO (GLUB)
ゴボッ
SHUBON (BLOOSH)
シュボン...
...WILL KEEP ON SLEEPING...
...IN HOPES THAT THEIR PRINCE WILL COME AND KISS THEM AWAKE AGAIN.

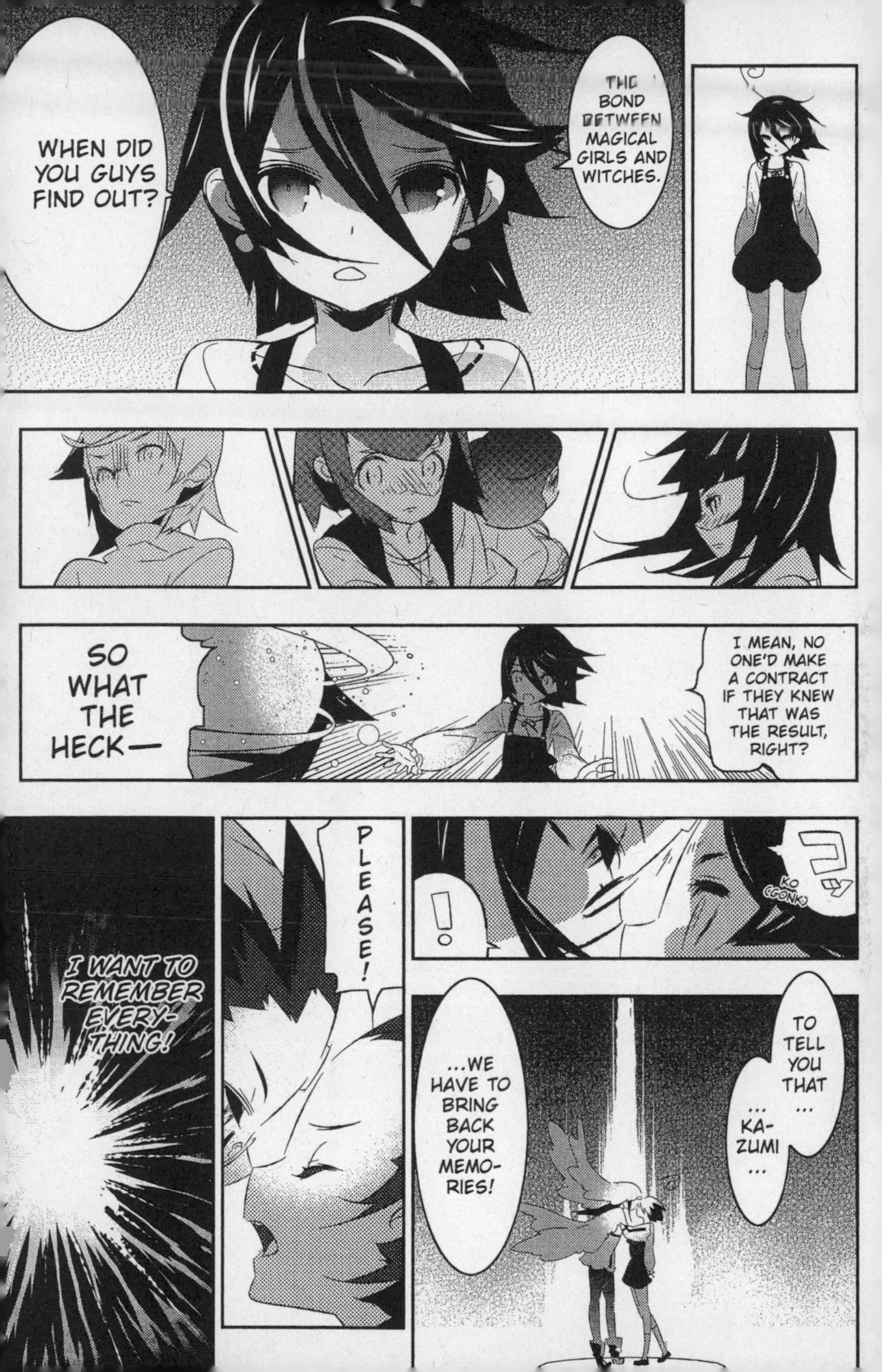
THE BOND BETWEEN MAGICAL GIRLS AND WITCHES.
WHEN DID YOU GUYS FIND OUT?
I MEAN, NO ONE'D MAKE A CONTRACT IF THEY KNEW THAT WAS THE RESULT, RIGHT?
SO WHAT THE HECK—
KO (GONK)
!
TO TELL YOU THAT... KA-ZUMI...
...WE HAVE TO BRING BACK YOUR MEMO-RIES!
PLEASE!
I WANT TO REMEMBER EVERY-THING!

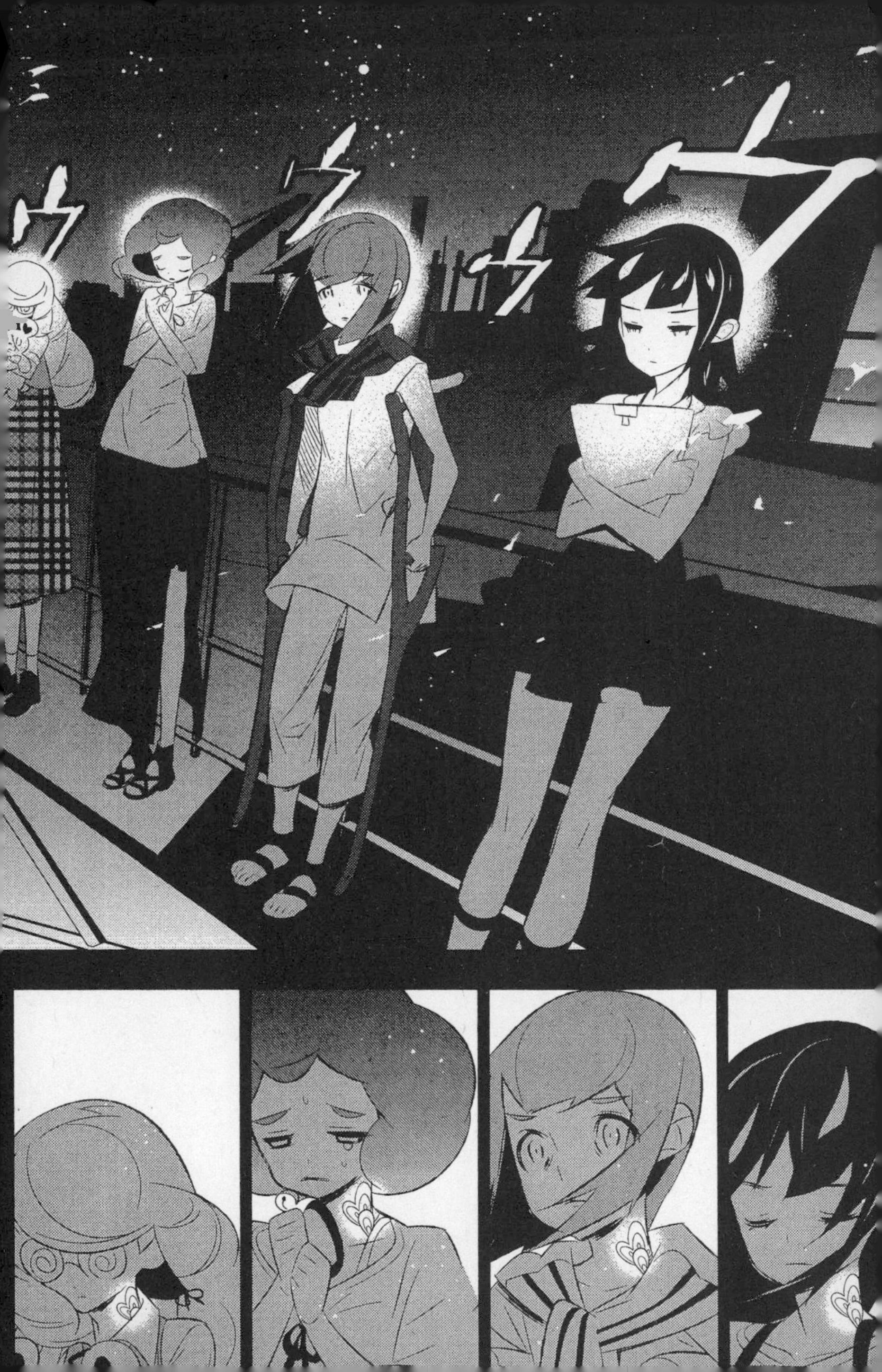

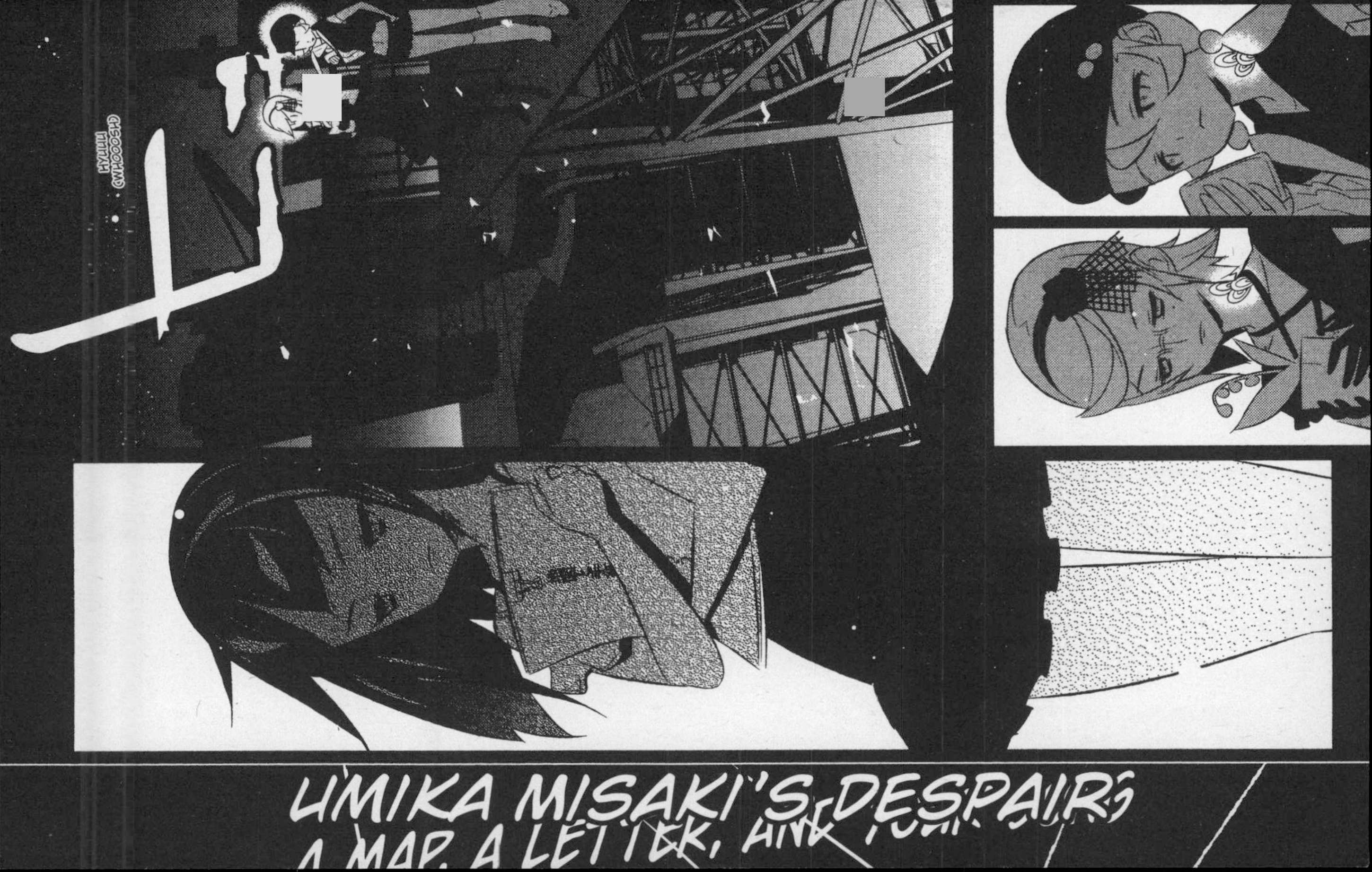
HYULLL
(WHOOOSH)
UMIKA MISAKI'S DESPAIR:
A MAP, A LETTER, AND

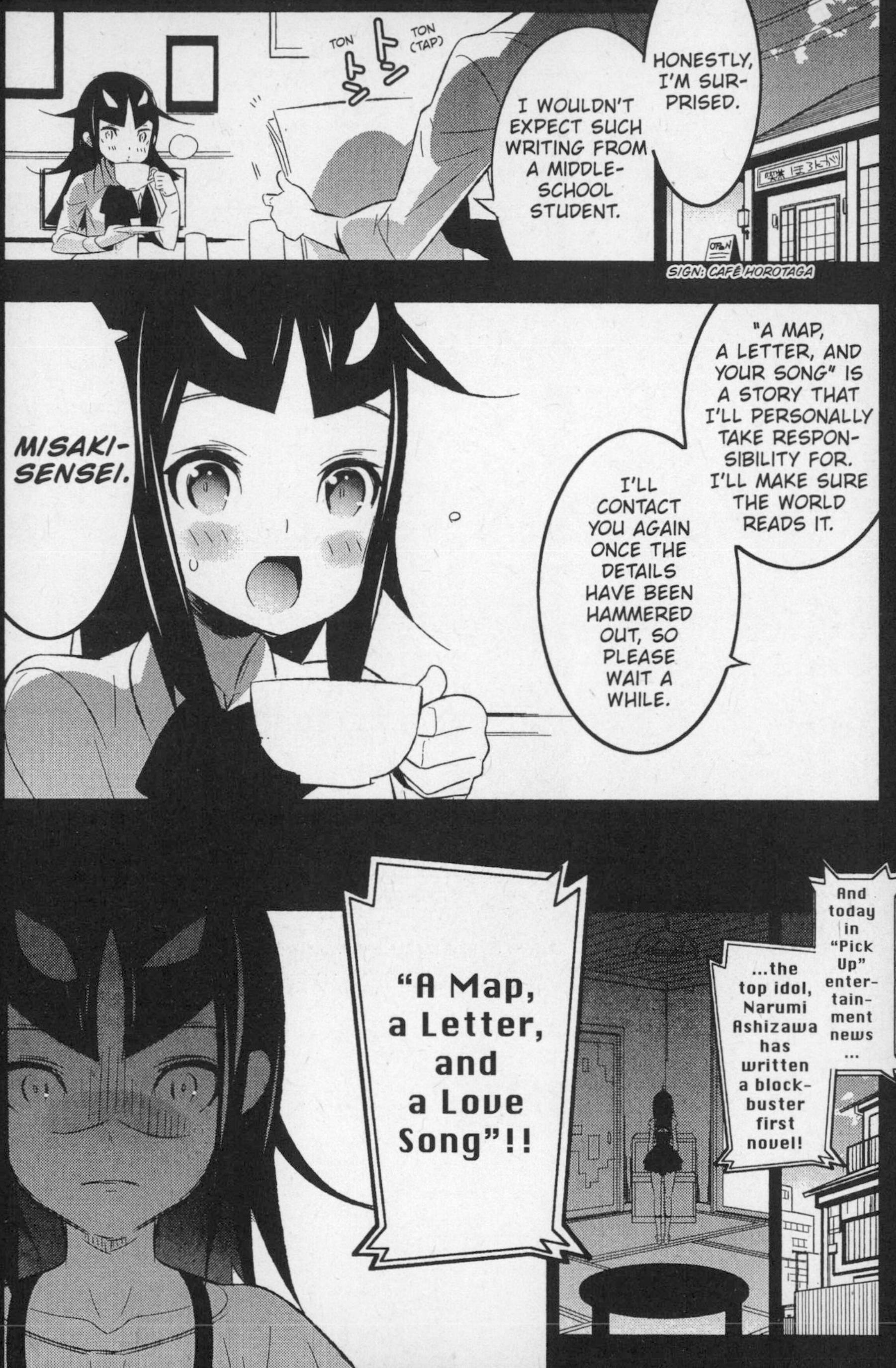
HONESTLY, I'M SUR-PRISED.
I WOULDN'T EXPECT SUCH WRITING FROM A MIDDLE-SCHOOL STUDENT.
TON TON (TAP)
SIGN: CAFÉ HOROTAGA
OPEN
"A MAP, A LETTER, AND YOUR SONG" IS A STORY THAT I'LL PERSONALLY TAKE RESPON-SIBILITY FOR. I'LL MAKE SURE THE WORLD READS IT.
I'LL CONTACT YOU AGAIN ONCE THE DETAILS HAVE BEEN HAMMERED OUT, SO PLEASE WAIT A WHILE.
MISAKI-SENSEI.
And today in "Pick Up" enter-tain-ment news...
...the top idol, Narumi Ashizawa has written a block-buster first novel!
"A Map, a Letter, and a Love Song"!!

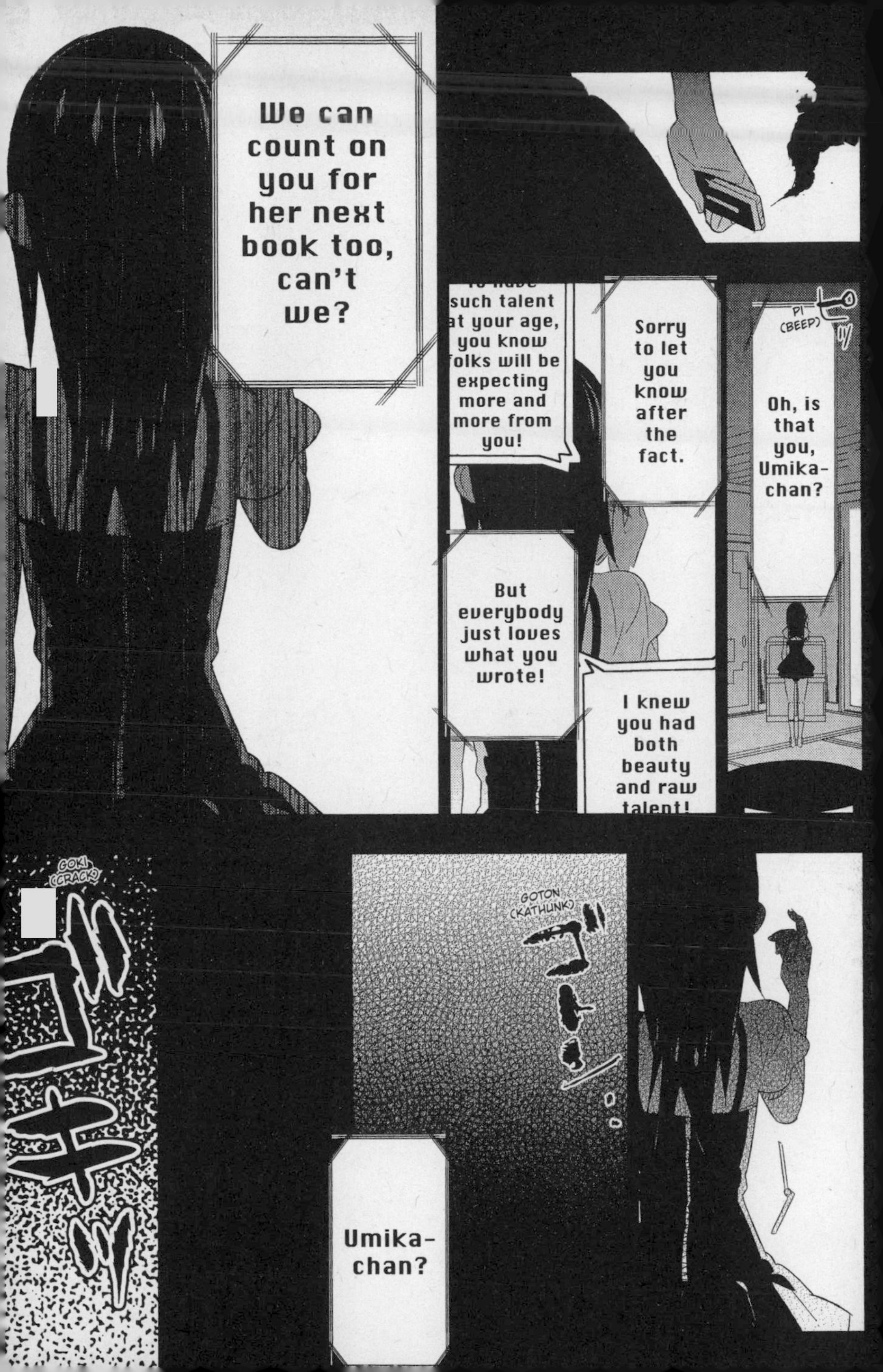
PI (BEEP)
Oh, is that you, Umika-chan?
Sorry to let you know after the fact.
such talent at your age, you know folks will be expecting more and more from you!
I knew you had both beauty and raw talent!
But everybody just loves what you wrote!
We can count on you for her next book too, can't we?
GOTON (KATHUNK)
Umika-chan?
GOKI (CRACK)

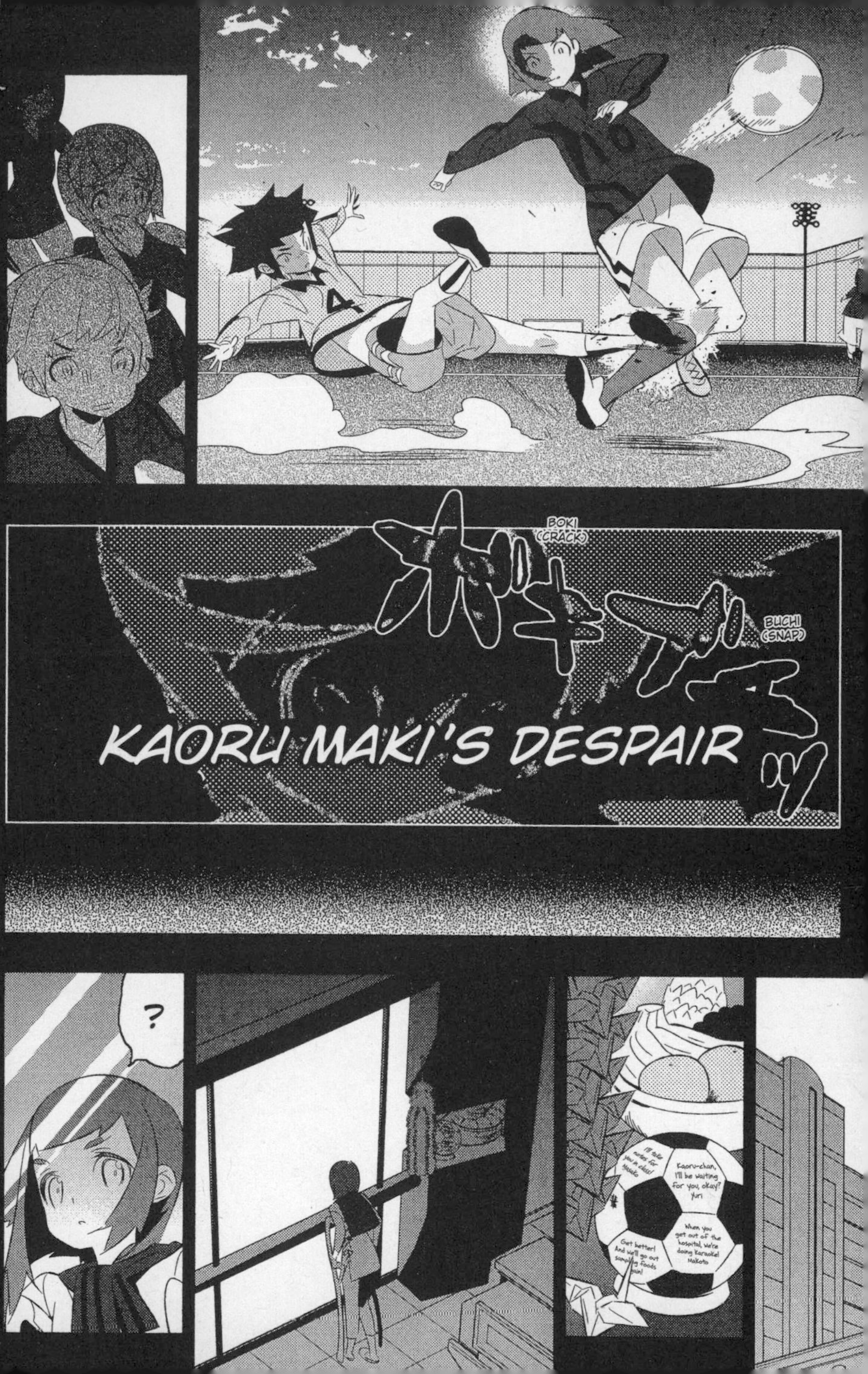
BOKI (CRACK)
BUCHI (SNAP)
KAORU MAKI'S DESPAIR
Kaoru-chan, I'll be waiting for you, okay? Yuri
I'll take notes for you in class! Yasuko
When you get out of the hospital, we're doing Karaoke! Makoto
Get better! And we'll go out sampling foods again!
?

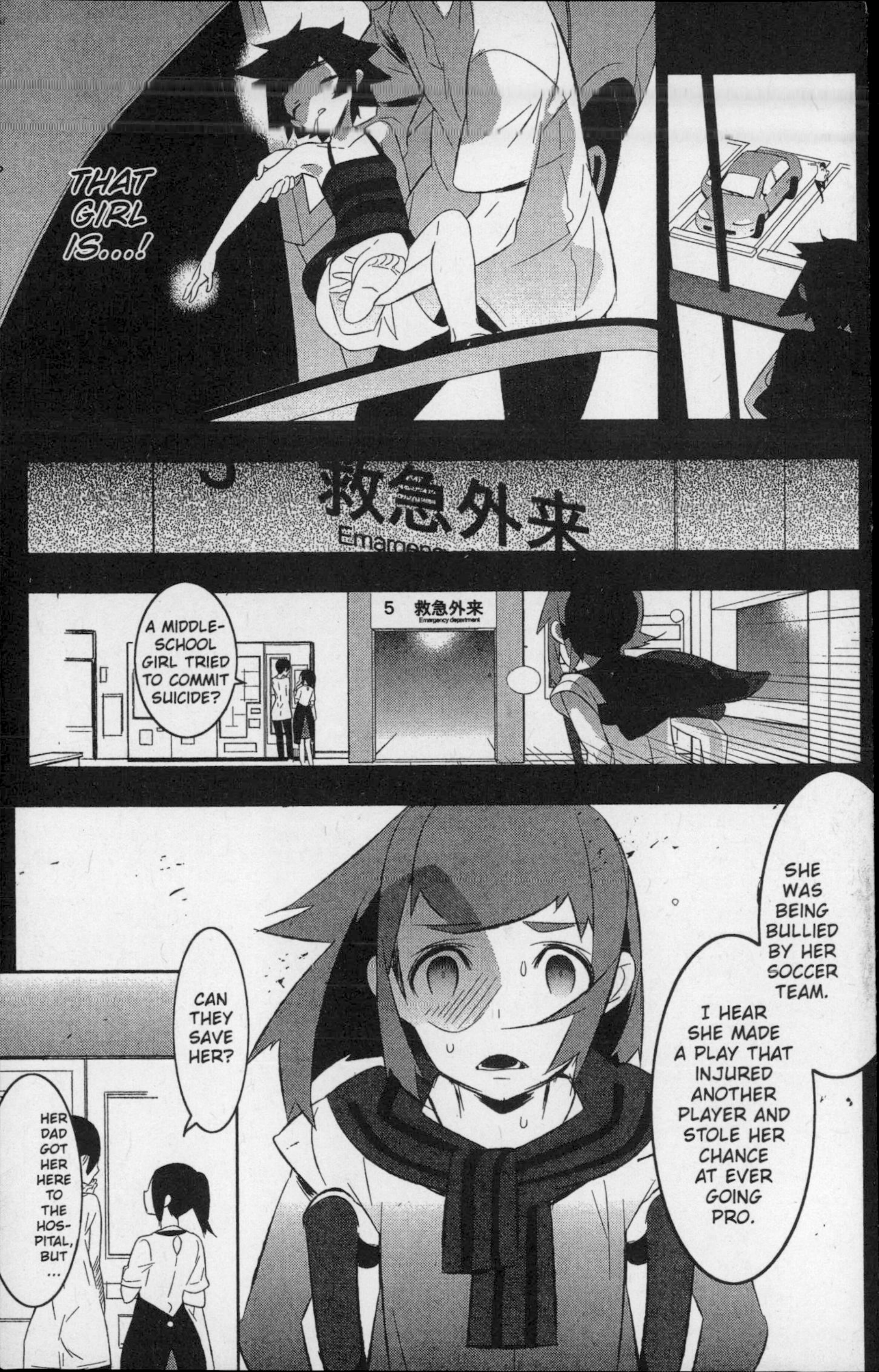
THAT GIRL IS...!
救急外来
5 救急外来
Emergency department
A MIDDLE-SCHOOL GIRL TRIED TO COMMIT SUICIDE?
SHE WAS BEING BULLIED BY HER SOCCER TEAM.
I HEAR SHE MADE A PLAY THAT INJURED ANOTHER PLAYER AND STOLE HER CHANCE AT EVER GOING PRO.
CAN THEY SAVE HER?
HER DAD GOT HER HERE TO THE HOS-PITAL, BUT ...

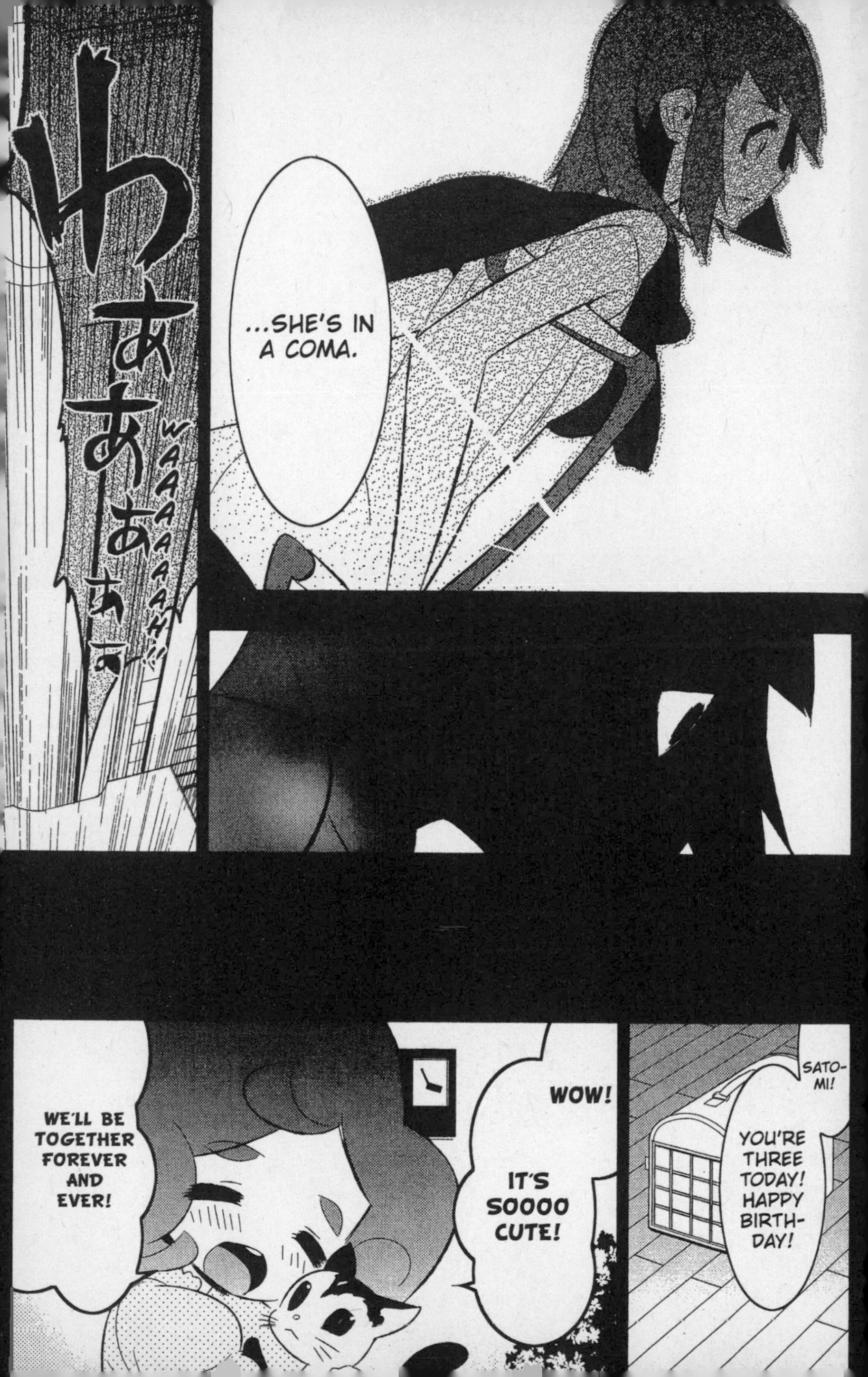
...SHE'S IN A COMA.
わあああああ
WAAAAAAAH!!
SATO-MI!
YOU'RE THREE TODAY! HAPPY BIRTH-DAY!
WOW!
IT'S SOOOO CUTE!
WE'LL BE TOGETHER FOREVER AND EVER!

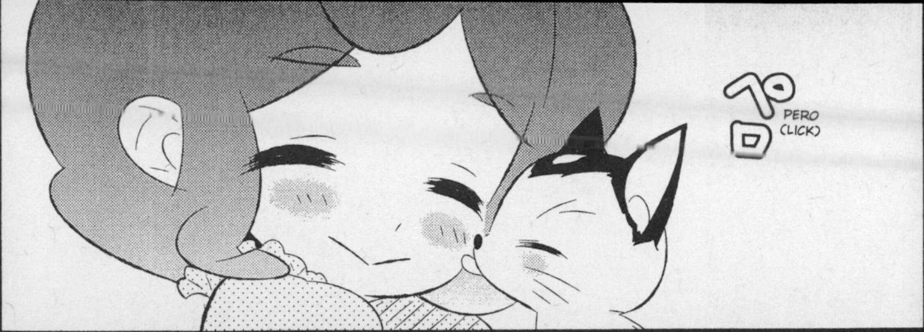
PERO (LICK)

SATOMI USAGI'S DESPAIR

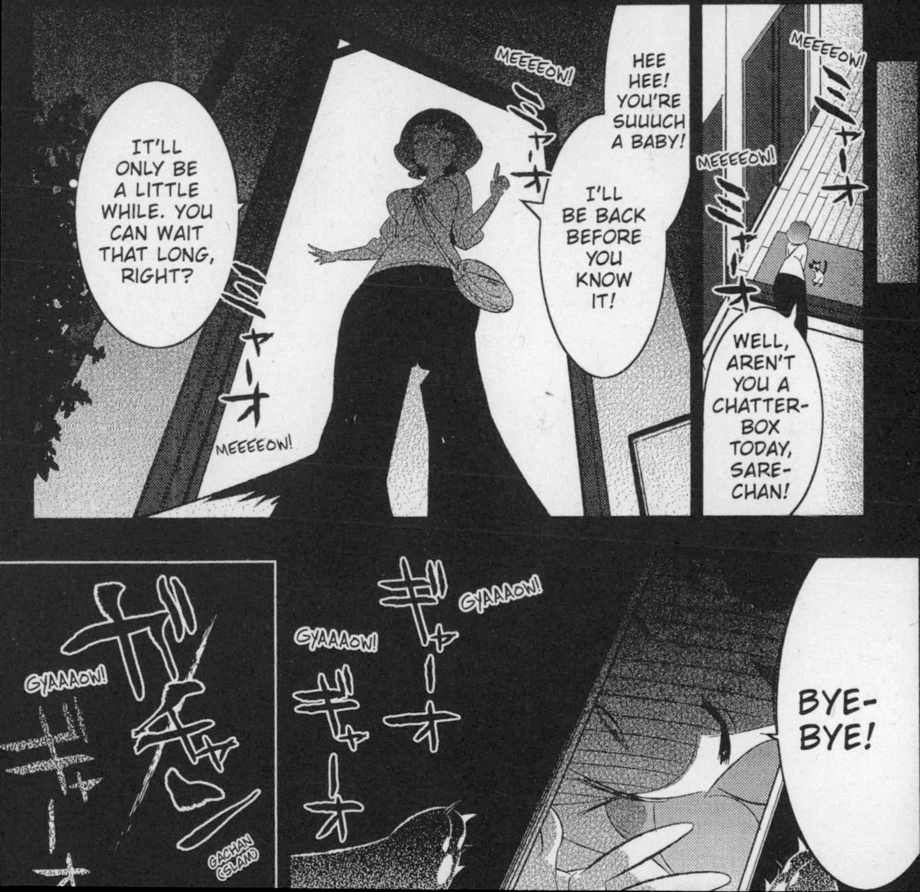
MEEEEOW!
MEEEEOW!
WELL, AREN'T YOU A CHATTER-BOX TODAY, SARE-CHAN!
MEEEEOW!
HEE HEE! YOU'RE SUUUCH A BABY!
I'LL BE BACK BEFORE YOU KNOW IT!
IT'LL ONLY BE A LITTLE WHILE. YOU CAN WAIT THAT LONG, RIGHT?
MEEEEOW!
BYE-BYE!
GYAAAOW!
GYAAAOW!
GYAAAOW!
GACHAN (SLAM)

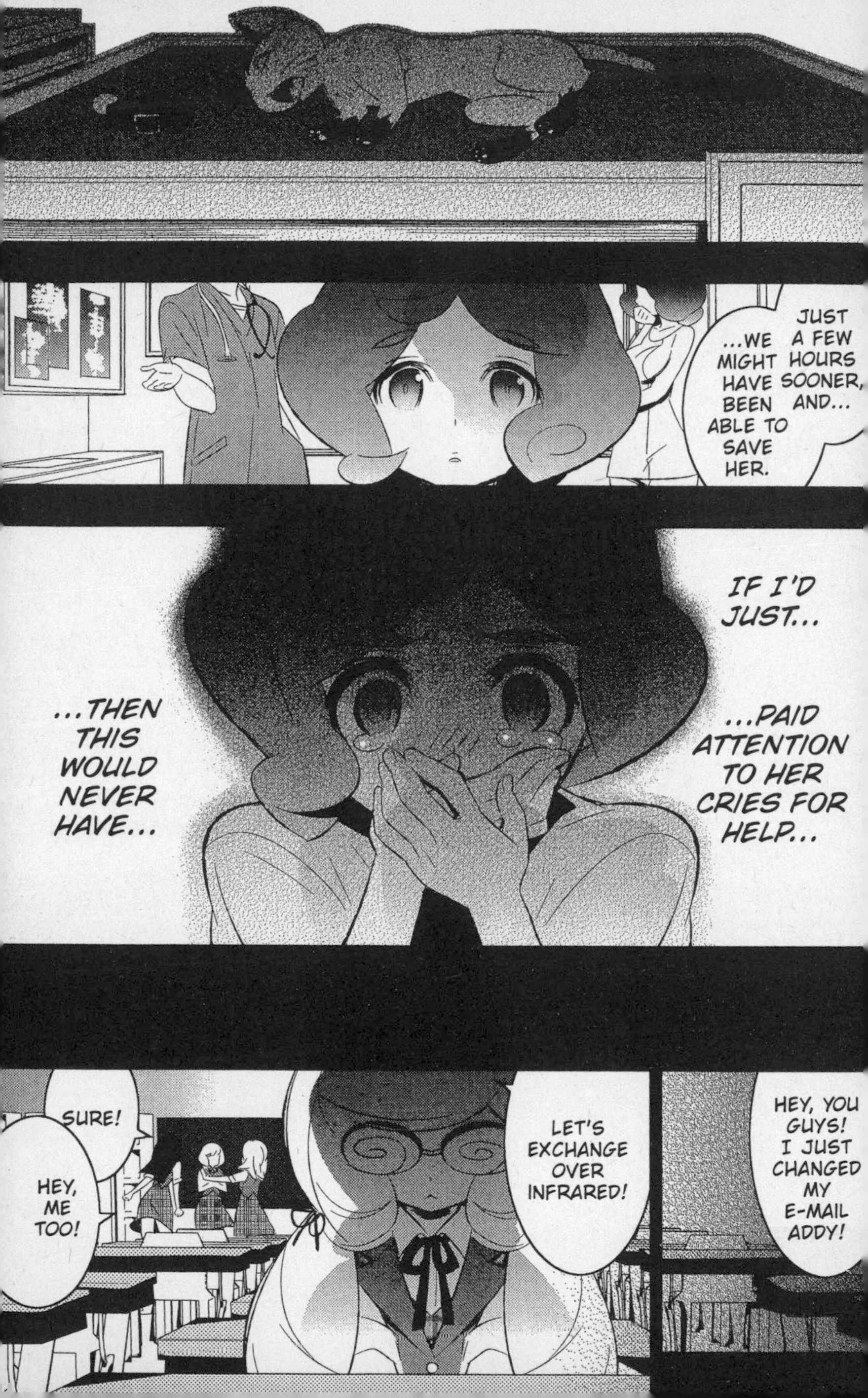
...WE MIGHT HAVE BEEN ABLE TO SAVE HER. JUST A FEW HOURS SOONER, AND...
IF I'D JUST...
...PAID ATTENTION TO HER CRIES FOR HELP...
...THEN THIS WOULD NEVER HAVE...
HEY, YOU GUYS! I JUST CHANGED MY E-MAIL ADDY!
LET'S EXCHANGE OVER INFRARED!
SURE!
HEY, ME TOO!

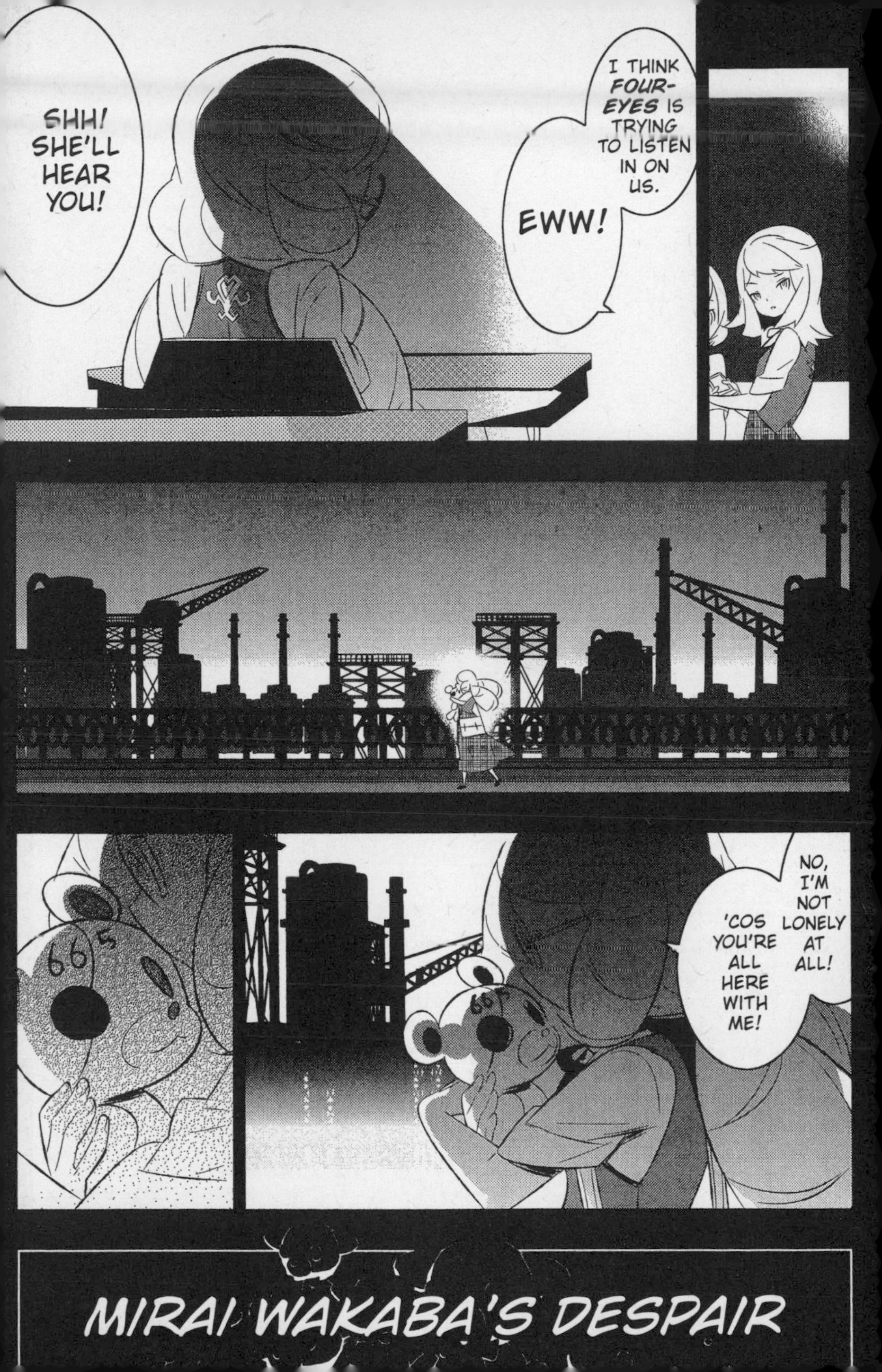
I THINK FOUR-EYES IS TRYING TO LISTEN IN ON US.
EWW!
SHH! SHE'LL HEAR YOU!
NO, I'M NOT LONELY AT ALL!
'COS YOU'RE ALL HERE WITH ME!
MIRAI WAKABA'S DESPAIR

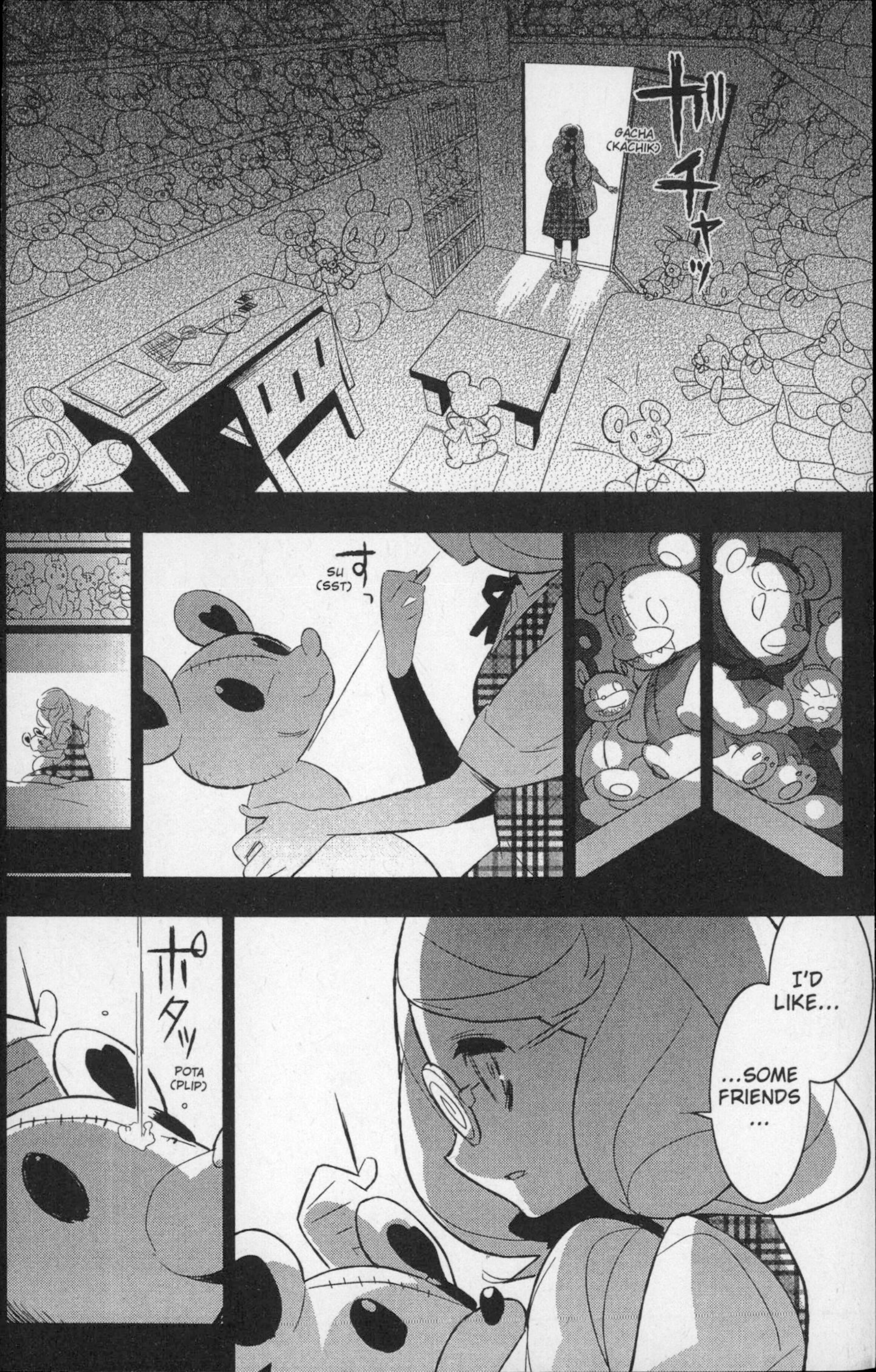
ガチャッ
GACHA (KACHIK)
すっ
SU (SST)
I'D LIKE...
...SOME FRIENDS ...
ポタッ
POTA (PLIP)

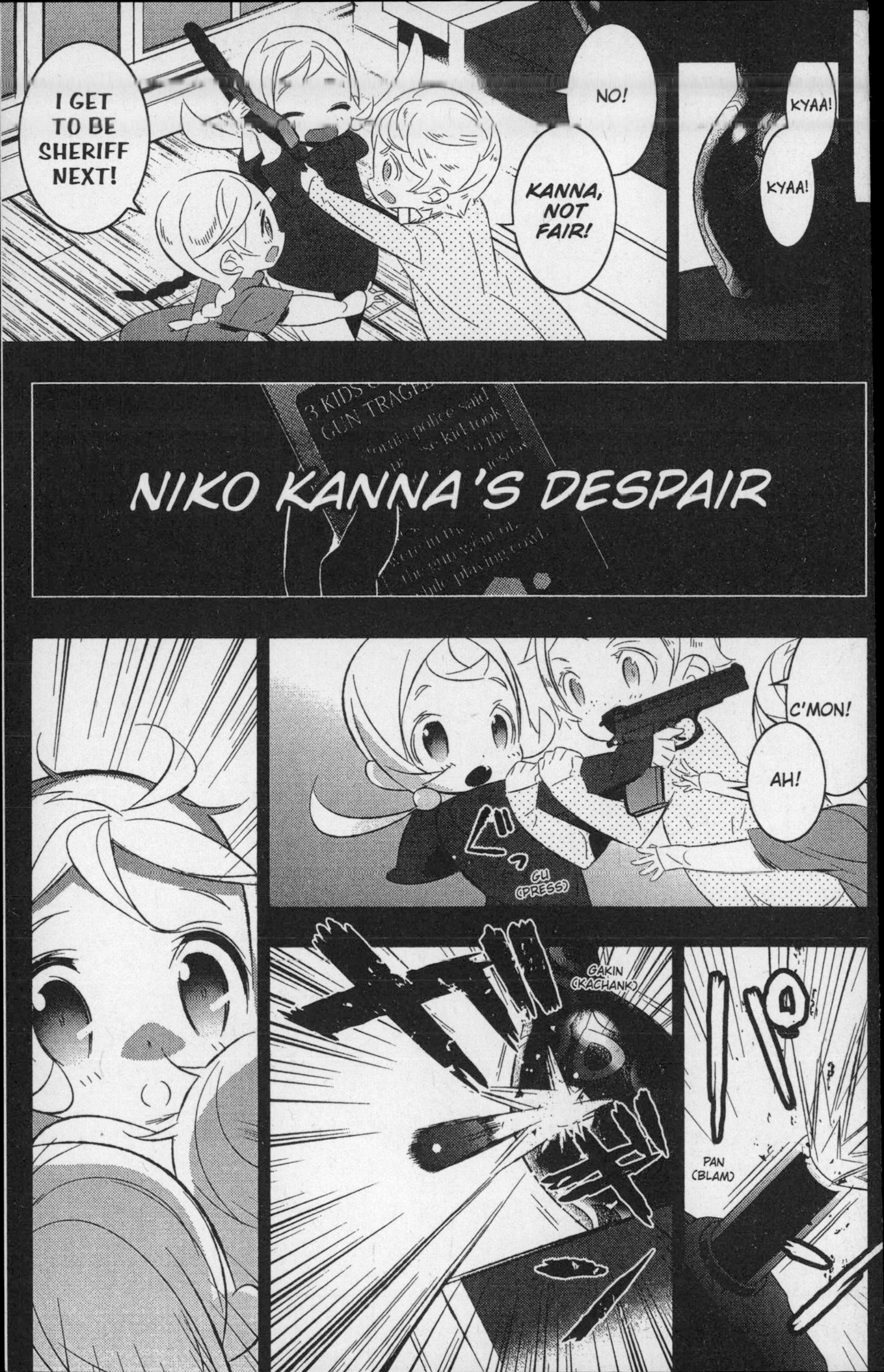
KYAA!
KYAA!
NO!
KANNA, NOT FAIR!
I GET TO BE SHERIFF NEXT!
NIKO KANNA'S DESPAIR
C'MON!
AH!
GU (PRESS)
PAN (BLAM)
GAKIN (KACHANK)

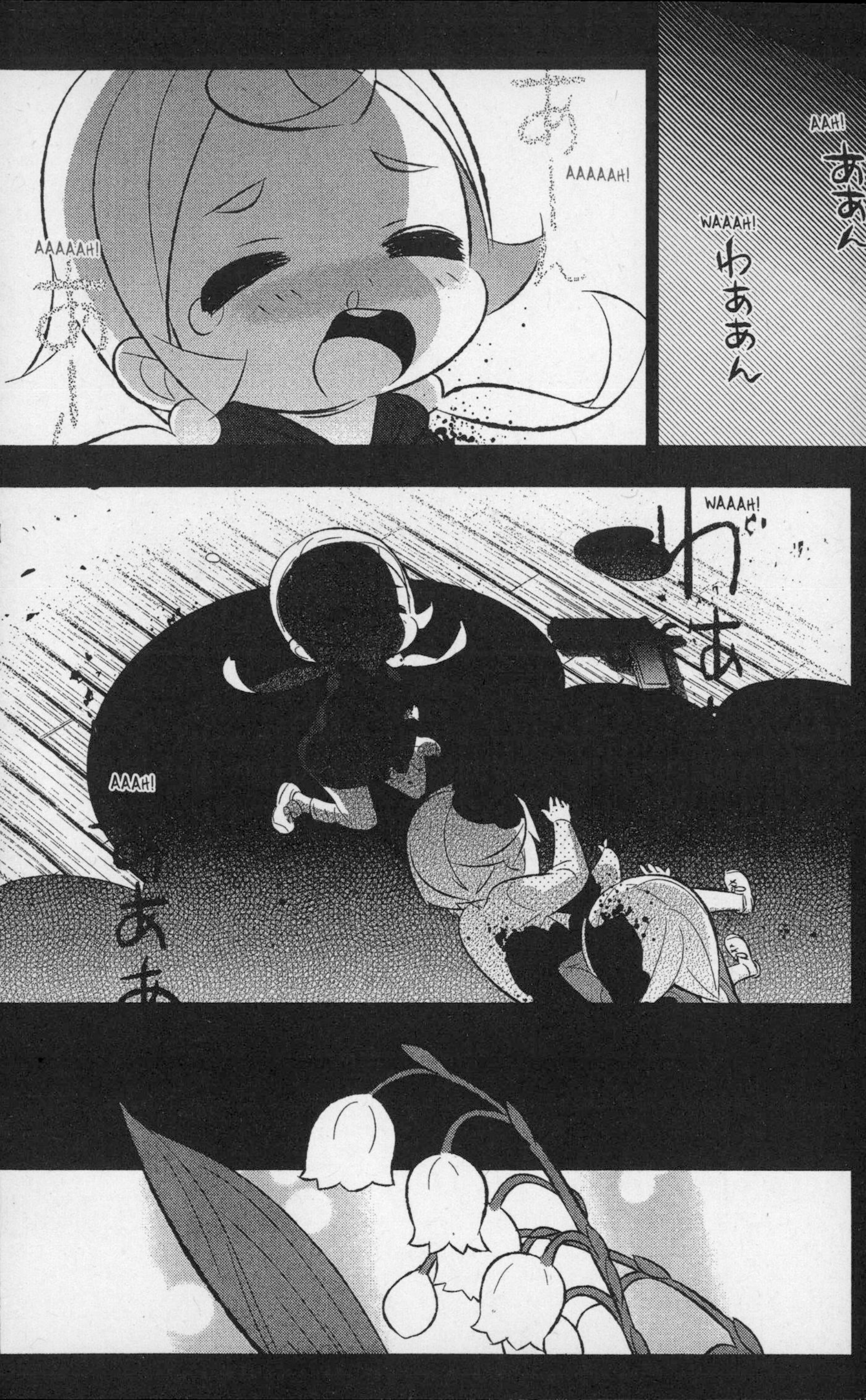
AAH!
ああん
WAAAH!
わあああん
AAAAAH!
AAAAAH!
WAAAH!
AAAH!

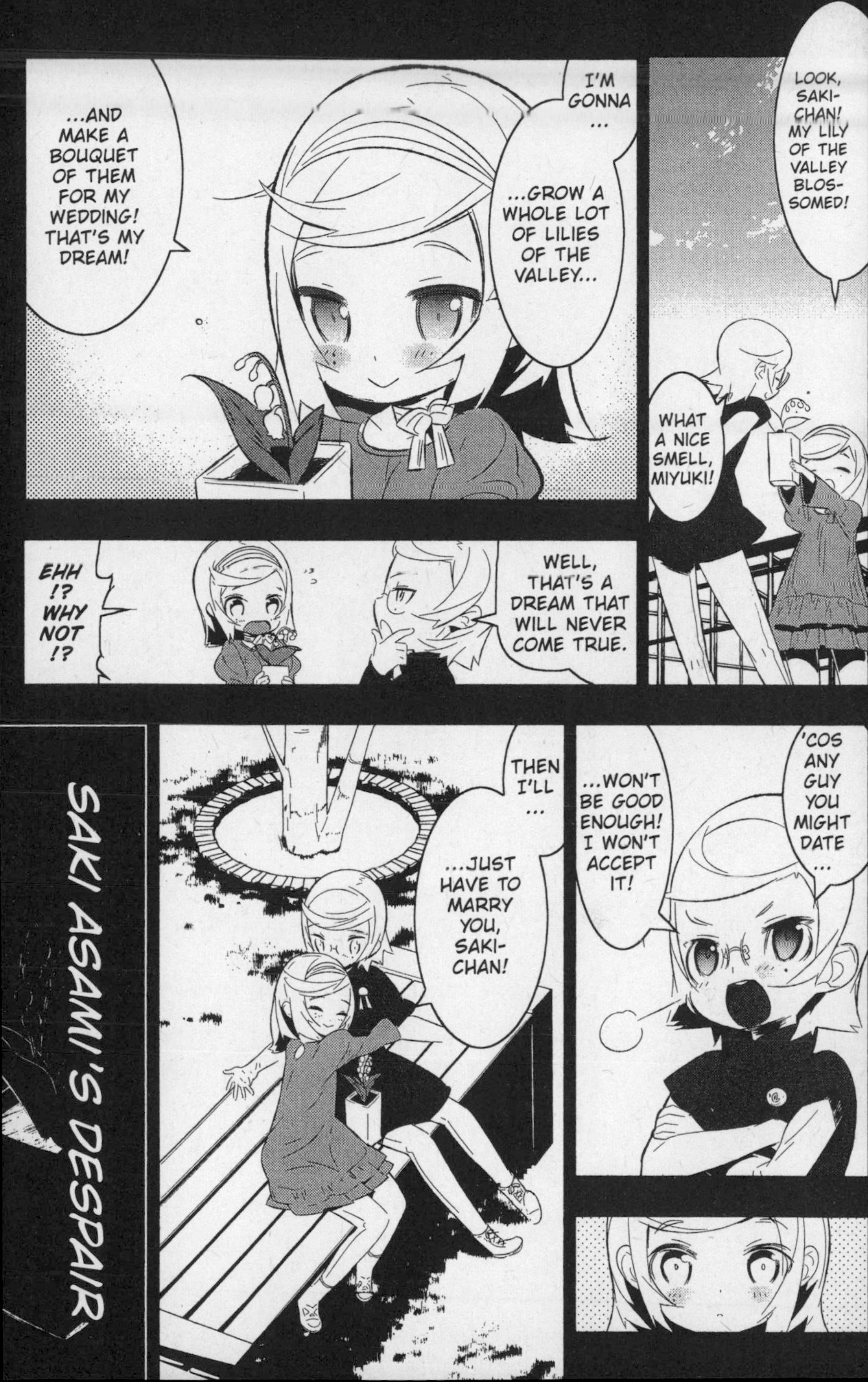
LOOK, SAKI-CHAN! MY LILY OF THE VALLEY BLOS-SOMED!
WHAT A NICE SMELL, MIYUKI!
I'M GONNA...
...GROW A WHOLE LOT OF LILIES OF THE VALLEY...
...AND MAKE A BOUQUET OF THEM FOR MY WEDDING! THAT'S MY DREAM!
WELL, THAT'S A DREAM THAT WILL NEVER COME TRUE.
EHH!? WHY NOT!?
'COS ANY GUY YOU MIGHT DATE...
...WON'T BE GOOD ENOUGH! I WON'T ACCEPT IT!
THEN I'LL...
...JUST HAVE TO MARRY YOU, SAKI-CHAN!
SAKI ASAMI'S DESPAIR

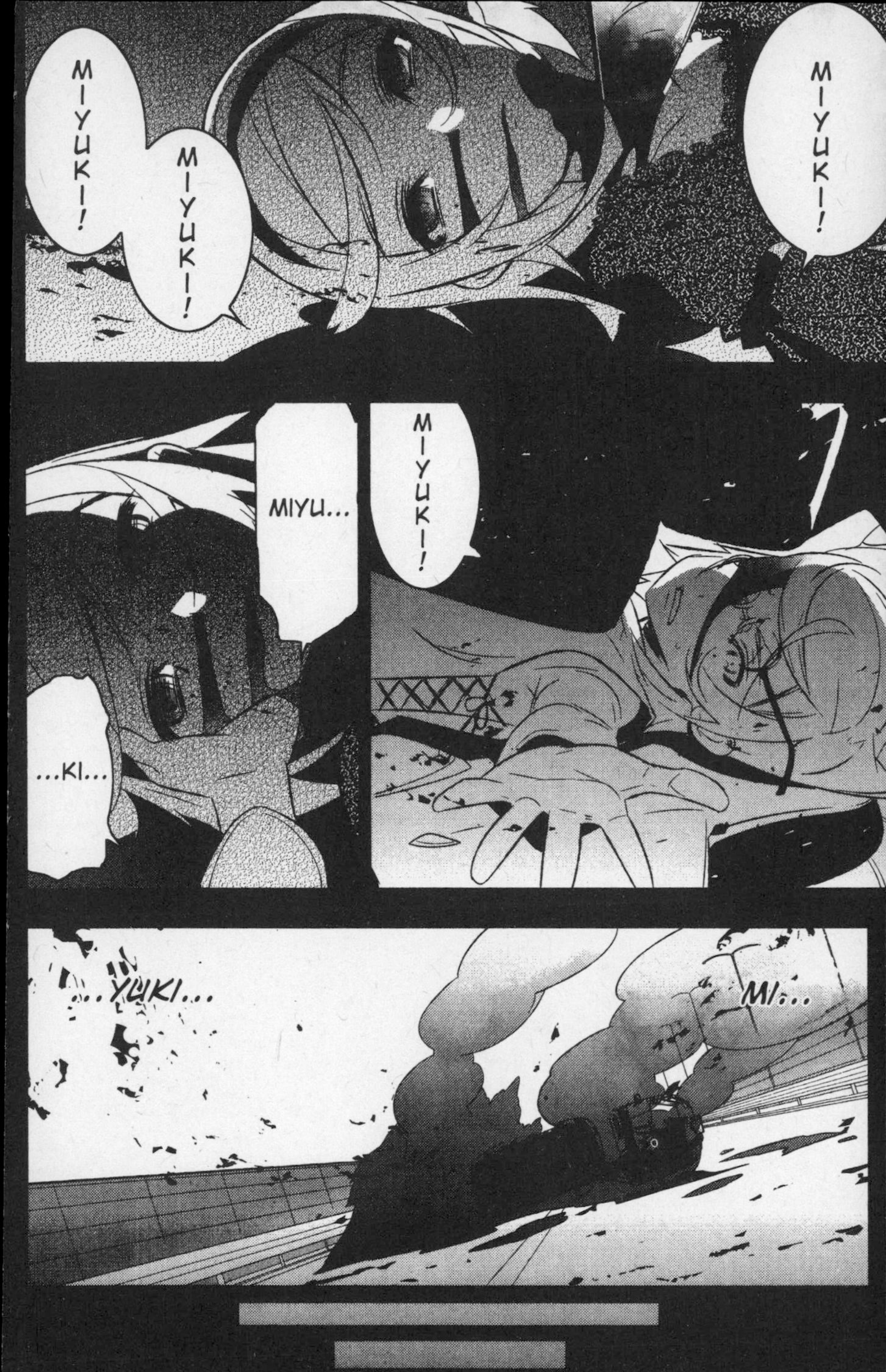
MIYUKI!
MIYUKI!
MIYUKI!
MIYUKI!
MIYU...
...KI...
MI...
...YUKI...

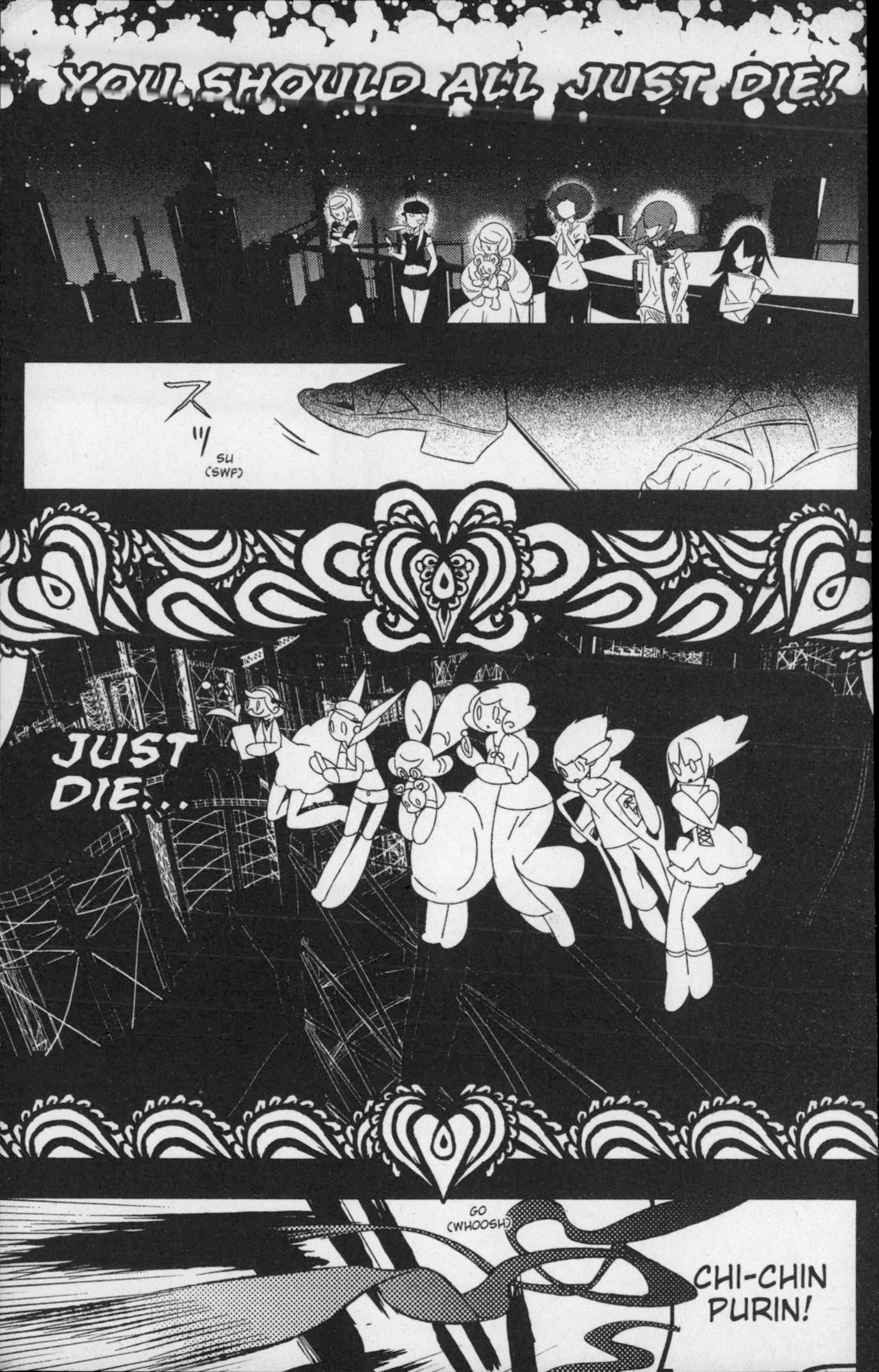
YOU SHOULD ALL JUST DIE!
スッ
SU
(SWP)
JUST DIE...
GO
(WHOOSH)
CHI-CHIN PURIN!

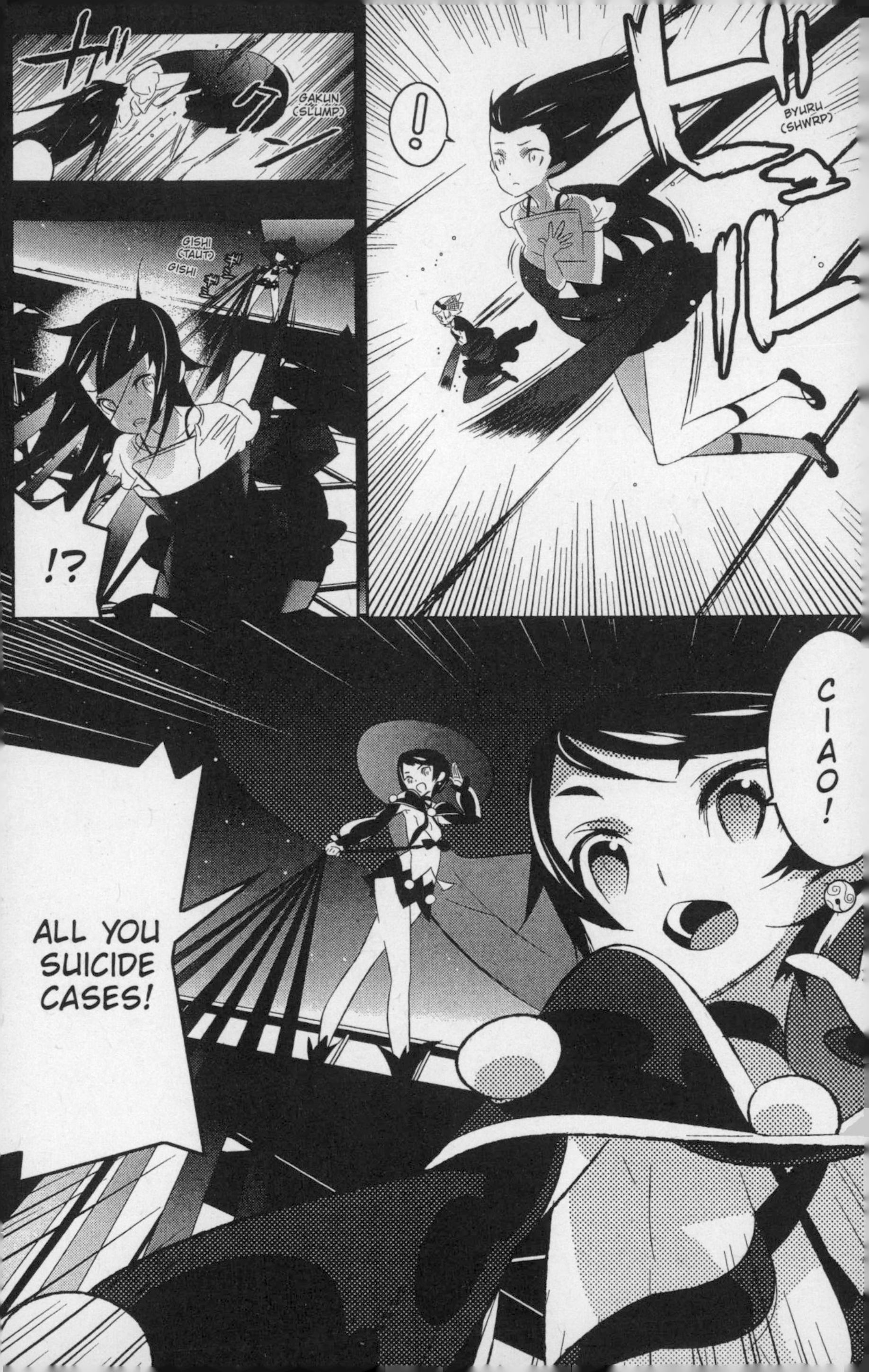
BYURU (SHWRP)
!
GAKUN (SLUMP)
GISHI (TAUT) GISHI
!?
CIAO!
ALL YOU SUICIDE CASES!

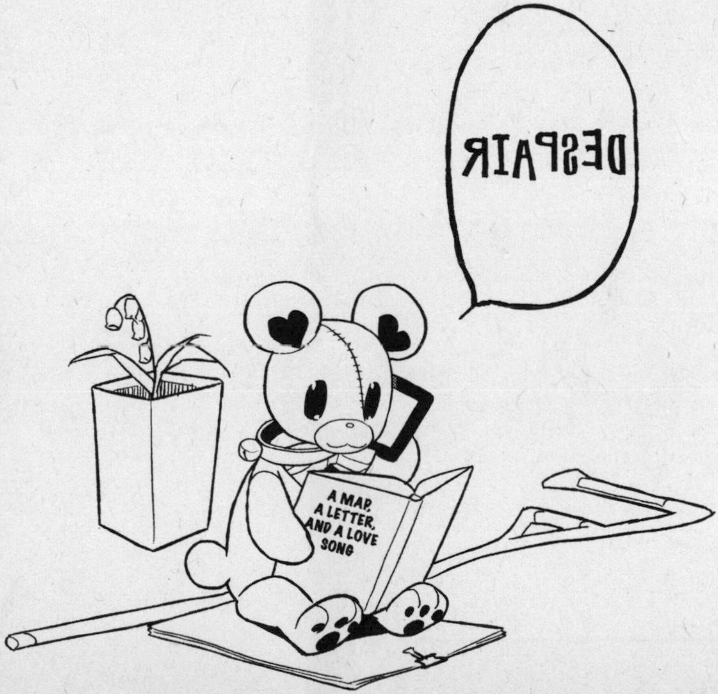
DESPAIR
A MAP, A LETTER, AND A LOVE SONG

PUELLA MAGI
KAZUMI ★ MAGICA
The innocent malice

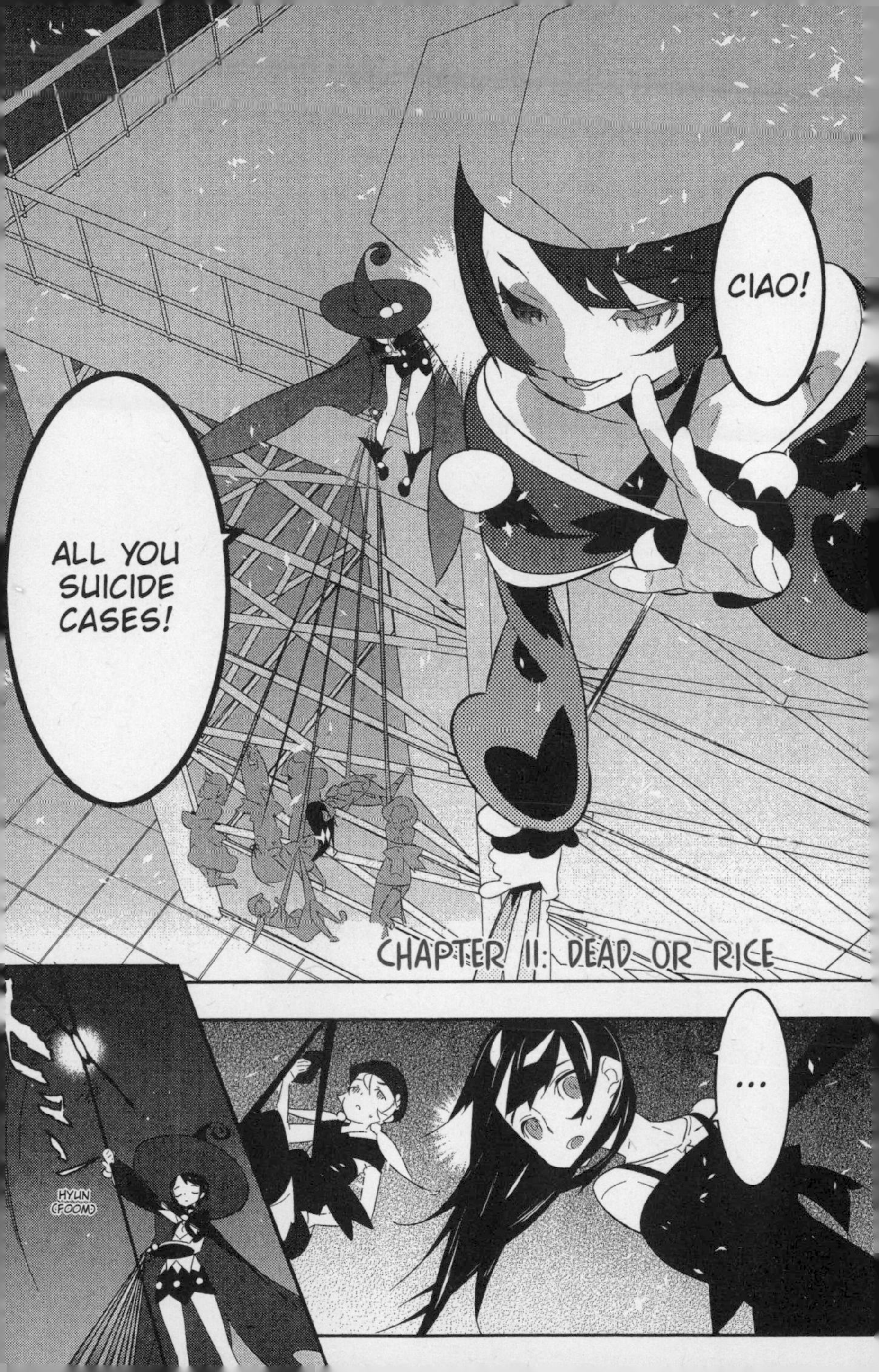
CIAO!
ALL YOU SUICIDE CASES!
CHAPTER 11: DEAD OR RICE
...
HYUN (FOOM)

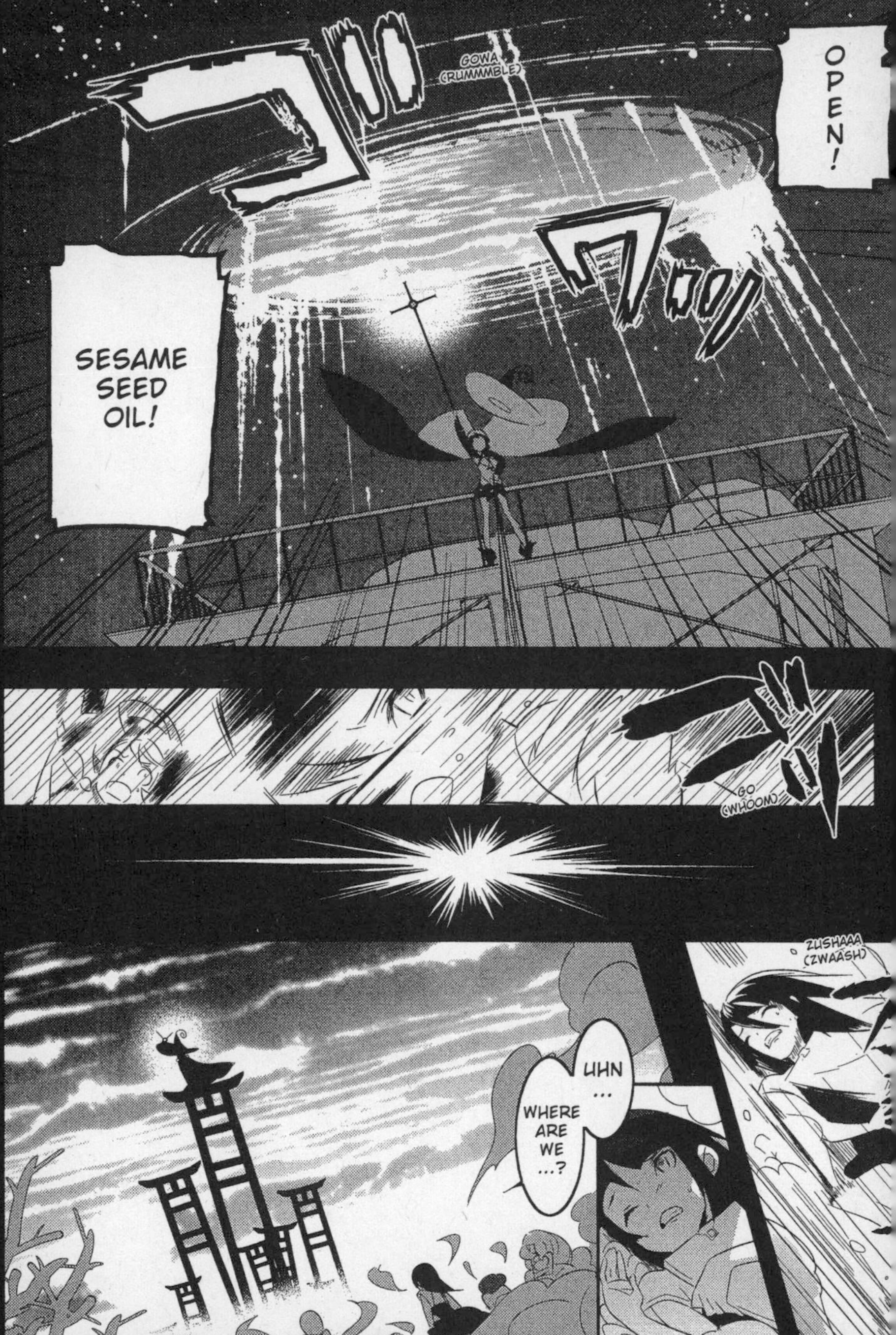
OPEN!
GOWA (RUMMMBLE)
SESAME SEED OIL!
GO (WHOOM)
ZUSHAAA (ZWAASH)
UHN ...
WHERE ARE WE ...?

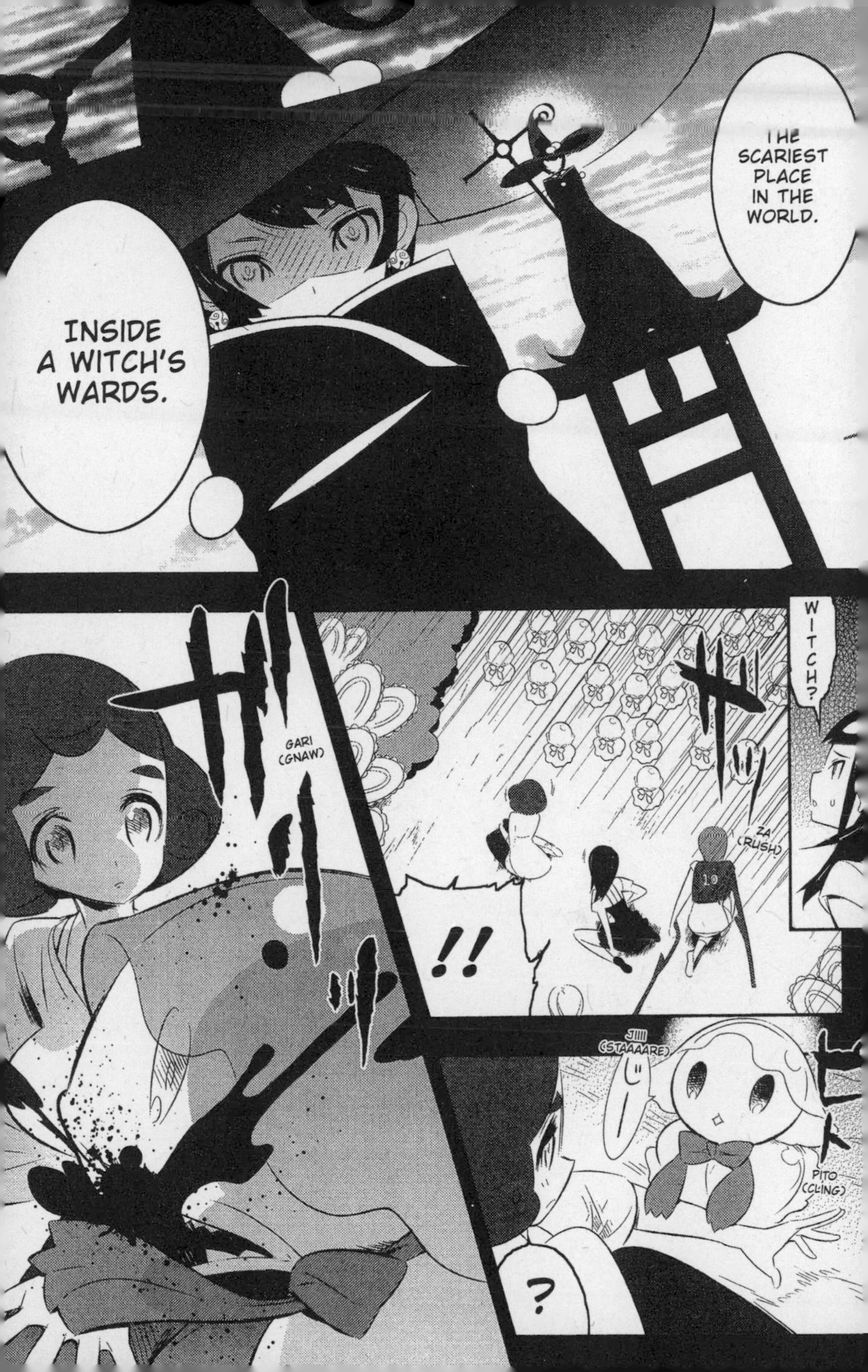

THE SCARIEST PLACE IN THE WORLD.
INSIDE A WITCH'S WARDS.
WITCH?
ZA (RUSH)
!!
JIIII (STAAAARE)
PITO (CLING)
?
GARI (GNAW)

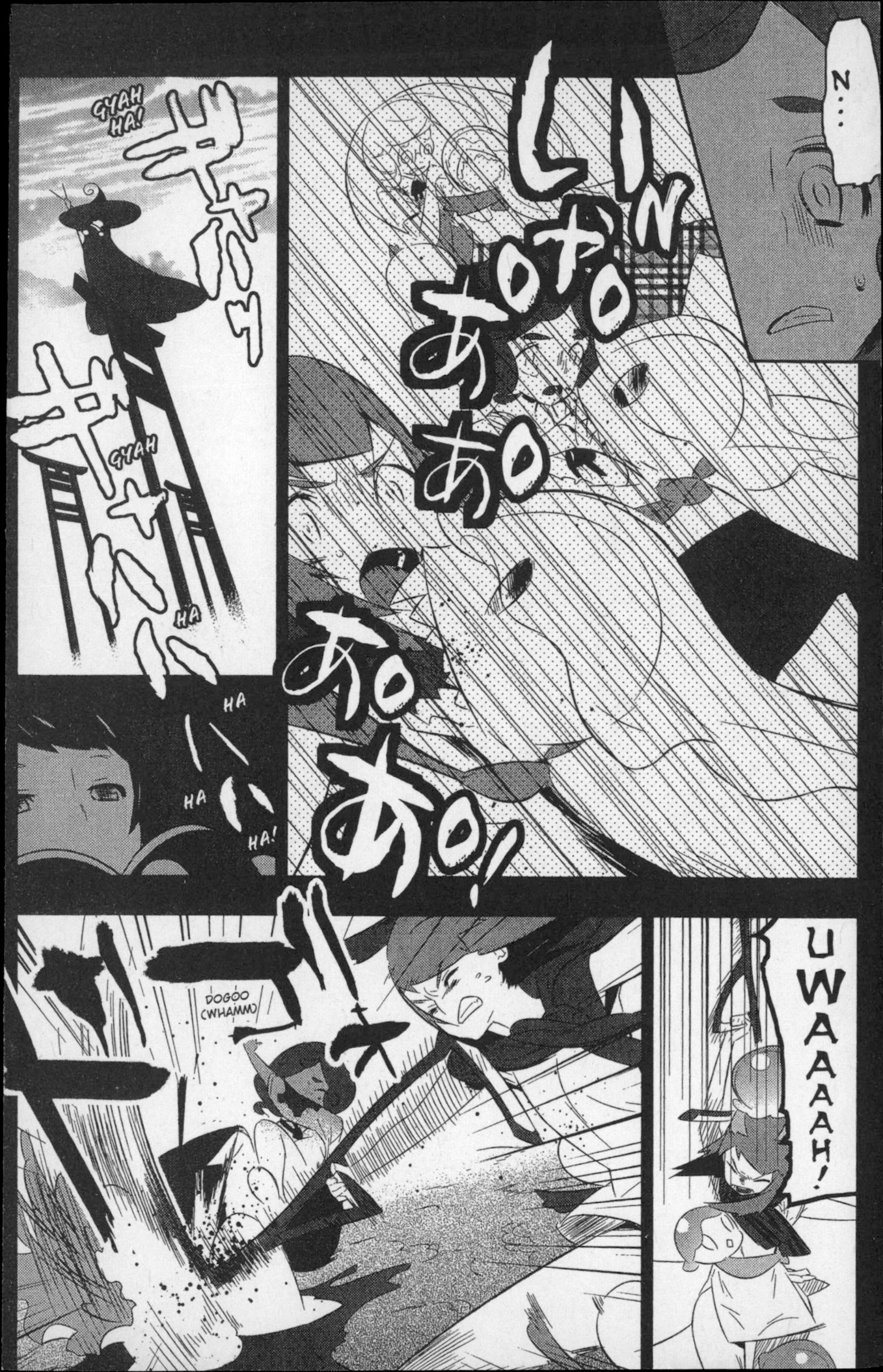
N...
GYAH HA!
GYAH
HA
HA
HA
HA!
UWAAAAH!
DOGOO (WHAMM)

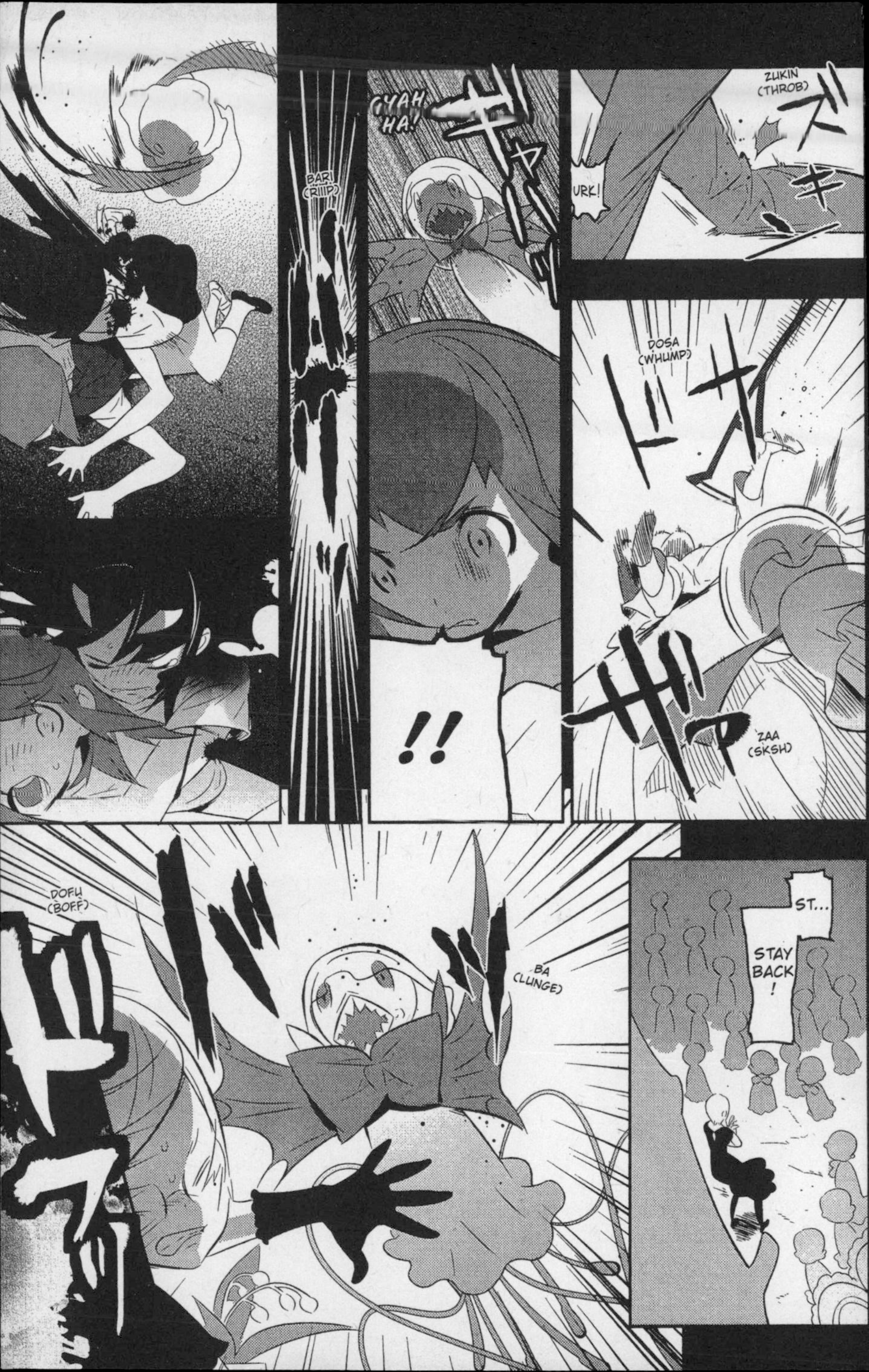
ZUKIN (THROB)
URK!
DOSA (WHUMP)
ZAA (SKSH)
YAH HA!
!!
BARI (RIIP)
ST...
STAY BACK!
BA (LUNGE)
DOFU (BOFF)

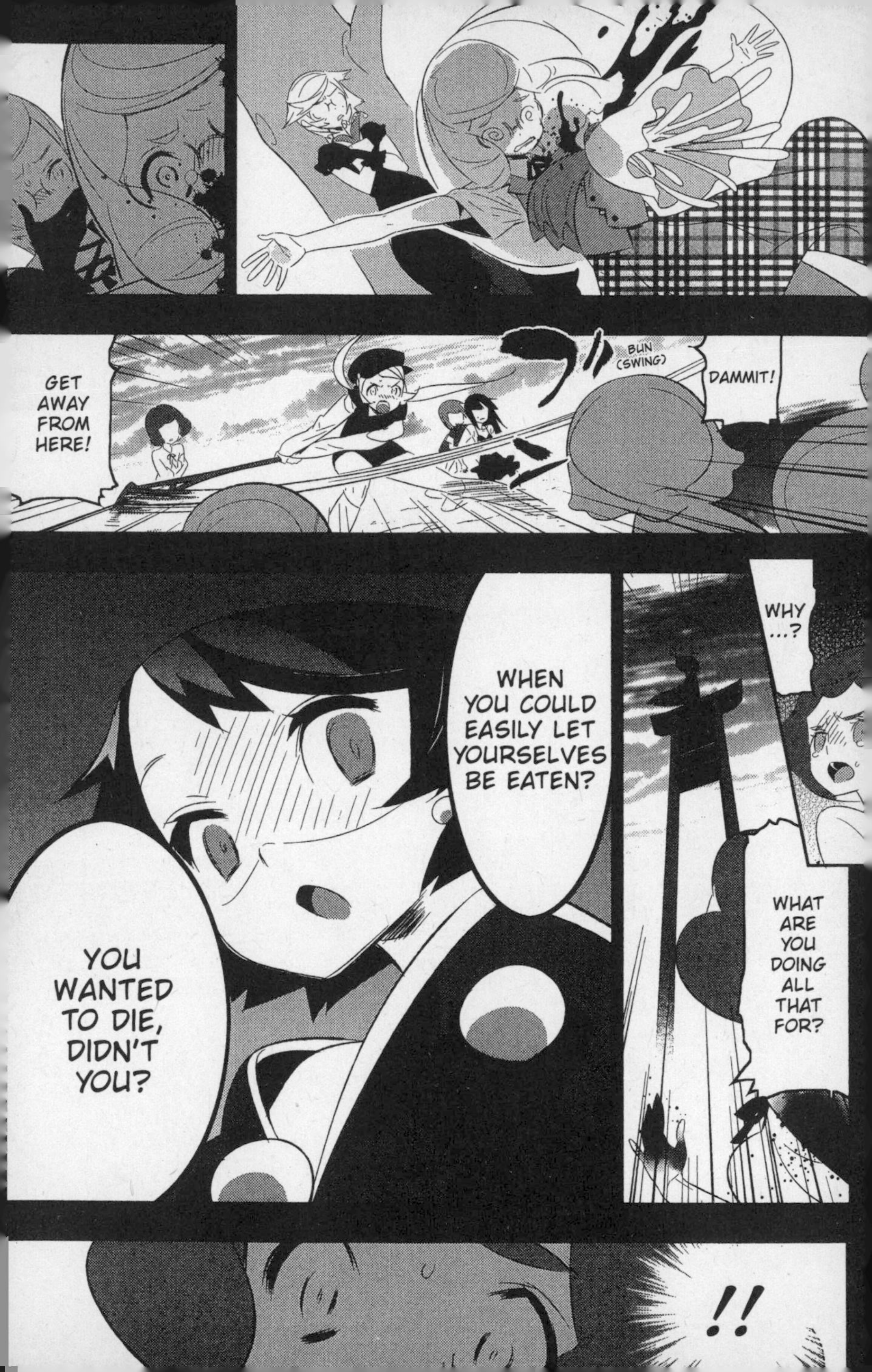
DAMMIT!
BUN (SWING)
GET AWAY FROM HERE!
WHY...?
WHAT ARE YOU DOING ALL THAT FOR?
WHEN YOU COULD EASILY LET YOURSELVES BE EATEN?
YOU WANTED TO DIE, DIDN'T YOU?
!!

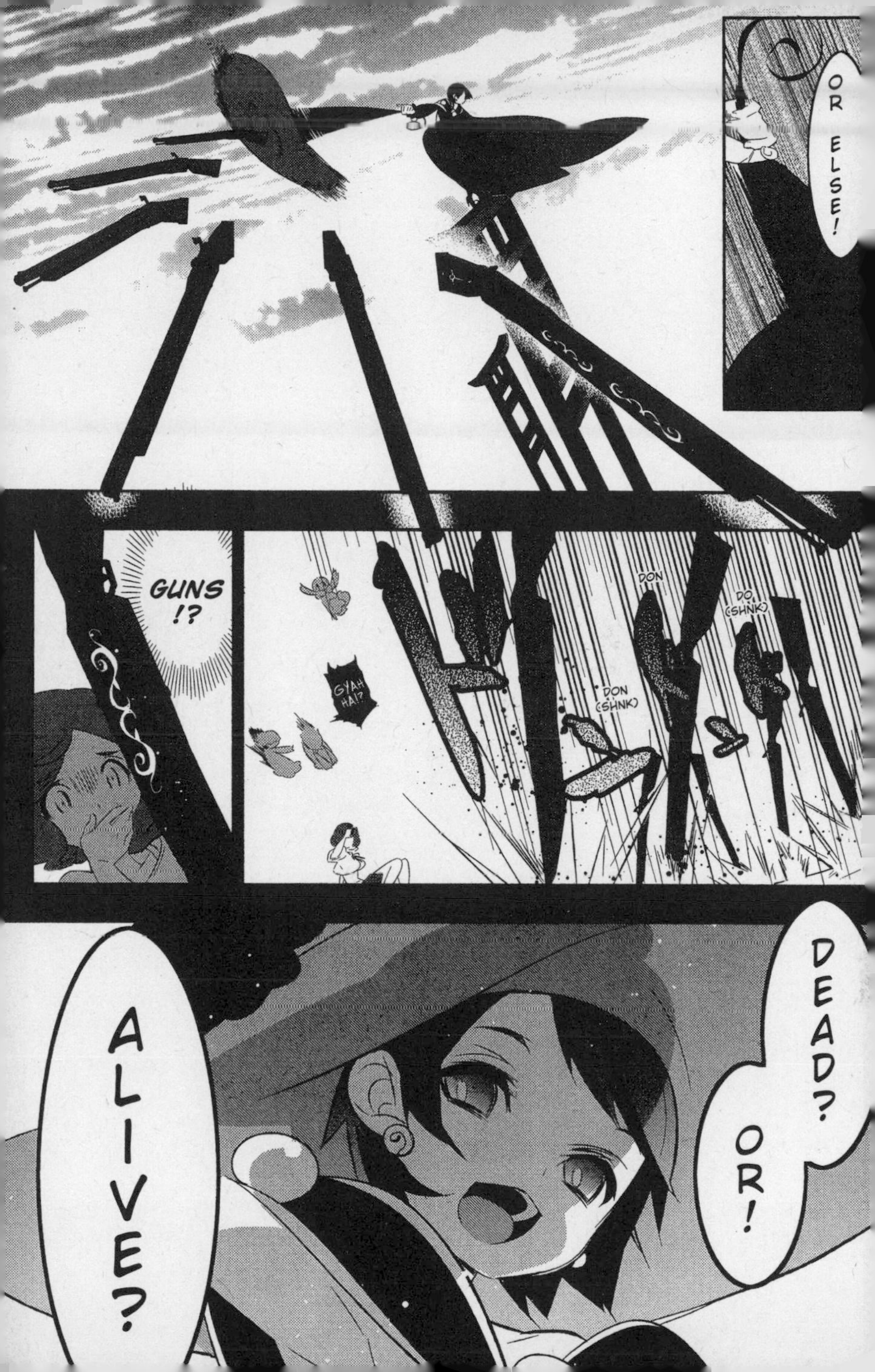
OR ELSE!
DO (SHNK)
DON
DON (SHNK)
GYAH HA!?
GUNS !?
DEAD? OR!
ALIVE?

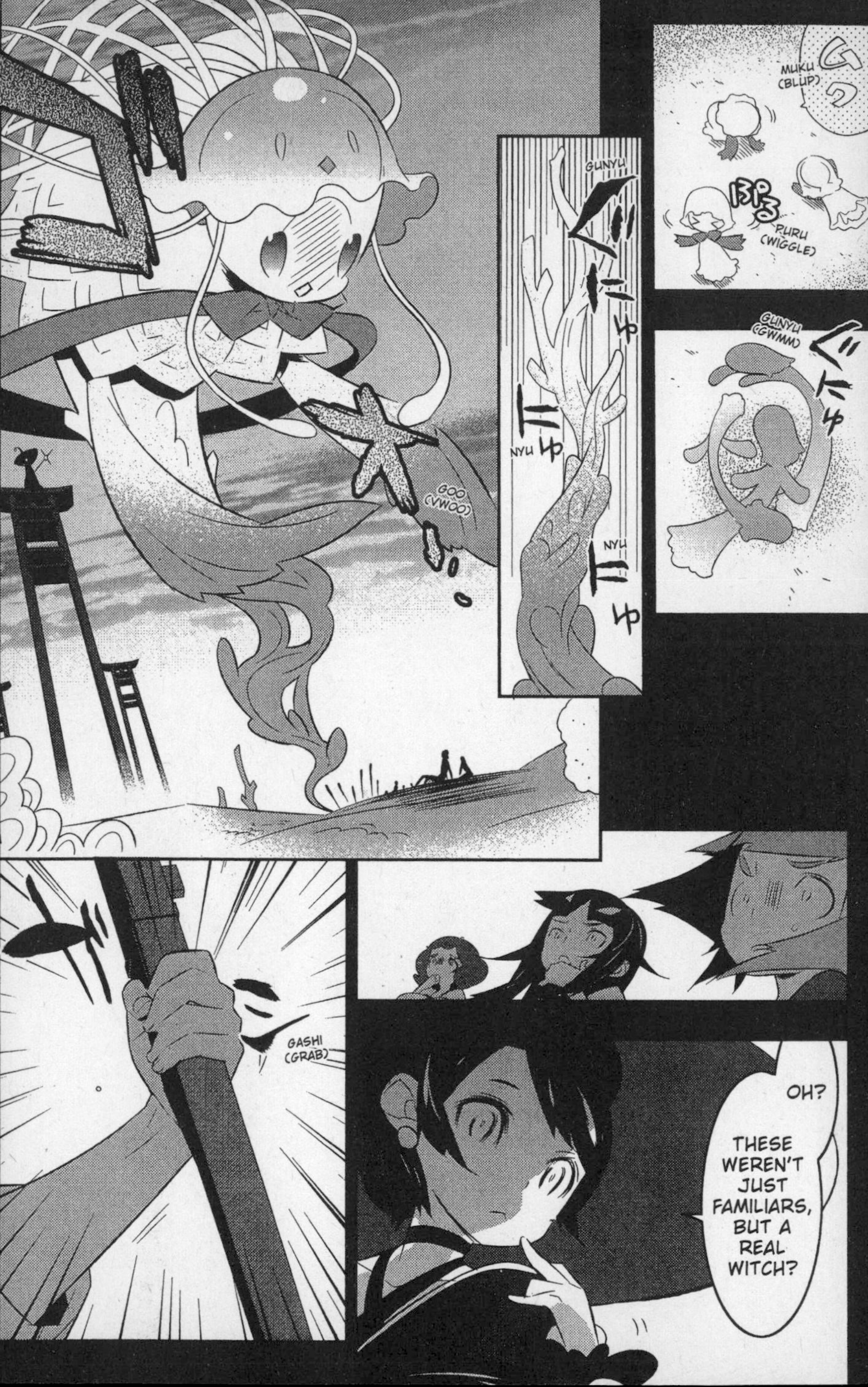
MUKU (BLUP)
PURU (WIGGLE)
GUNYU (GWMM)
GUNYU
NYU
NYU
GOO (VWOO)
OH?
THESE WEREN'T JUST FAMILIARS, BUT A REAL WITCH?
GASHI (GRAB)

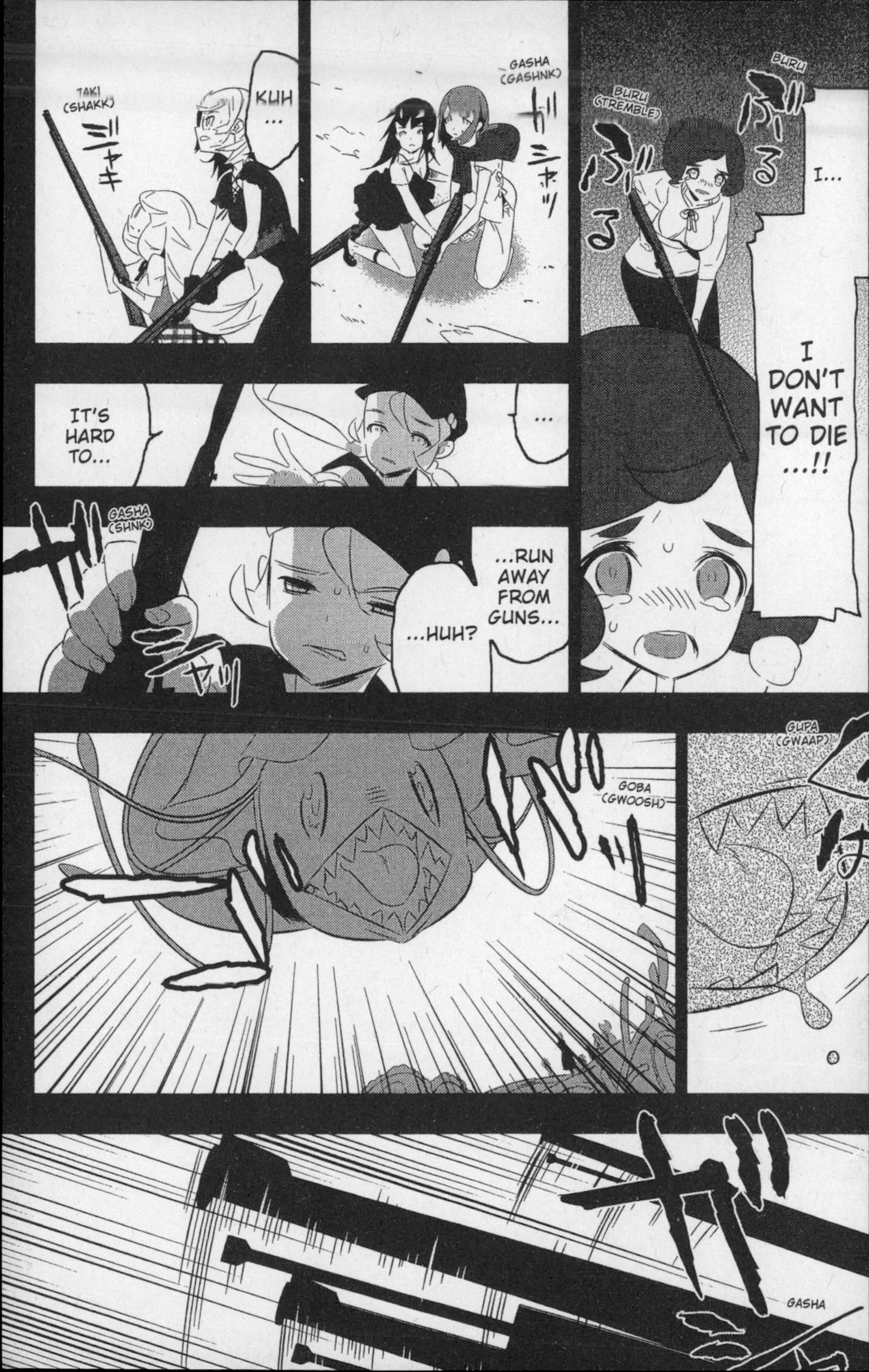
BURU
BURU (TREMBLE)
I...
GASHA (GASHNK)
KUH...
TAKI (SHAKK)
I DON'T WANT TO DIE...!!
...
IT'S HARD TO...
...RUN AWAY FROM GUNS...
...HUH?
GASHA (SHNK)
GUPA (GWAAP)
GOBA (GWOOSH)
GASHA

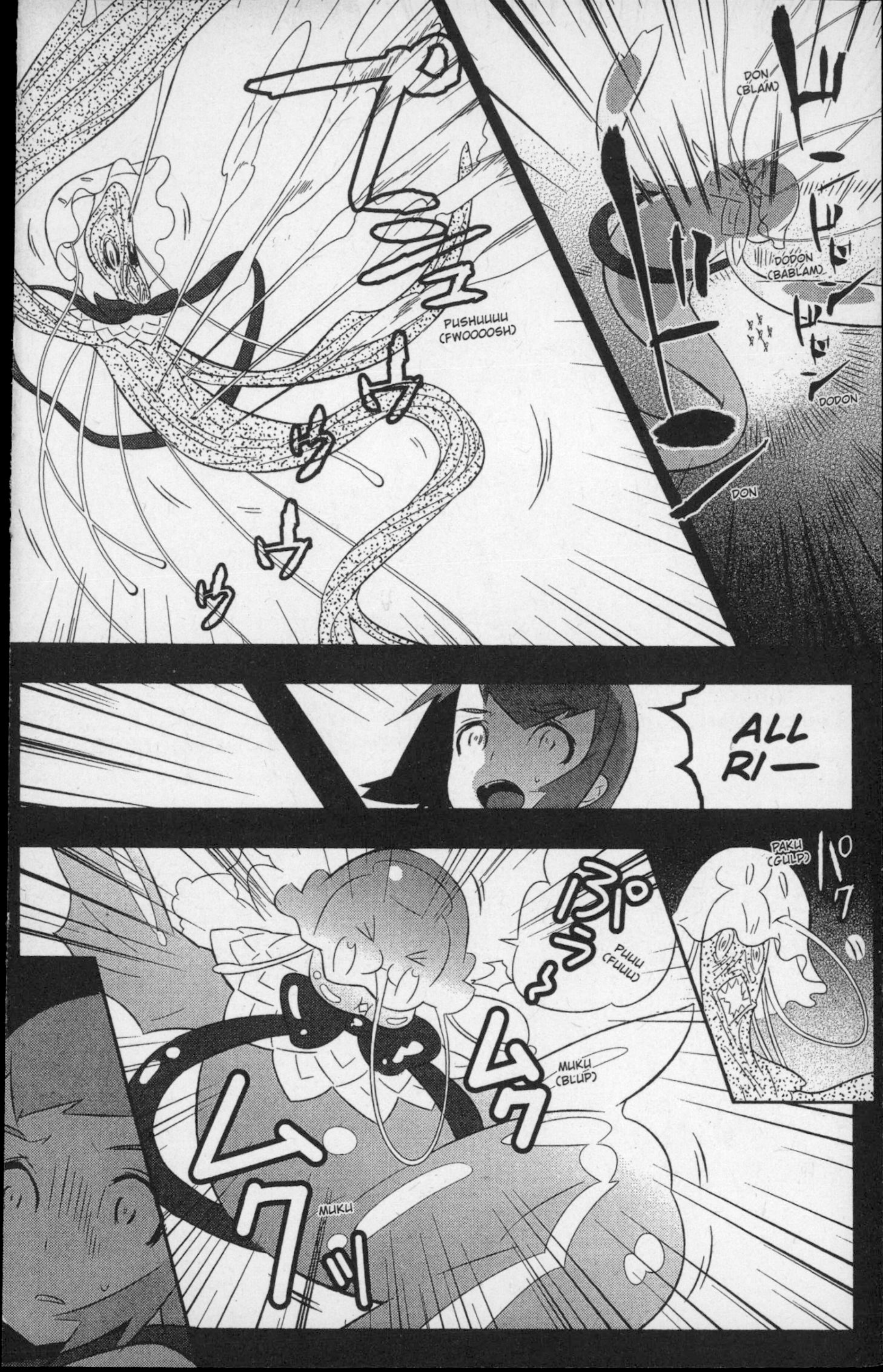
DON
(BLAM)
DODON
(BABLAM)
DODON
DON
PUSHUUUU
(FWOOOOSH)
ALL
RI—
PAKU
(GULP)
PUUU
(FUUU)
MUKU
(BLUP)
MUKU

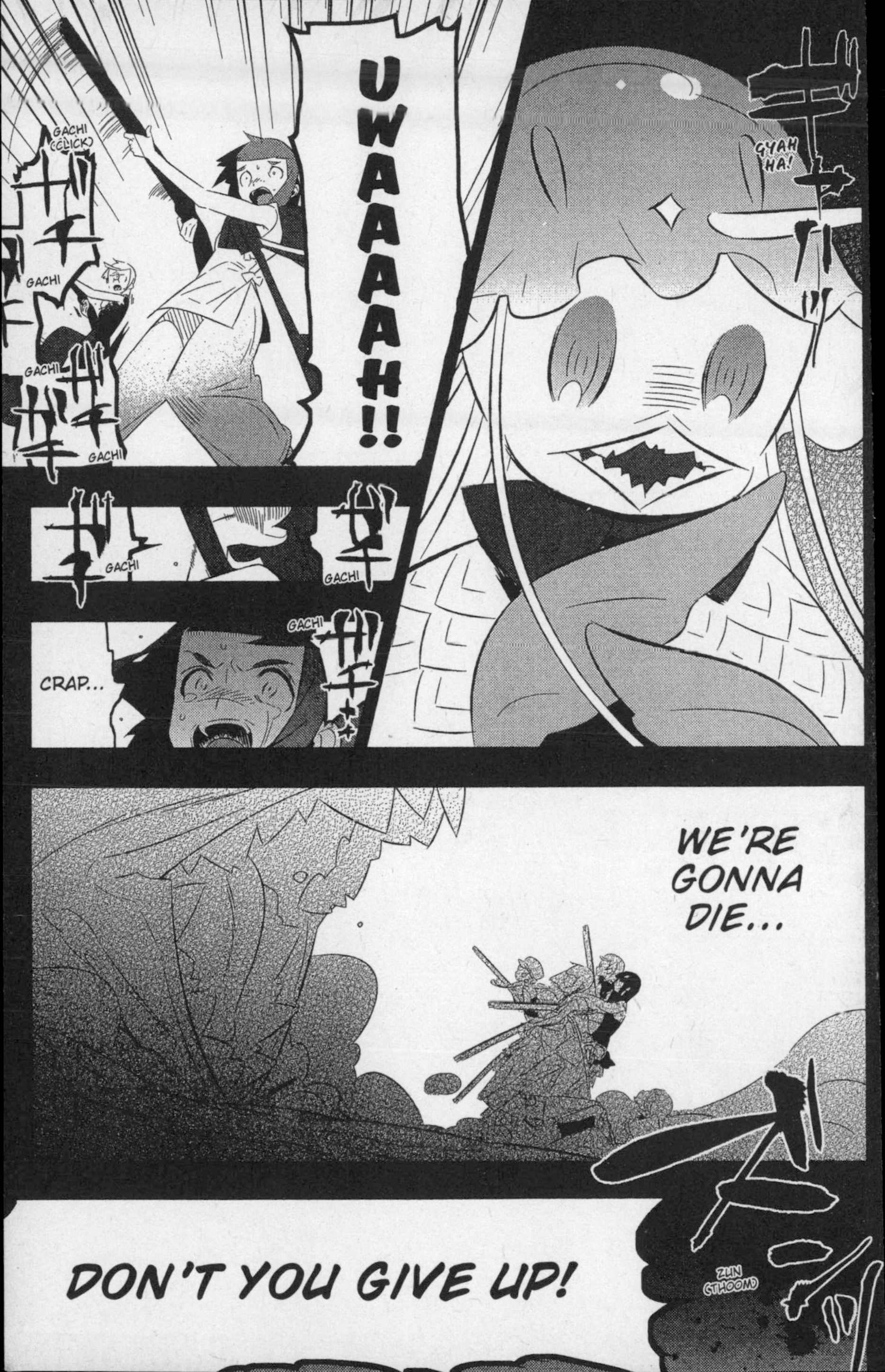
GYAH HA!
UWAAAAAH!!
GACHI (CLICK)
GACHI
GACHI
GACHI
GACHI
GACHI
GACHI
CRAP...
WE'RE GONNA DIE...
ZUN (THOOM)
DON'T YOU GIVE UP!

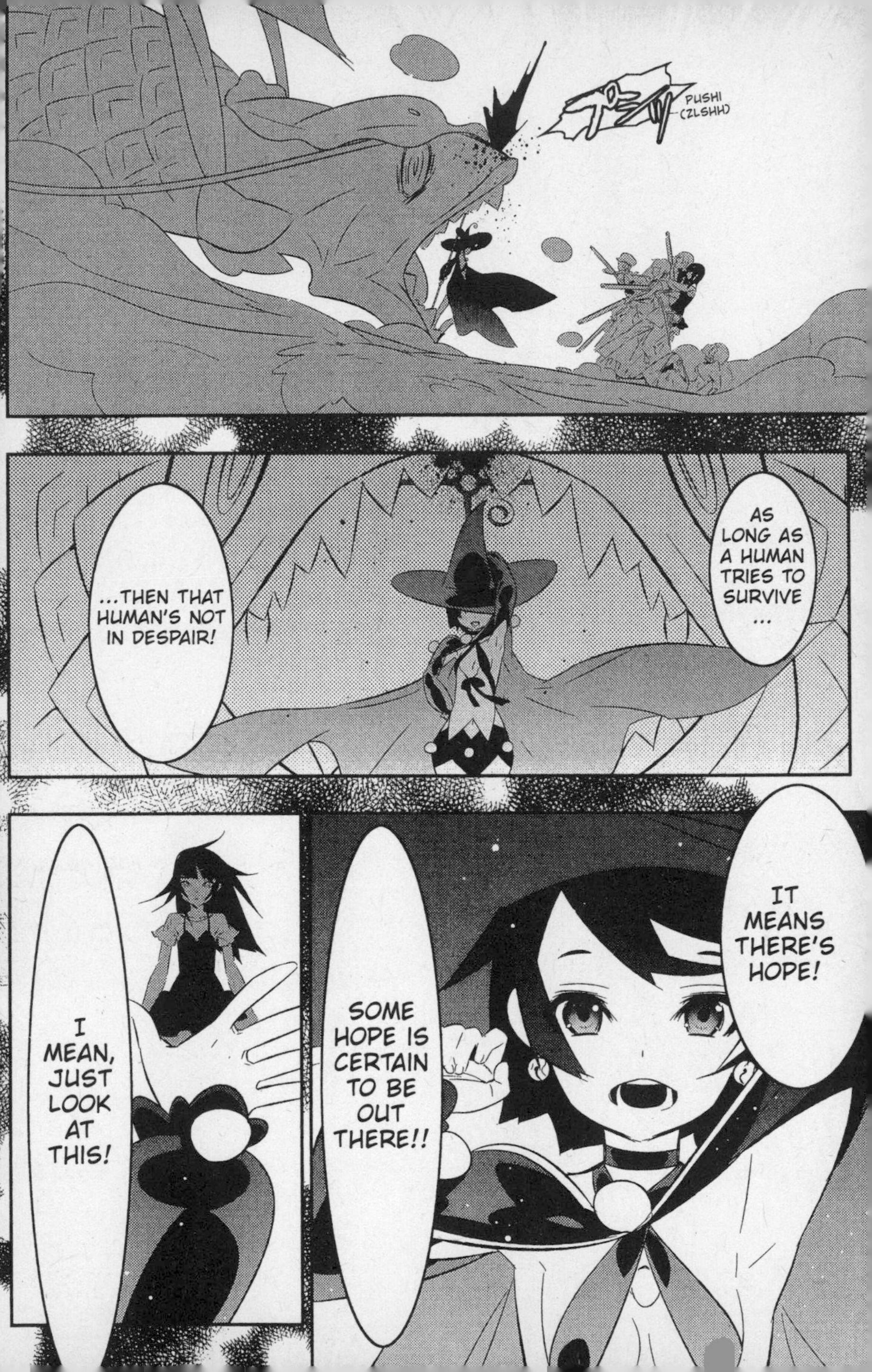
PUSHI (ZLSHH)
AS LONG AS A HUMAN TRIES TO SURVIVE ...
...THEN THAT HUMAN'S NOT IN DESPAIR!
IT MEANS THERE'S HOPE!
SOME HOPE IS CERTAIN TO BE OUT THERE!!
I MEAN, JUST LOOK AT THIS!

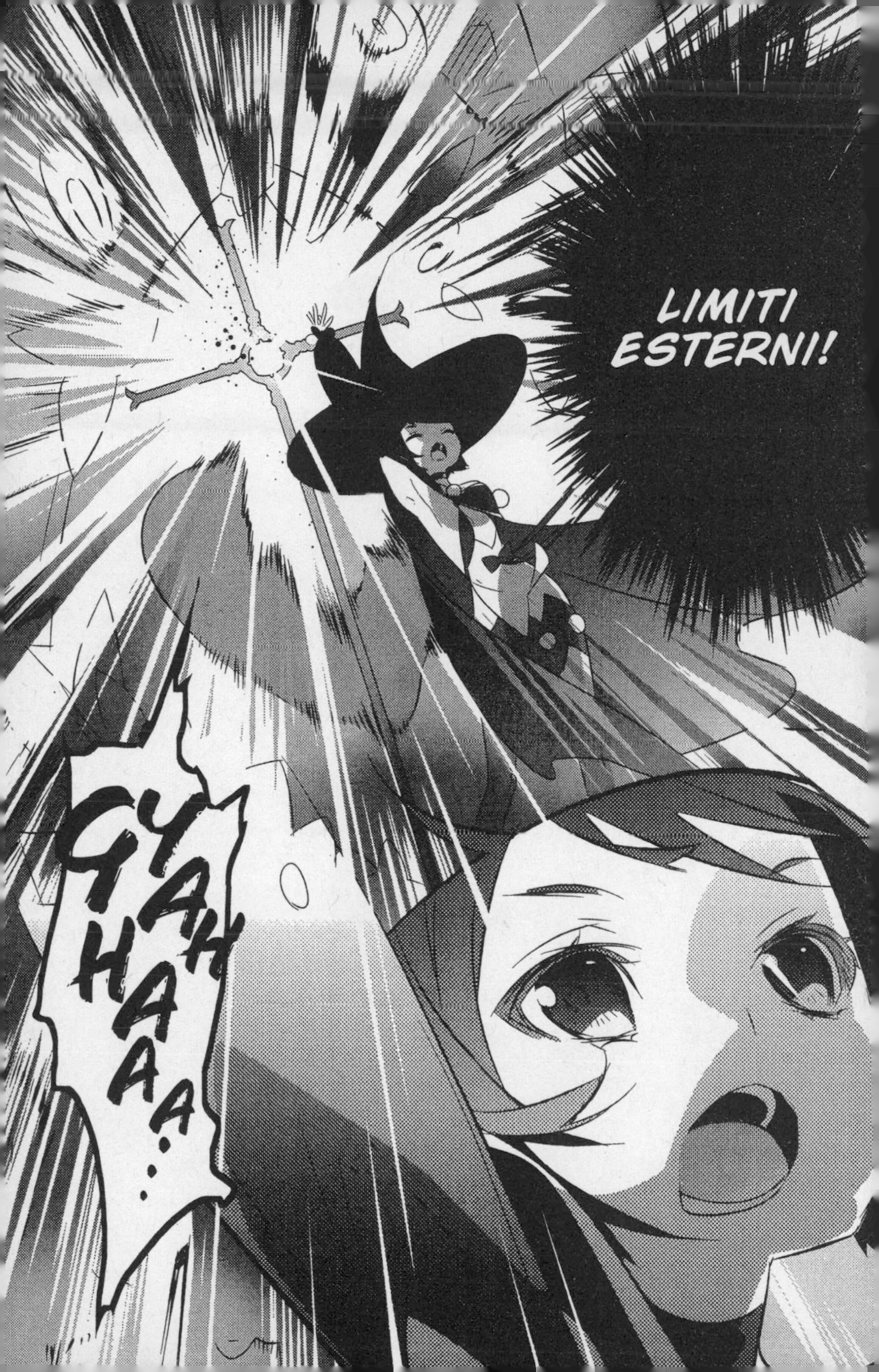
LIMITI ESTERNI!
GYAAHHAAAA?!...

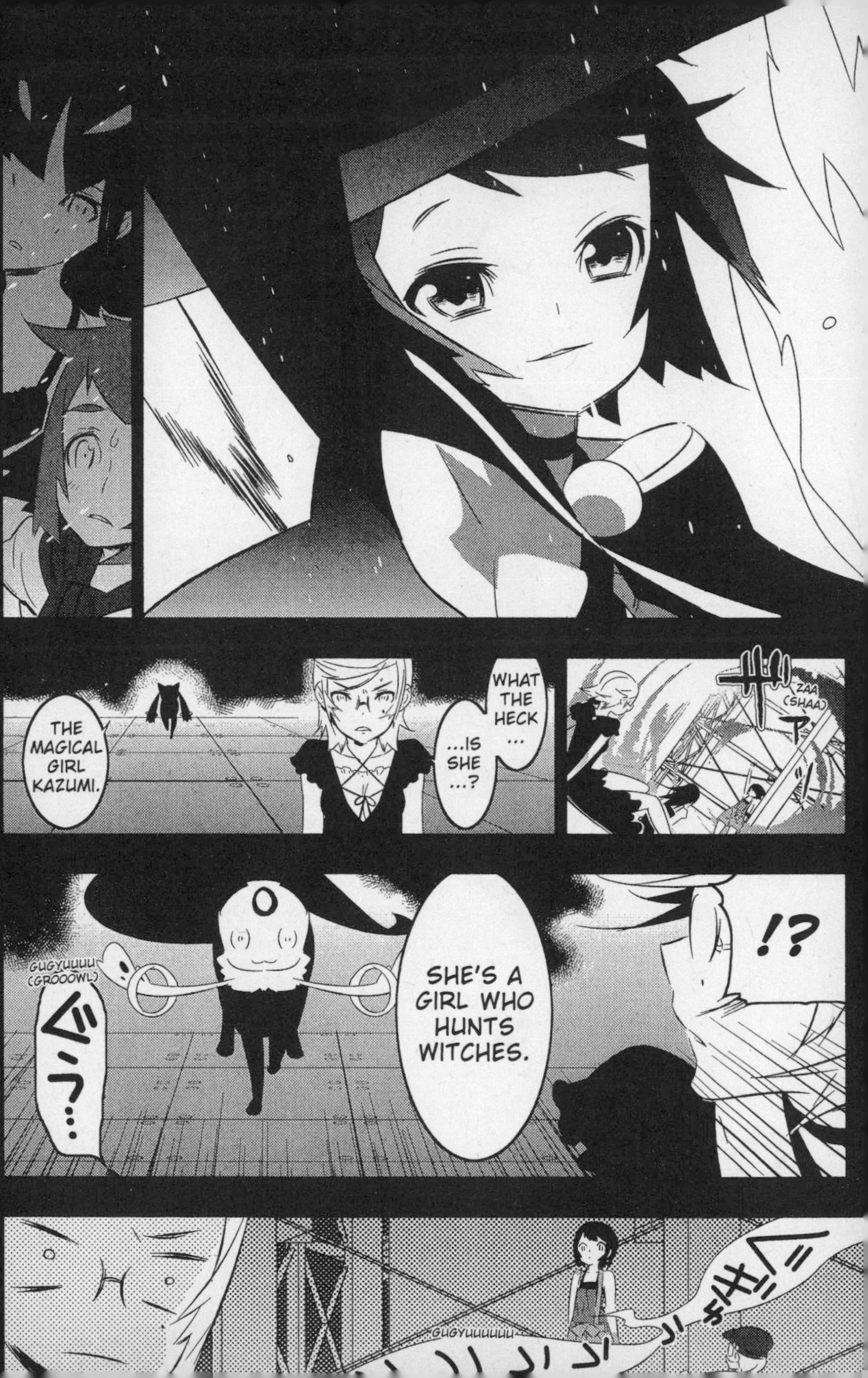
ZAA (SHAA)
WHAT THE HECK ...
...IS SHE ...?
THE MAGICAL GIRL KAZUMI.
!?
SHE'S A GIRL WHO HUNTS WITCHES.
GUGYUUUU (GROOOWL)
GUGYUUUUUU

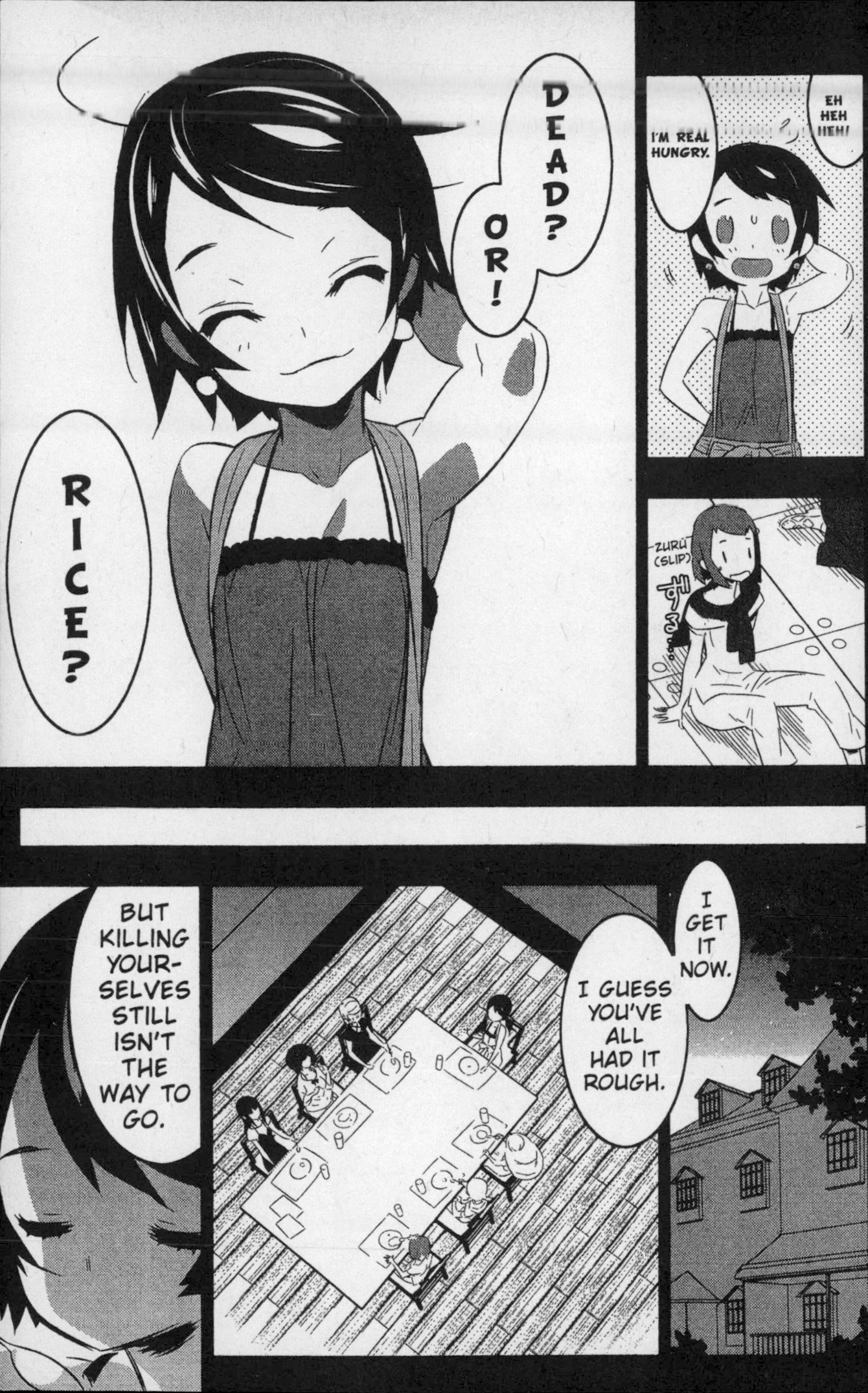
EH HEH HEH!
I'M REAL HUNGRY.
ZURU (SLIP)
ずる…
DEAD?
OR!
RICE?
I GET IT NOW.
I GUESS YOU'VE ALL HAD IT ROUGH.
BUT KILLING YOURSELVES STILL ISN'T THE WAY TO GO.

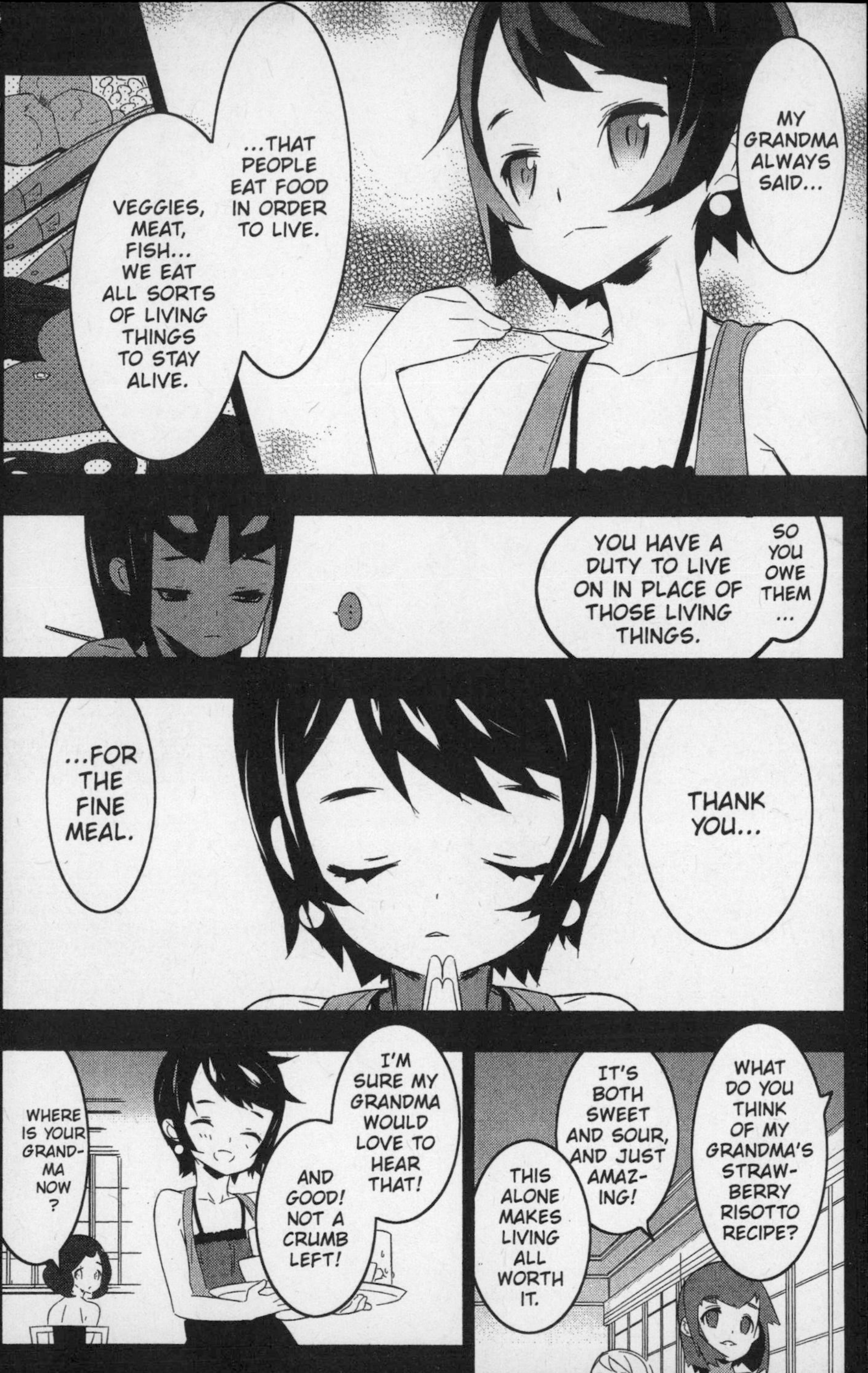
MY GRANDMA ALWAYS SAID...
...THAT PEOPLE EAT FOOD IN ORDER TO LIVE.
VEGGIES, MEAT, FISH... WE EAT ALL SORTS OF LIVING THINGS TO STAY ALIVE.
SO YOU OWE THEM ...
YOU HAVE A DUTY TO LIVE ON IN PLACE OF THOSE LIVING THINGS.
...
THANK YOU...
...FOR THE FINE MEAL.
WHAT DO YOU THINK OF MY GRANDMA'S STRAWBERRY RISOTTO RECIPE?
IT'S BOTH SWEET AND SOUR, AND JUST AMAZING!
THIS ALONE MAKES LIVING ALL WORTH IT.
I'M SURE MY GRANDMA WOULD LOVE TO HEAR THAT!
AND GOOD! NOT A CRUMB LEFT!
WHERE IS YOUR GRANDMA NOW?

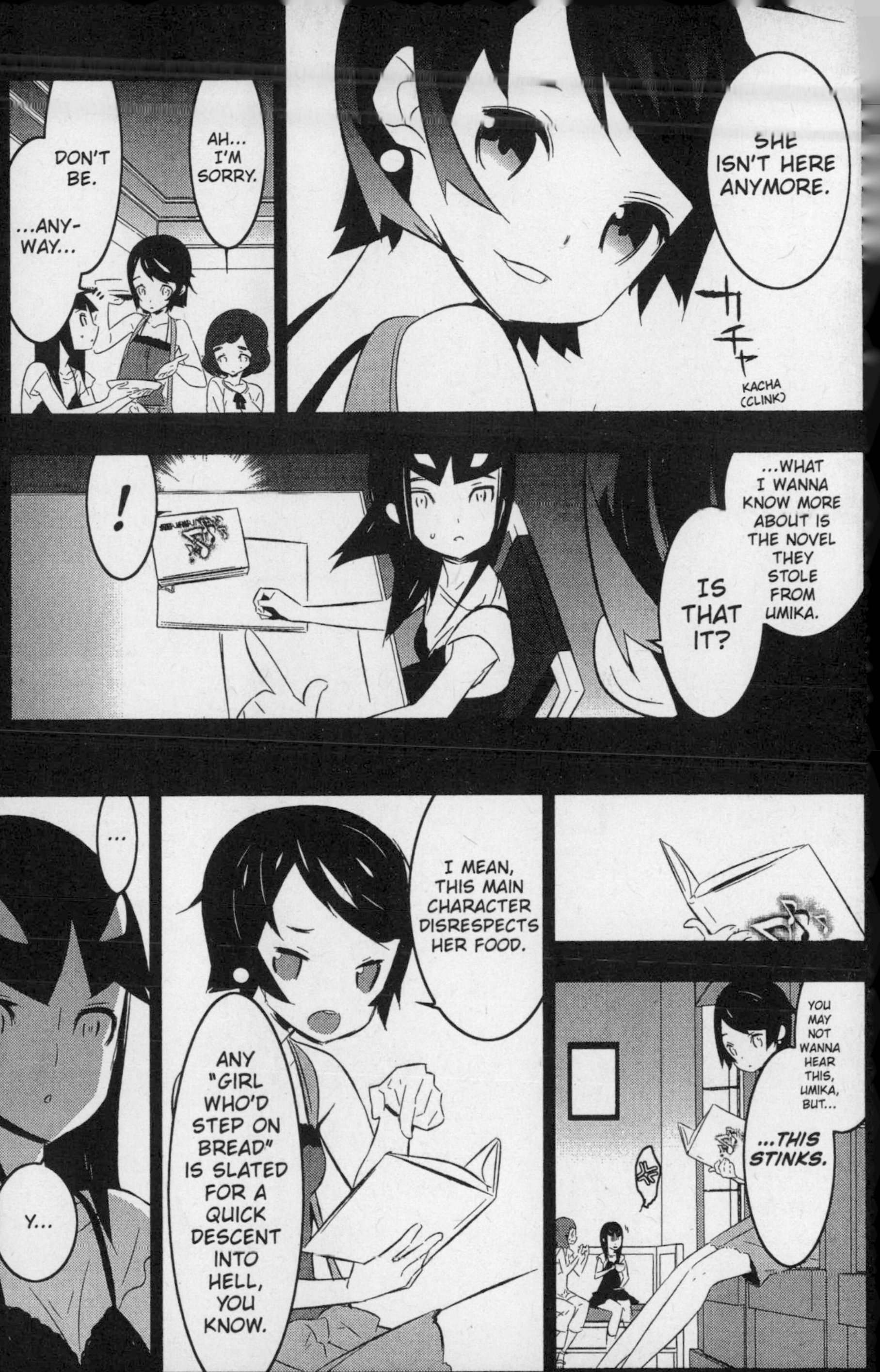
SHE ISN'T HERE ANYMORE.
KACHA (CLINK)
AH... I'M SORRY.
DON'T BE.
...ANY-WAY...
...WHAT I WANNA KNOW MORE ABOUT IS THE NOVEL THEY STOLE FROM UMIKA.
IS THAT IT?
!
YOU MAY NOT WANNA HEAR THIS, UMIKA, BUT...
...THIS STINKS.
I MEAN, THIS MAIN CHARACTER DISRESPECTS HER FOOD.
ANY "GIRL WHO'D STEP ON BREAD" IS SLATED FOR A QUICK DESCENT INTO HELL, YOU KNOW.
...
Y...

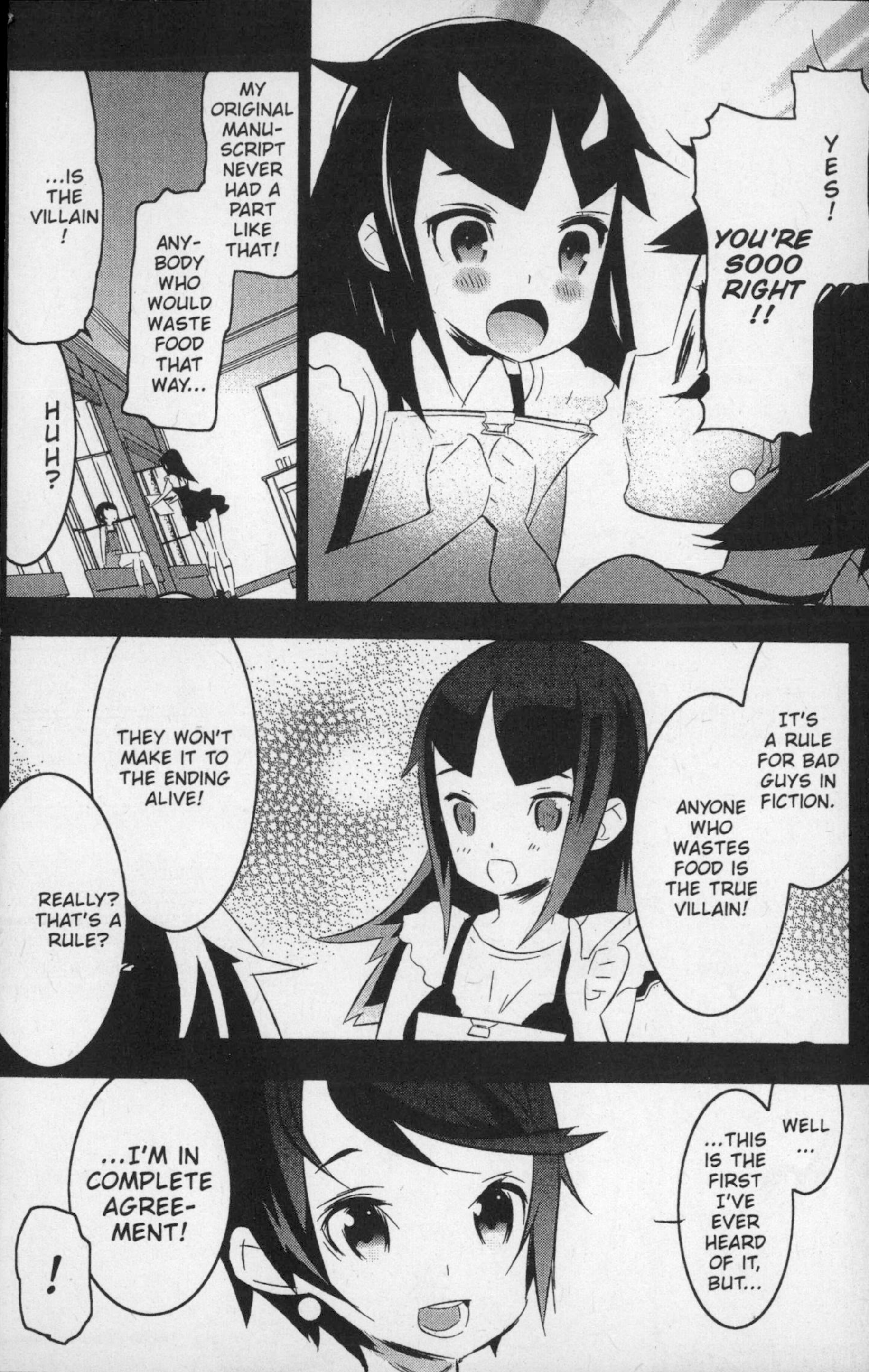
YES!
YOU'RE SOOO RIGHT!!
MY ORIGINAL MANUSCRIPT NEVER HAD A PART LIKE THAT!
ANYBODY WHO WOULD WASTE FOOD THAT WAY...
...IS THE VILLAIN!
HUH?
IT'S A RULE FOR BAD GUYS IN FICTION.
ANYONE WHO WASTES FOOD IS THE TRUE VILLAIN!
THEY WON'T MAKE IT TO THE ENDING ALIVE!
REALLY? THAT'S A RULE?
WELL...
...THIS IS THE FIRST I'VE EVER HEARD OF IT, BUT...
...I'M IN COMPLETE AGREEMENT!
!

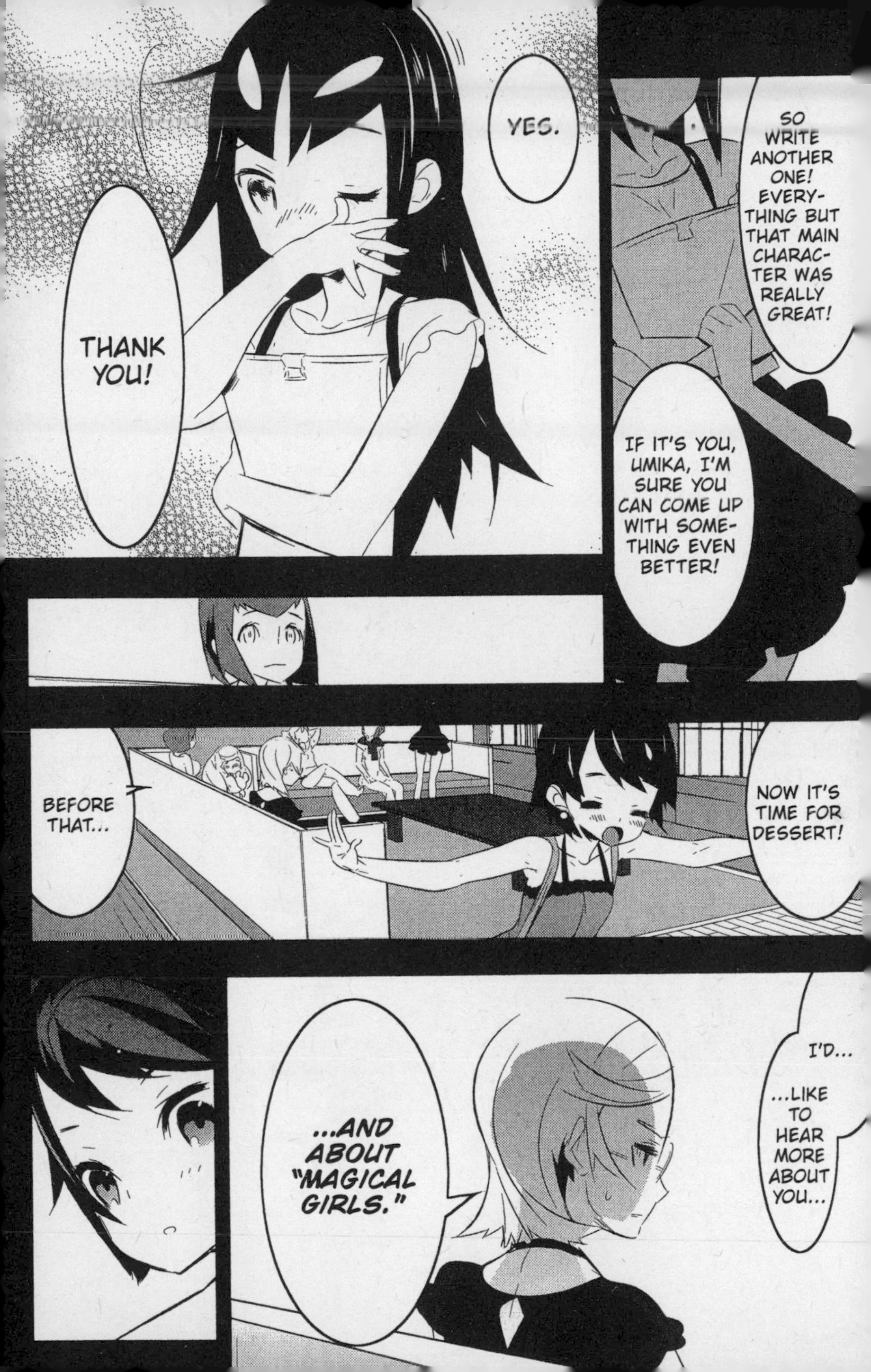
SO WRITE ANOTHER ONE! EVERYTHING BUT THAT MAIN CHARACTER WAS REALLY GREAT!
IF IT'S YOU, UMIKA, I'M SURE YOU CAN COME UP WITH SOMETHING EVEN BETTER!
YES.
THANK YOU!
NOW IT'S TIME FOR DESSERT!
BEFORE THAT...
I'D...
...LIKE TO HEAR MORE ABOUT YOU...
...AND ABOUT "MAGICAL GIRLS."

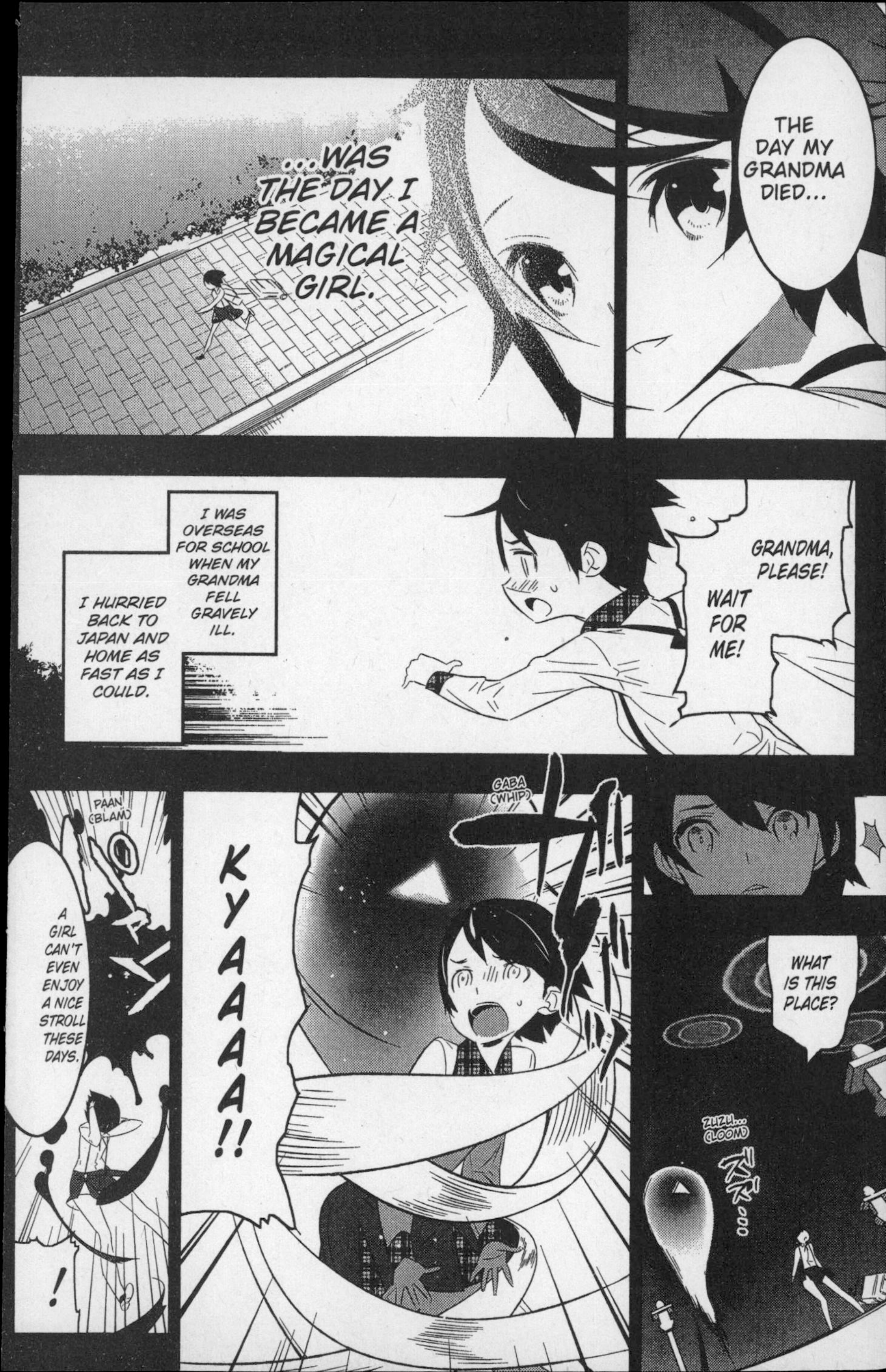
THE DAY MY GRANDMA DIED...
...WAS THE DAY I BECAME A MAGICAL GIRL.
GRANDMA, PLEASE!
WAIT FOR ME!
I WAS OVERSEAS FOR SCHOOL WHEN MY GRANDMA FELL GRAVELY ILL.
I HURRIED BACK TO JAPAN AND HOME AS FAST AS I COULD.
WHAT IS THIS PLACE?
ZUZU... (LOOM)
GABA (WHIP)
KYAAAAA!!
PAAN (BLAM)
A GIRL CAN'T EVEN ENJOY A NICE STROLL THESE DAYS.
!

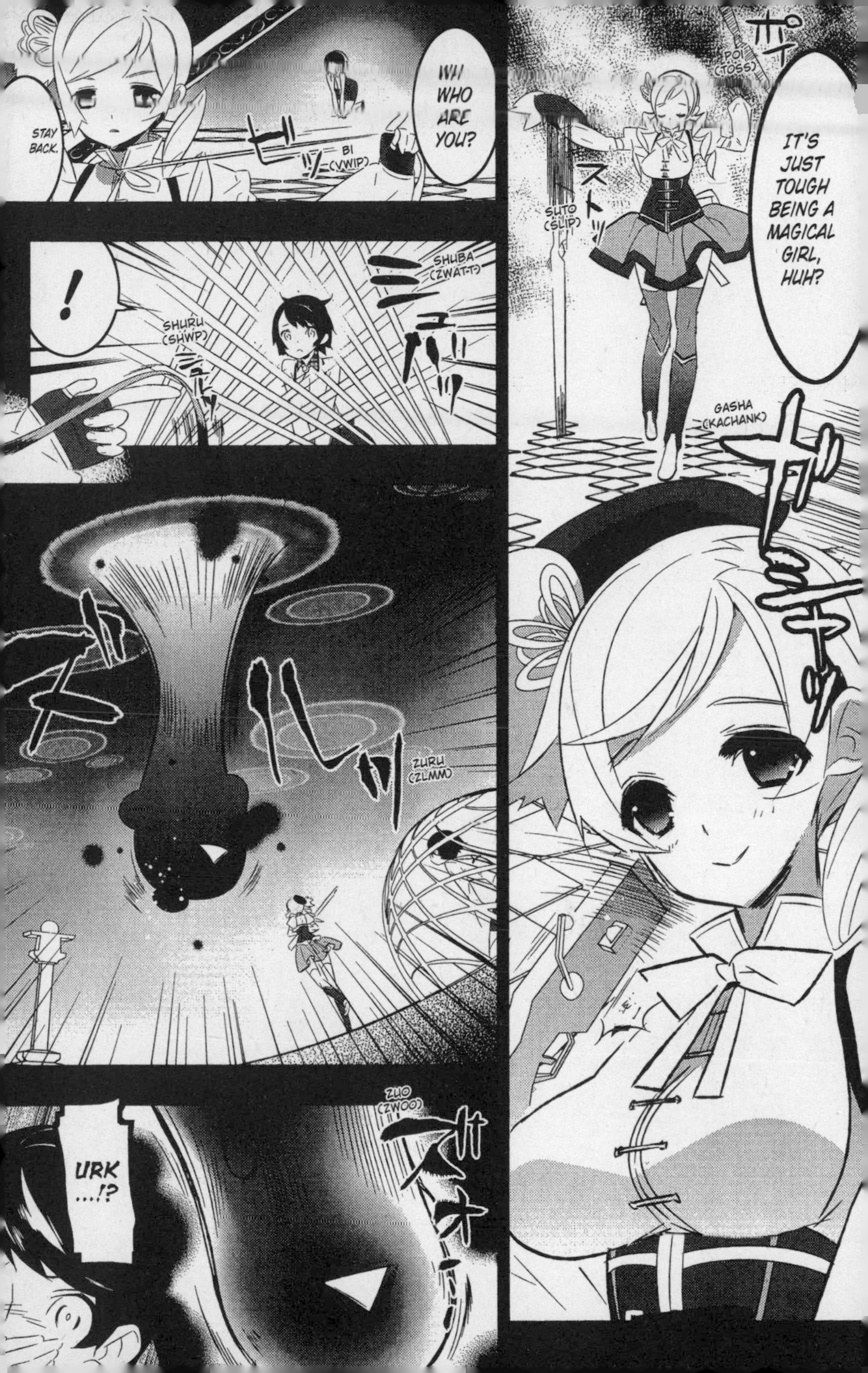
POI (TOSS)
IT'S JUST TOUGH BEING A MAGICAL GIRL, HUH?
SUTO (SLIP)
GASHA (KACHANK)
WH WHO ARE YOU?
BI (VWIP)
STAY BACK.
SHUBA (ZWAT-T-)
!
SHURU (SHWP)
ZURU (ZLMM)
ZUO (ZWOO)
URK ...!?

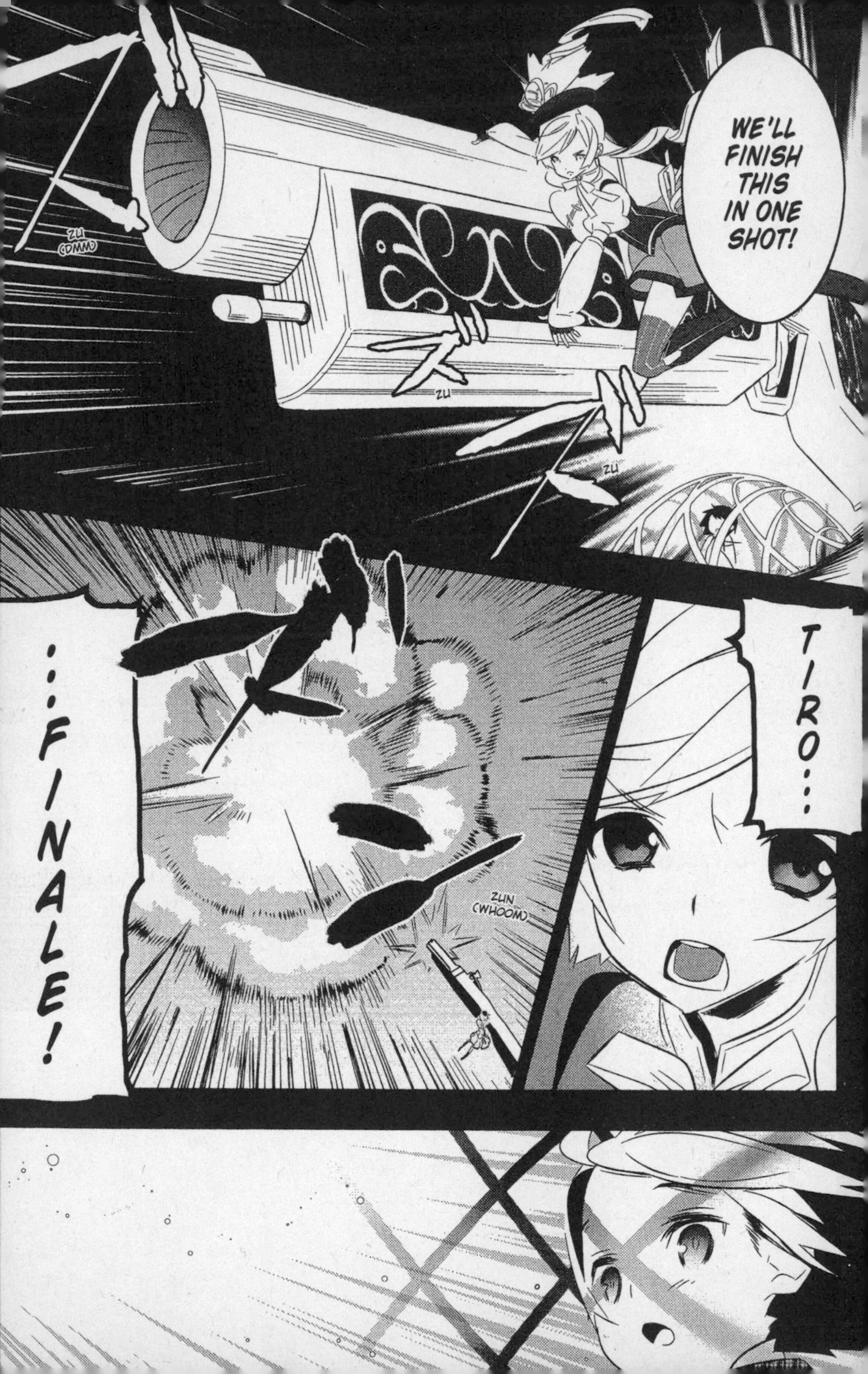
WE'LL FINISH THIS IN ONE SHOT!
ZU (DMM)
ZU
ZU
TIRO...
...FINALE!
ZUN (WHOOM)

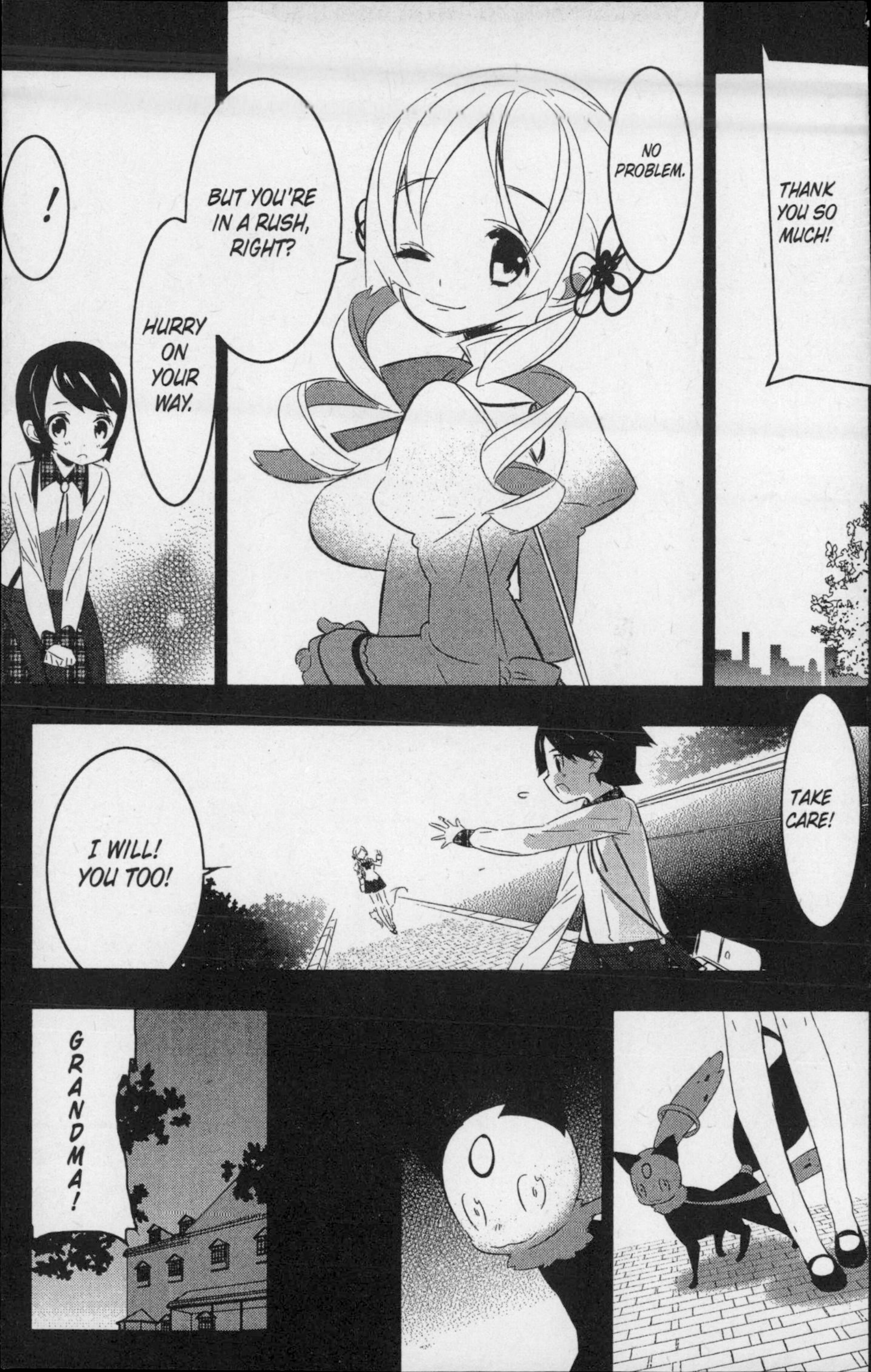
THANK YOU SO MUCH!
NO PROBLEM.
BUT YOU'RE IN A RUSH, RIGHT?
HURRY ON YOUR WAY.
!
TAKE CARE!
I WILL! YOU TOO!
GRANDMA!

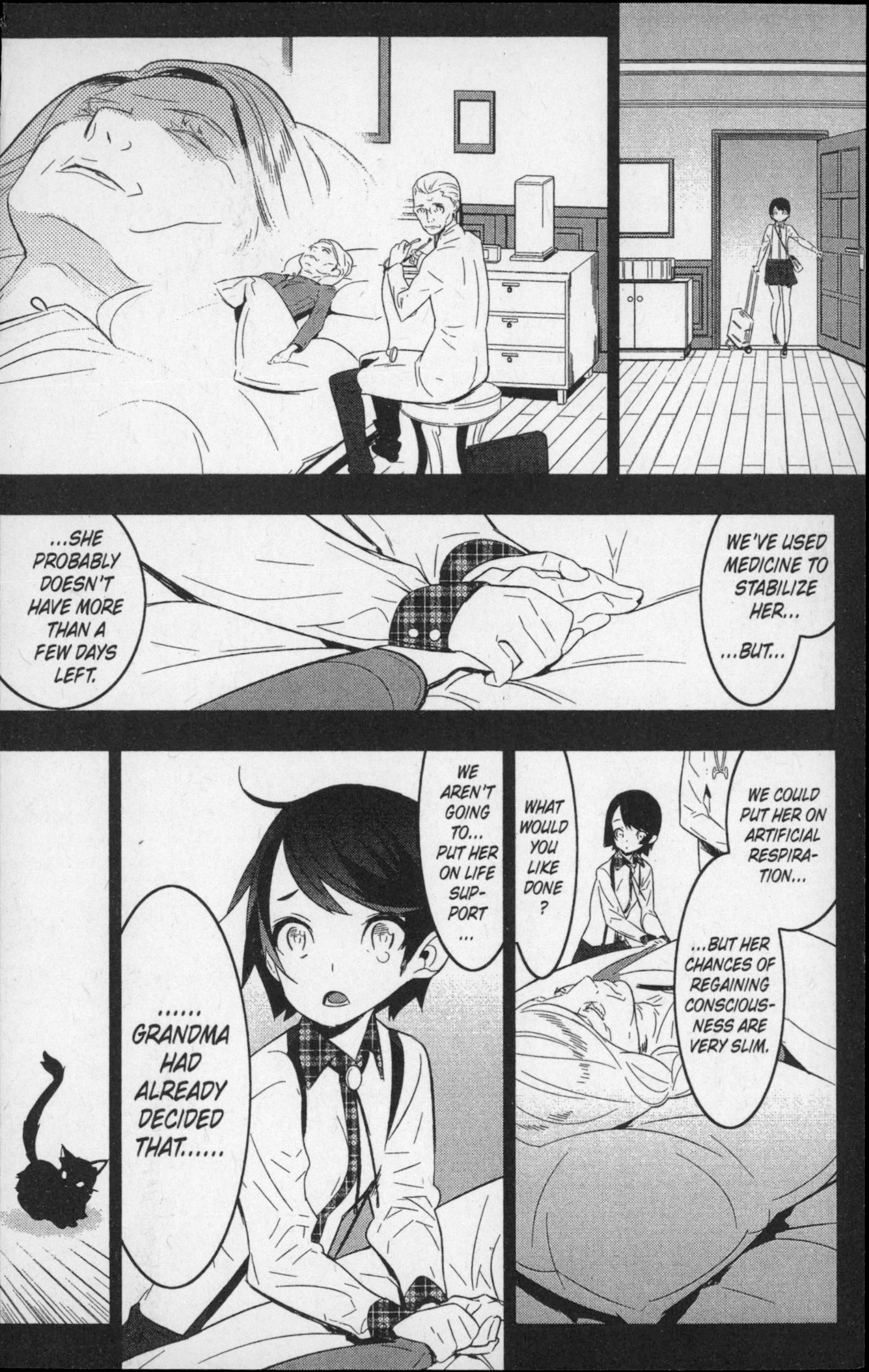
WE'VE USED MEDICINE TO STABILIZE HER... ...BUT...
...SHE PROBABLY DOESN'T HAVE MORE THAN A FEW DAYS LEFT.
WE COULD PUT HER ON ARTIFICIAL RESPIRA-TION...
...BUT HER CHANCES OF REGAINING CONSCIOUS-NESS ARE VERY SLIM.
WHAT WOULD YOU LIKE DONE?
WE AREN'T GOING TO... PUT HER ON LIFE SUP-PORT...
......GRANDMA HAD ALREADY DECIDED THAT......

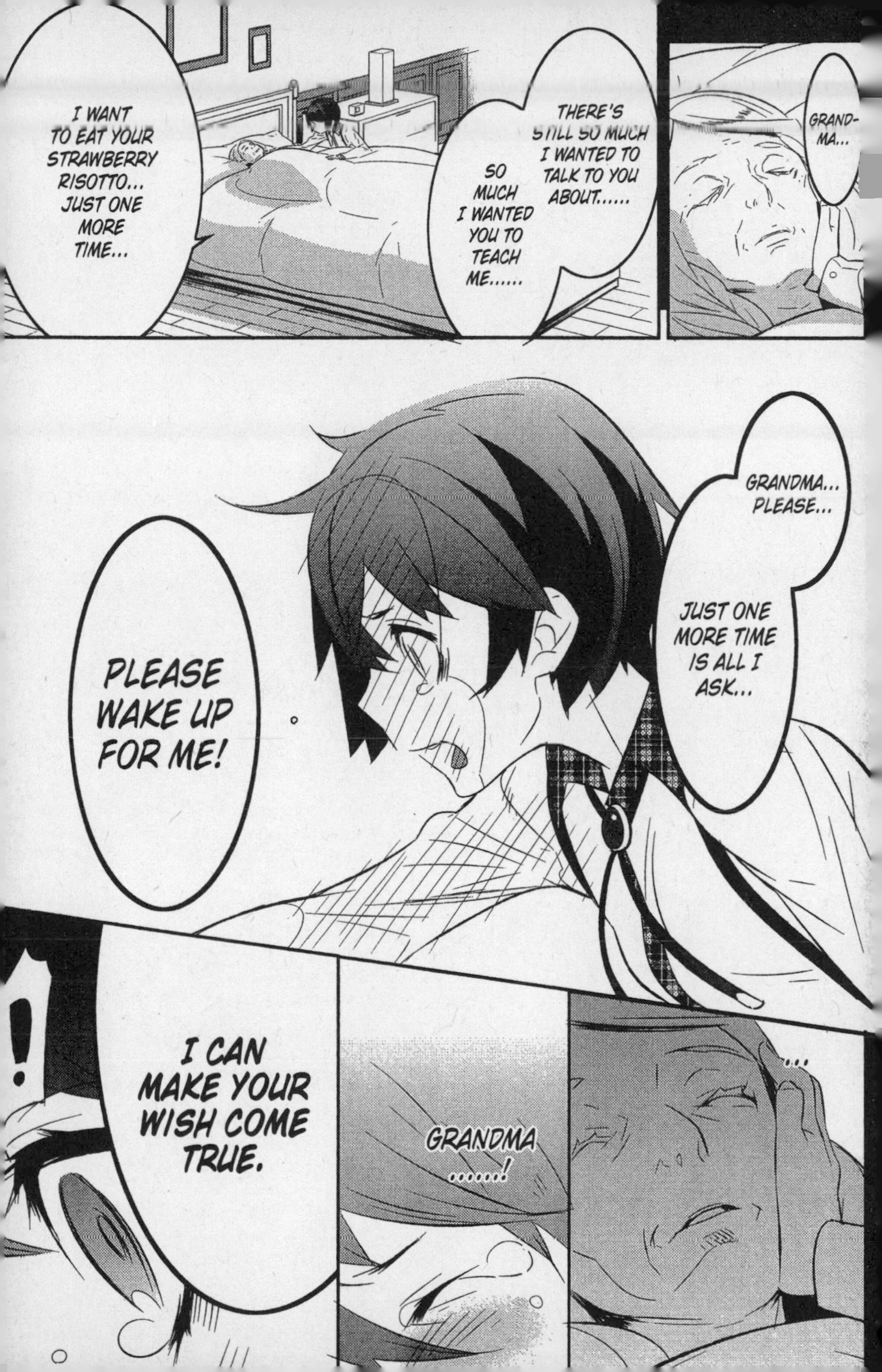
GRAND-MA...
THERE'S STILL SO MUCH I WANTED TO TALK TO YOU ABOUT......
SO MUCH I WANTED YOU TO TEACH ME......
I WANT TO EAT YOUR STRAWBERRY RISOTTO... JUST ONE MORE TIME...
GRANDMA... PLEASE...
JUST ONE MORE TIME IS ALL I ASK...
PLEASE WAKE UP FOR ME!
...
GRANDMA ......!
I CAN MAKE YOUR WISH COME TRUE.
!

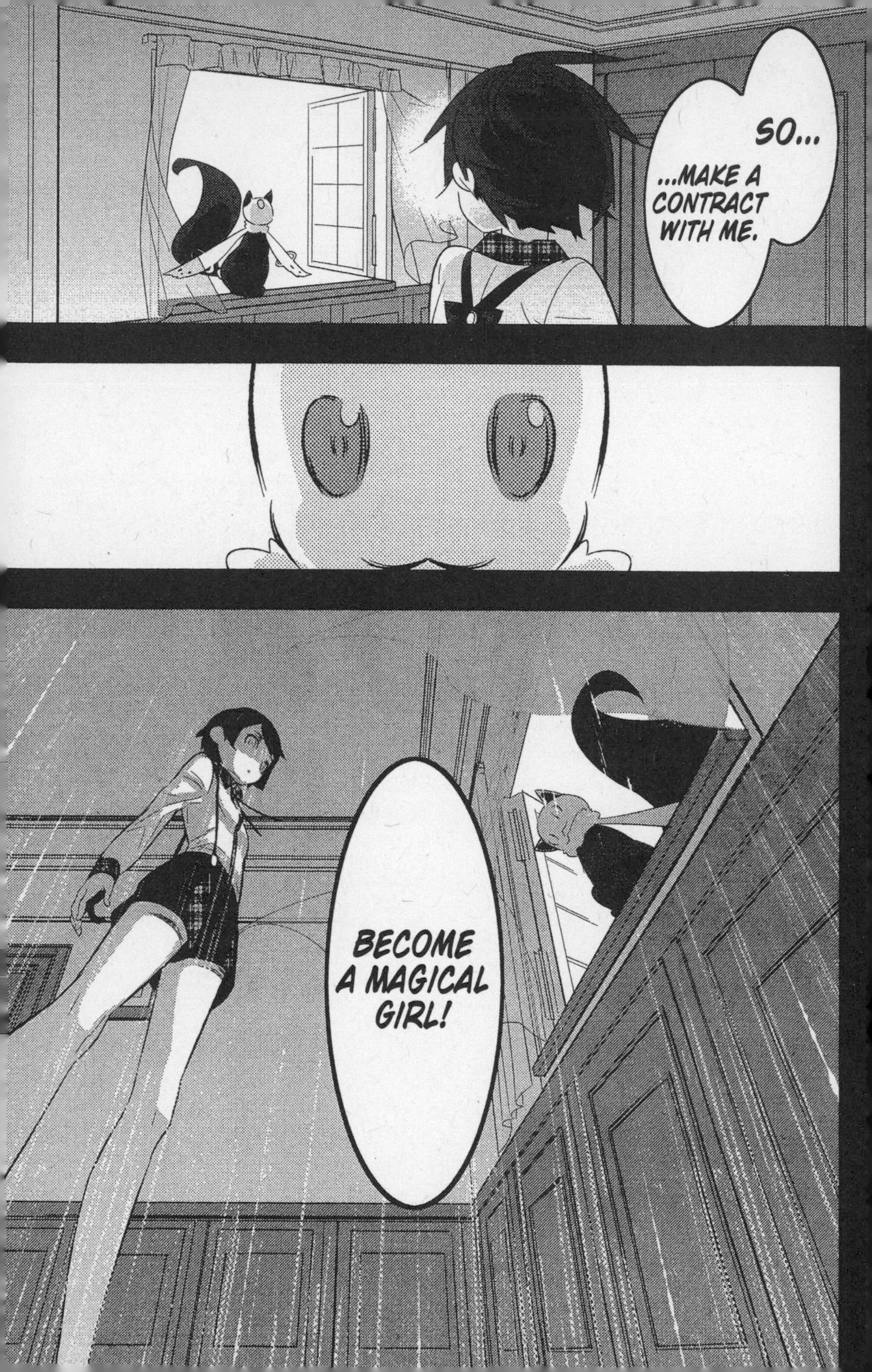
SO...
...MAKE A CONTRACT WITH ME.
BECOME A MAGICAL GIRL!

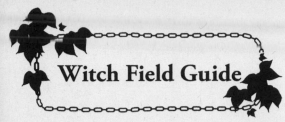

Witch Field Guide

Like a Sea Witch from an ancient era. Her aspect is that of the lonely girl.

She reminds you of life-forms that live and act in great numbers such as jellyfish and coral. The familiars combine to form the witch. It is unknown whether they are independent familiars or just parts of her body. Since she is a mass-body, she can be hurt if one part of her is destroyed, but she cannot be killed in this manner. All her parts must be destroyed at once. She may look cute, but she is a very dangerous witch.

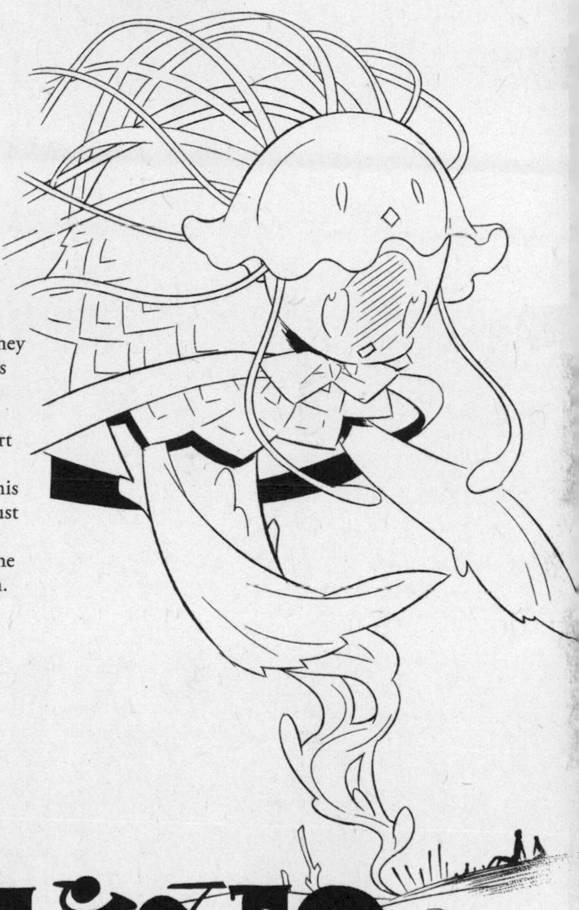

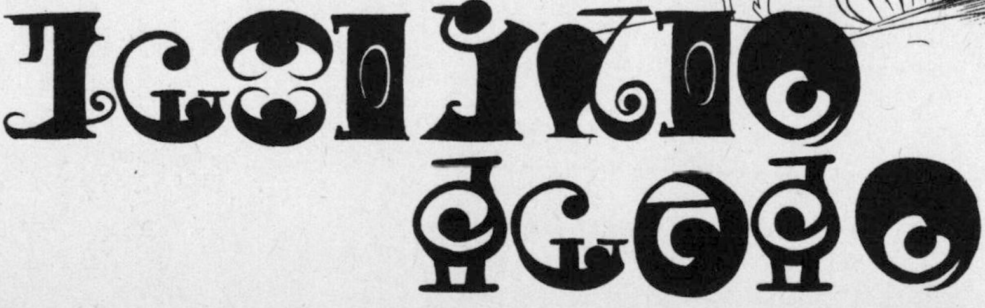

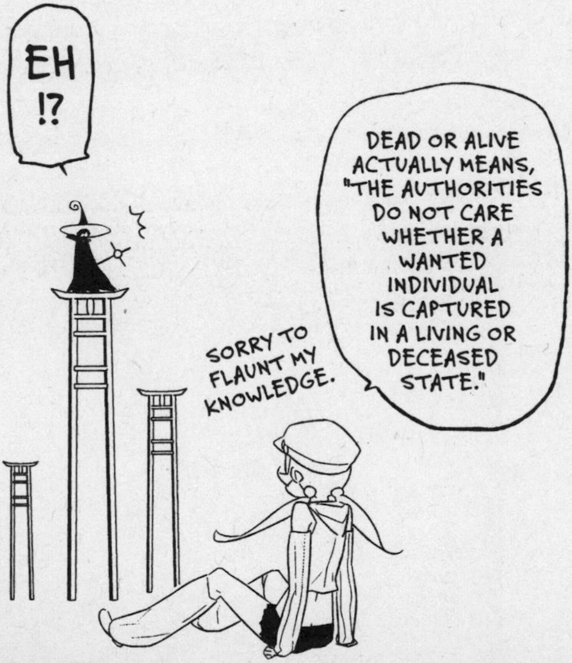
DEAD OR ALIVE ACTUALLY MEANS, "THE AUTHORITIES DO NOT CARE WHETHER A WANTED INDIVIDUAL IS CAPTURED IN A LIVING OR DECEASED STATE."
SORRY TO FLAUNT MY KNOWLEDGE.
EH !?

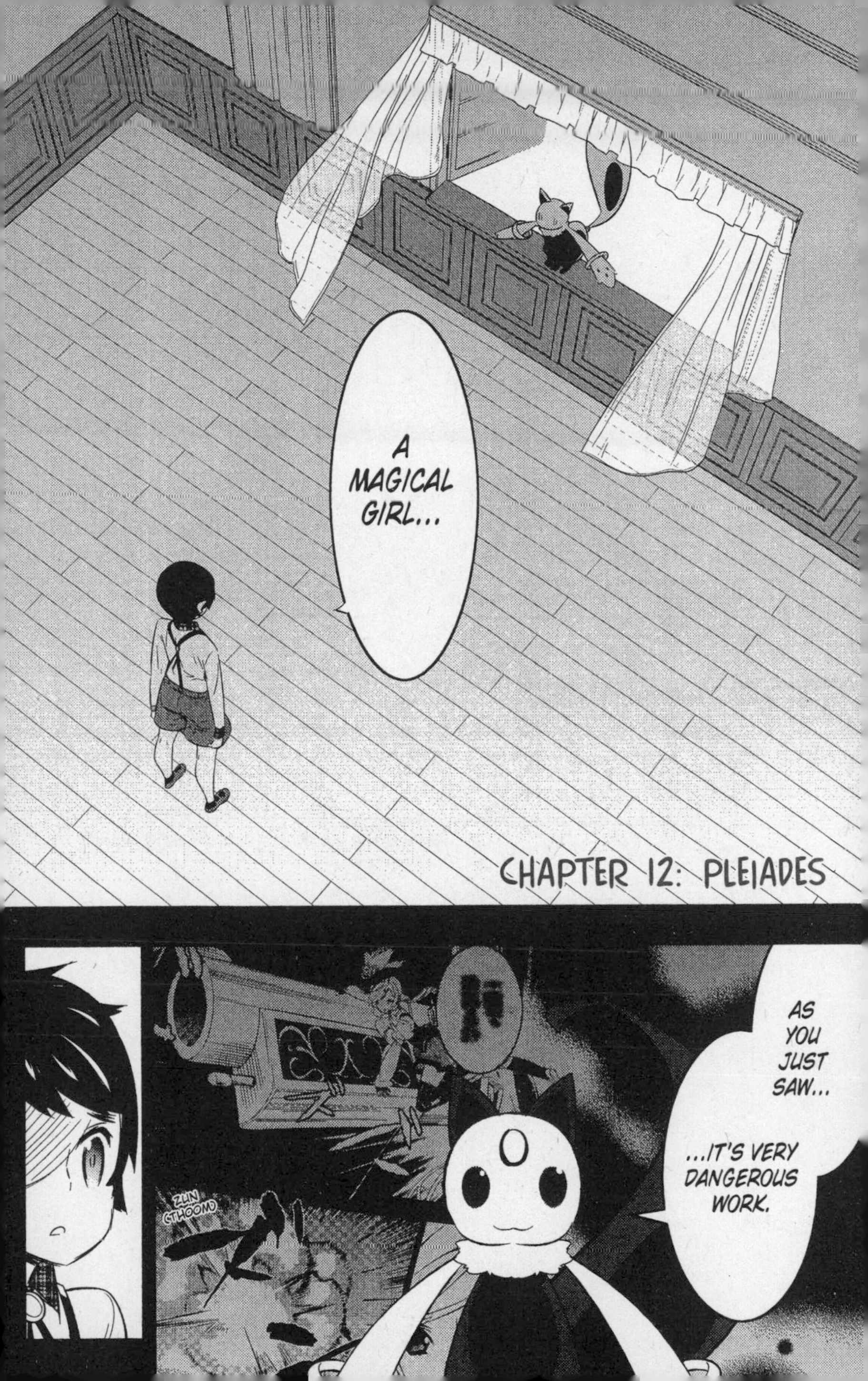
A MAGICAL GIRL...
CHAPTER 12: PLEIADES
AS YOU JUST SAW...
...IT'S VERY DANGEROUS WORK.
ZUN (THOOM)

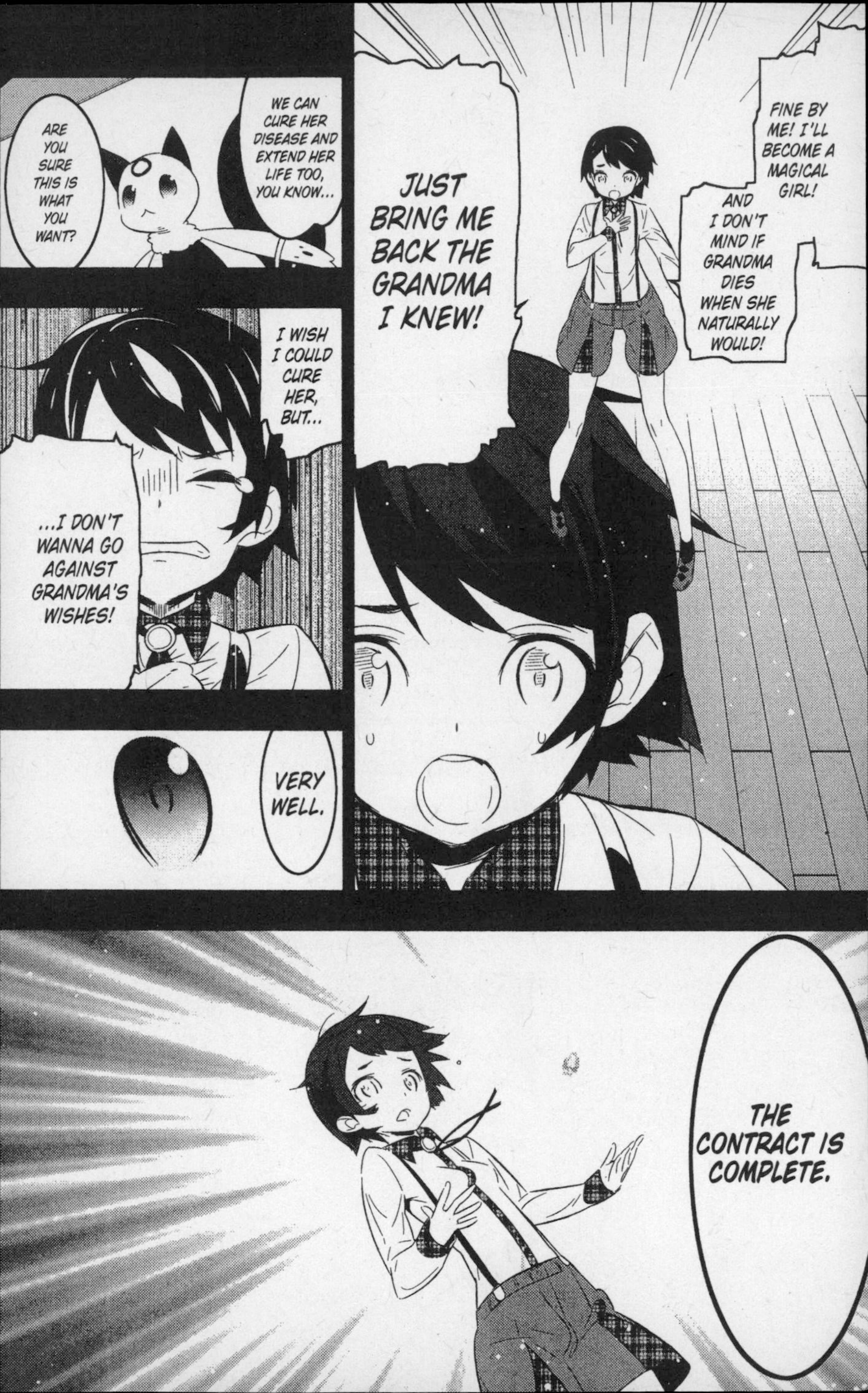
FINE BY ME! I'LL BECOME A MAGICAL GIRL!
AND I DON'T MIND IF GRANDMA DIES WHEN SHE NATURALLY WOULD!
JUST BRING ME BACK THE GRANDMA I KNEW!
WE CAN CURE HER DISEASE AND EXTEND HER LIFE TOO, YOU KNOW...
ARE YOU SURE THIS IS WHAT YOU WANT?
I WISH I COULD CURE HER, BUT...
...I DON'T WANNA GO AGAINST GRANDMA'S WISHES!
VERY WELL.
THE CONTRACT IS COMPLETE.

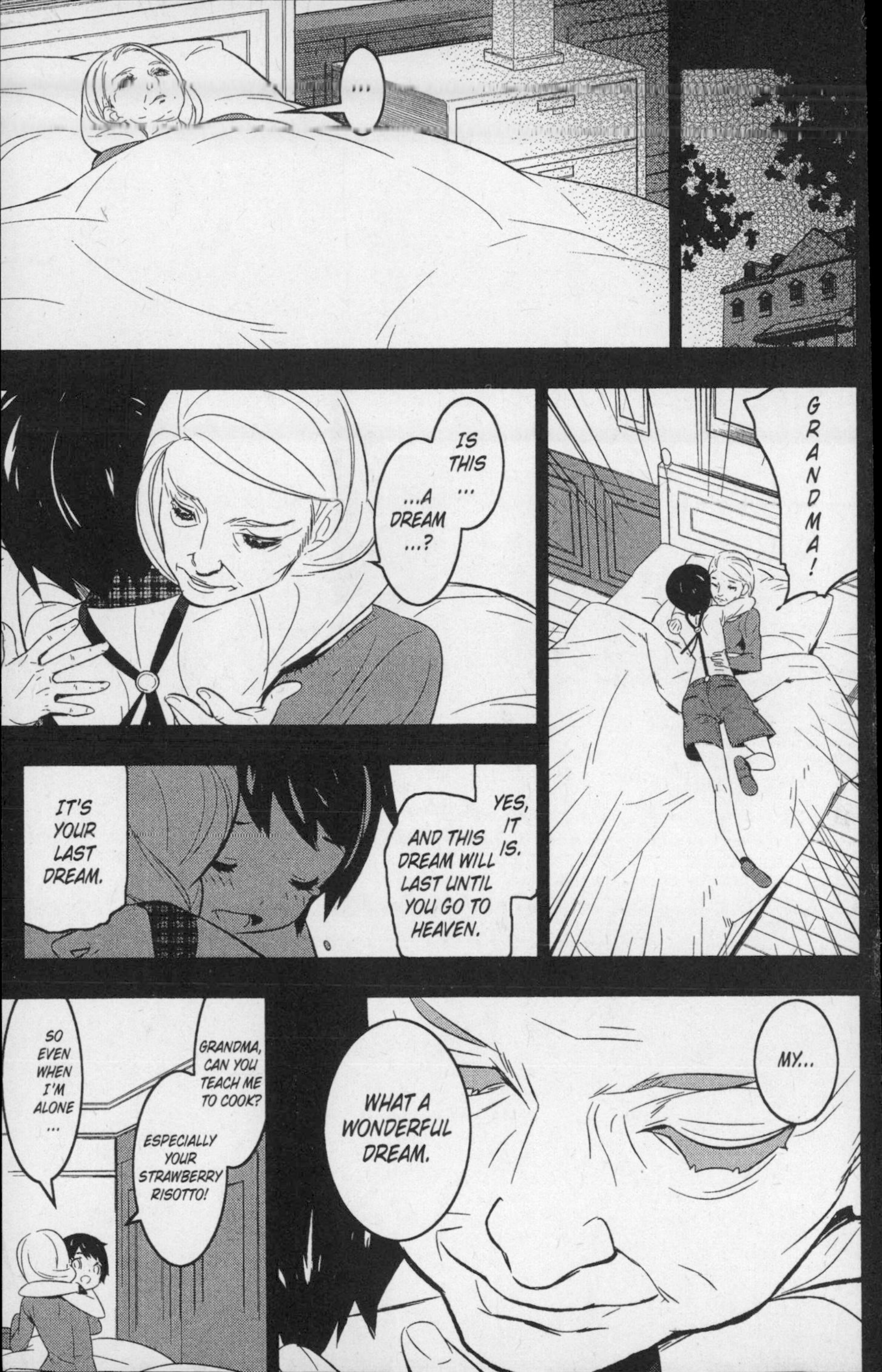
...
GRANDMA!
IS THIS ... ...A DREAM ...?
YES, IT IS.
AND THIS DREAM WILL LAST UNTIL YOU GO TO HEAVEN.
IT'S YOUR LAST DREAM.
MY...
WHAT A WONDERFUL DREAM.
GRANDMA, CAN YOU TEACH ME TO COOK?
ESPECIALLY YOUR STRAWBERRY RISOTTO!
SO EVEN WHEN I'M ALONE ...

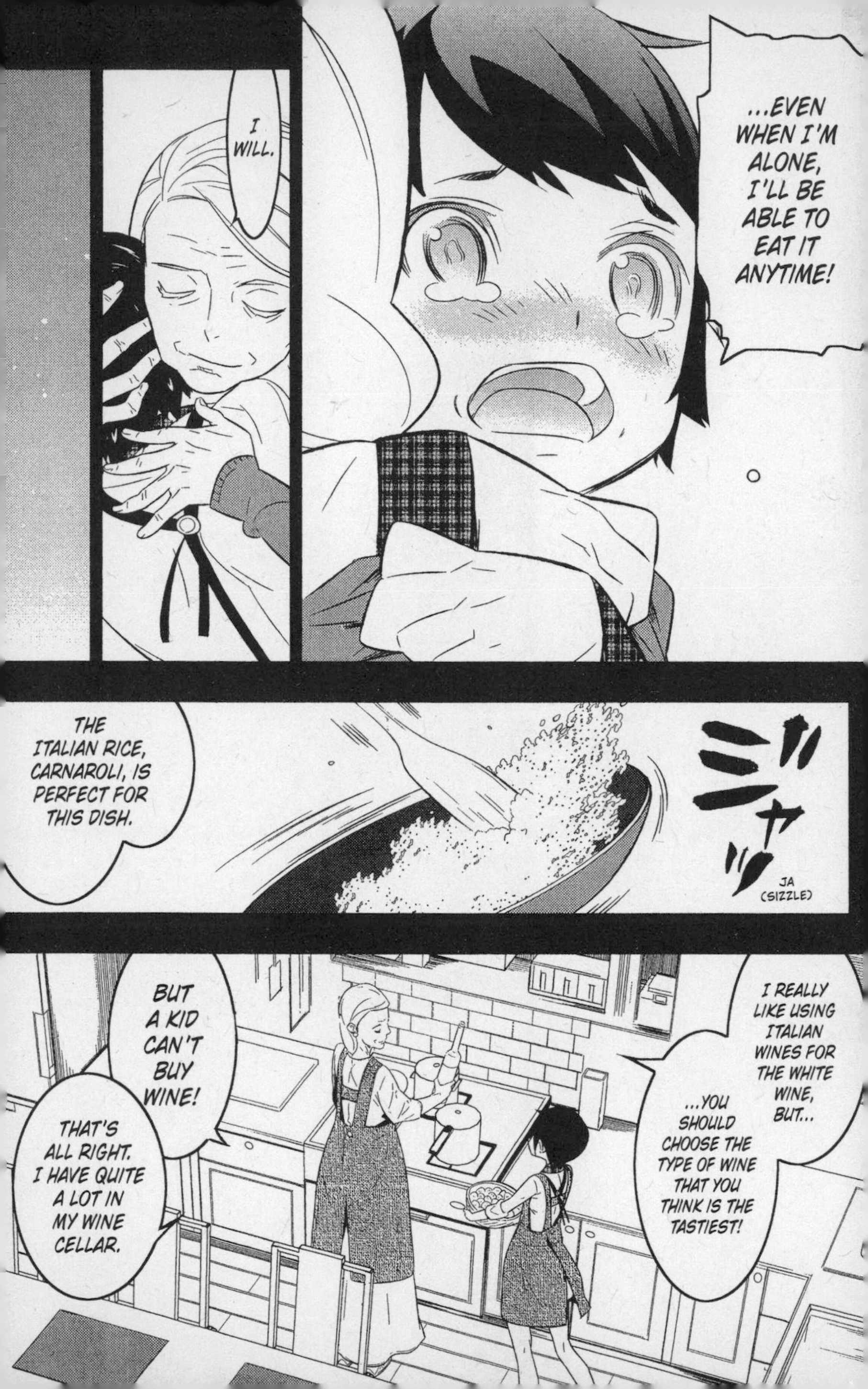
...EVEN WHEN I'M ALONE, I'LL BE ABLE TO EAT IT ANYTIME!
I WILL.
ジャッ
JA (SIZZLE)
THE ITALIAN RICE, CARNAROLI, IS PERFECT FOR THIS DISH.
I REALLY LIKE USING ITALIAN WINES FOR THE WHITE WINE, BUT...
...YOU SHOULD CHOOSE THE TYPE OF WINE THAT YOU THINK IS THE TASTIEST!
BUT A KID CAN'T BUY WINE!
THAT'S ALL RIGHT. I HAVE QUITE A LOT IN MY WINE CELLAR.

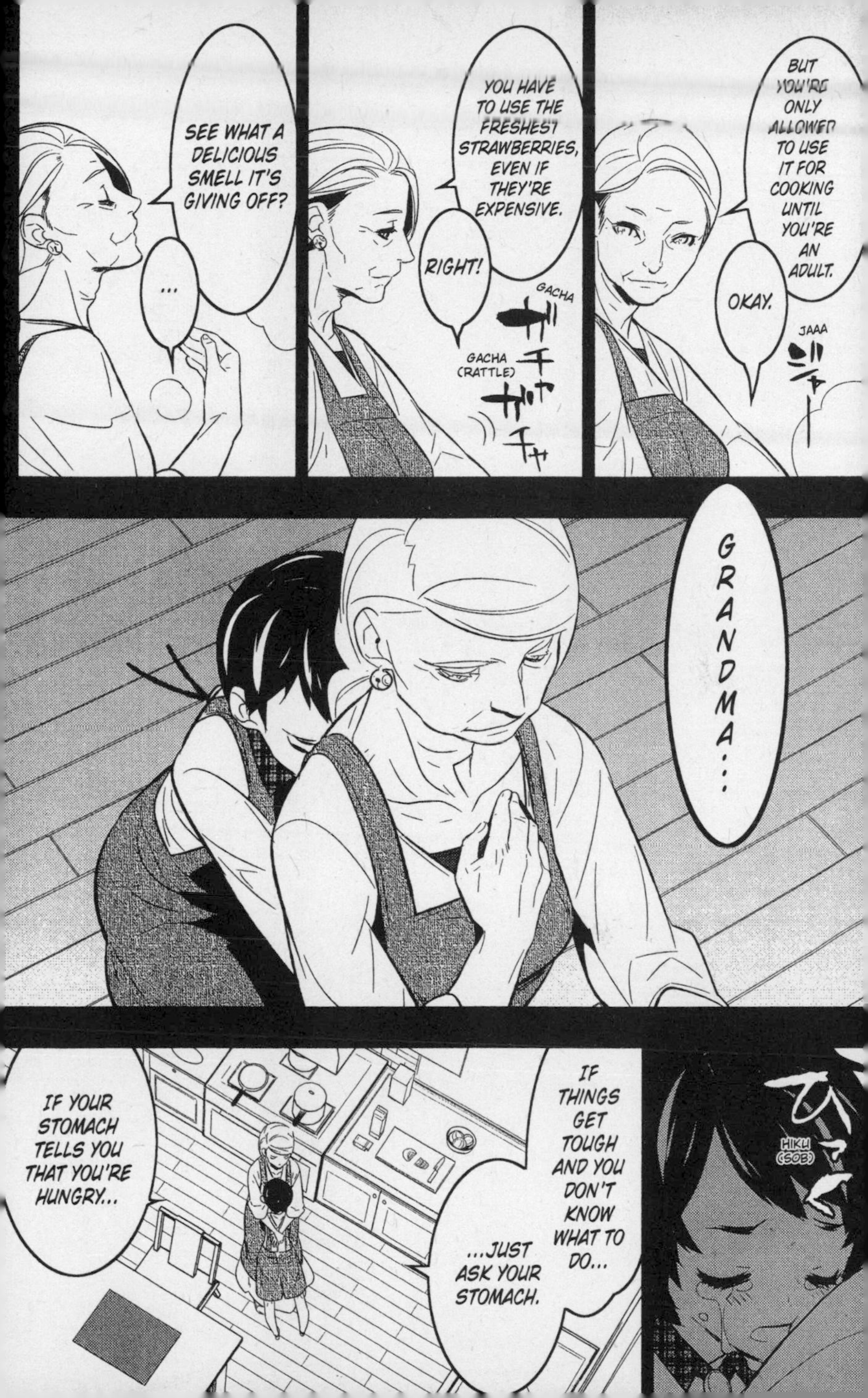
BUT YOU'RE ONLY ALLOWED TO USE IT FOR COOKING UNTIL YOU'RE AN ADULT.
OKAY.
JAAA
YOU HAVE TO USE THE FRESHEST STRAWBERRIES, EVEN IF THEY'RE EXPENSIVE.
RIGHT!
GACHA
GACHA (RATTLE)
SEE WHAT A DELICIOUS SMELL IT'S GIVING OFF?
...
GRANDMA...
HIKU (SOB)
IF THINGS GET TOUGH AND YOU DON'T KNOW WHAT TO DO...
...JUST ASK YOUR STOMACH.
IF YOUR STOMACH TELLS YOU THAT YOU'RE HUNGRY...

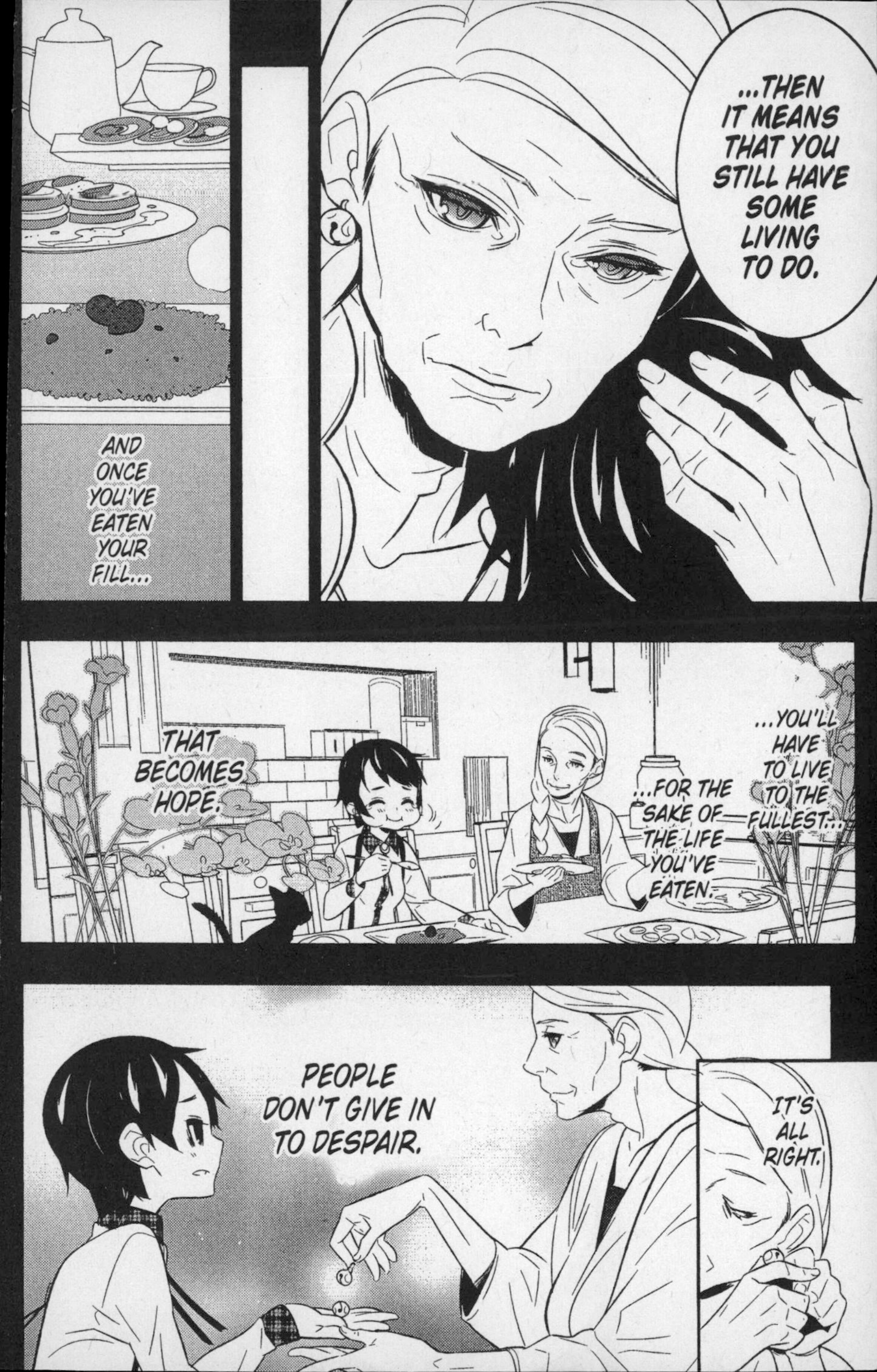
...THEN IT MEANS THAT YOU STILL HAVE SOME LIVING TO DO.
AND ONCE YOU'VE EATEN YOUR FILL...
...YOU'LL HAVE TO LIVE TO THE FULLEST...
...FOR THE SAKE OF THE LIFE YOU'VE EATEN.
THAT BECOMES HOPE.
IT'S ALL RIGHT.
PEOPLE DON'T GIVE IN TO DESPAIR.

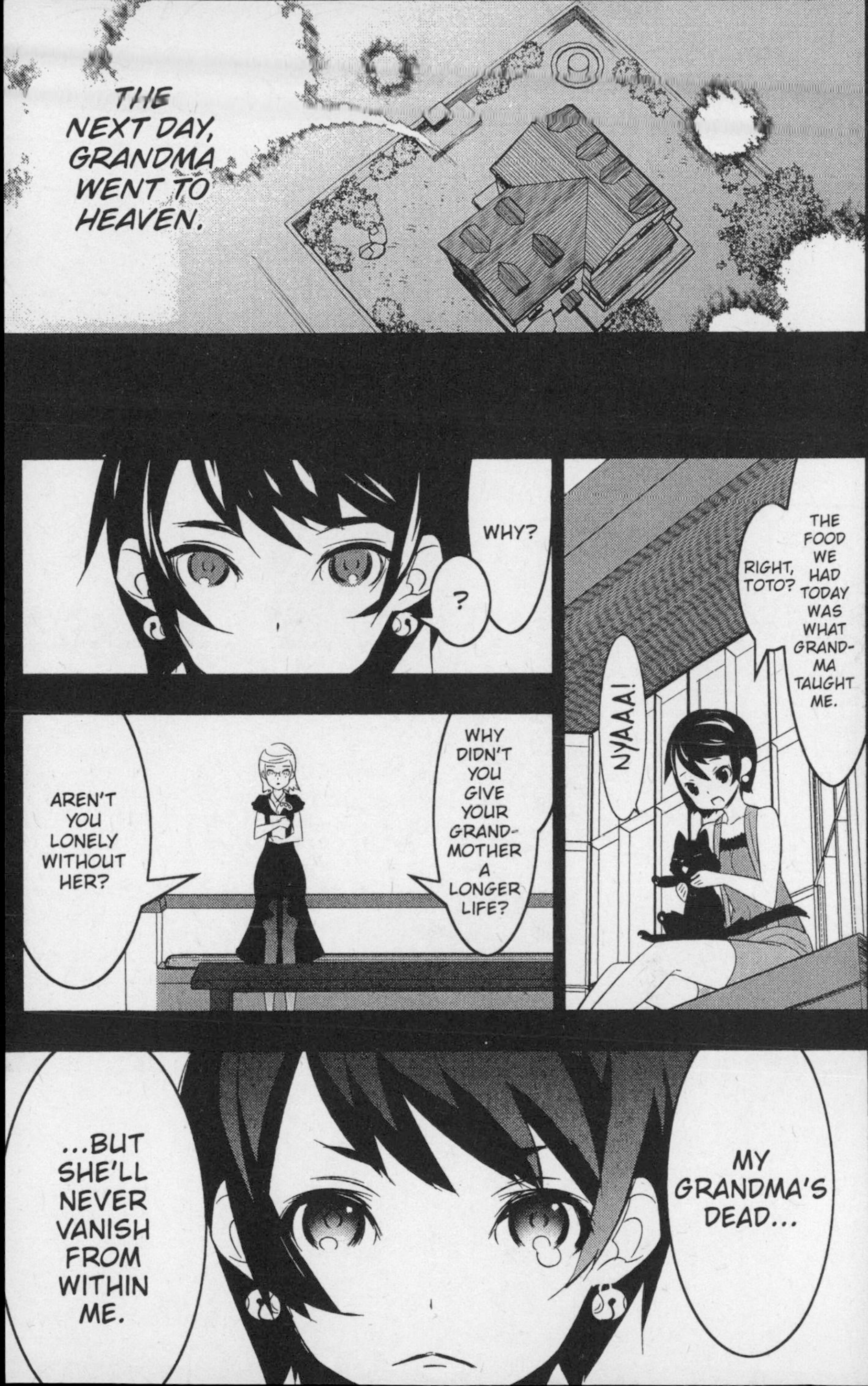
THE NEXT DAY, GRANDMA WENT TO HEAVEN.
THE FOOD WE HAD TODAY WAS WHAT GRANDMA TAUGHT ME.
RIGHT, TOTO?
NYAAAA!
WHY?
?
WHY DIDN'T YOU GIVE YOUR GRANDMOTHER A LONGER LIFE?
AREN'T YOU LONELY WITHOUT HER?
MY GRANDMA'S DEAD...
...BUT SHE'LL NEVER VANISH FROM WITHIN ME.

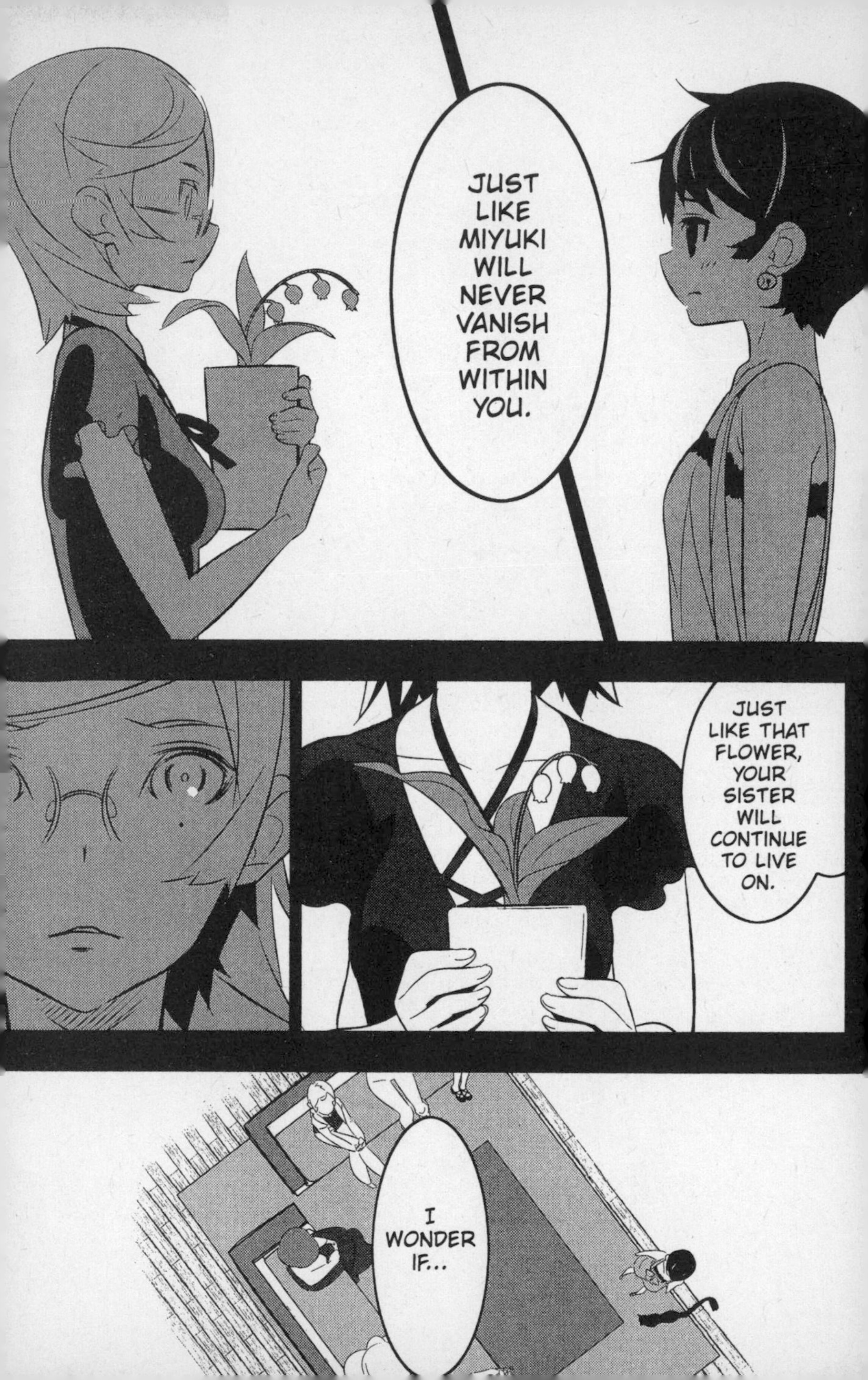
JUST LIKE MIYUKI WILL NEVER VANISH FROM WITHIN YOU.
JUST LIKE THAT FLOWER, YOUR SISTER WILL CONTINUE TO LIVE ON.
I WONDER IF...

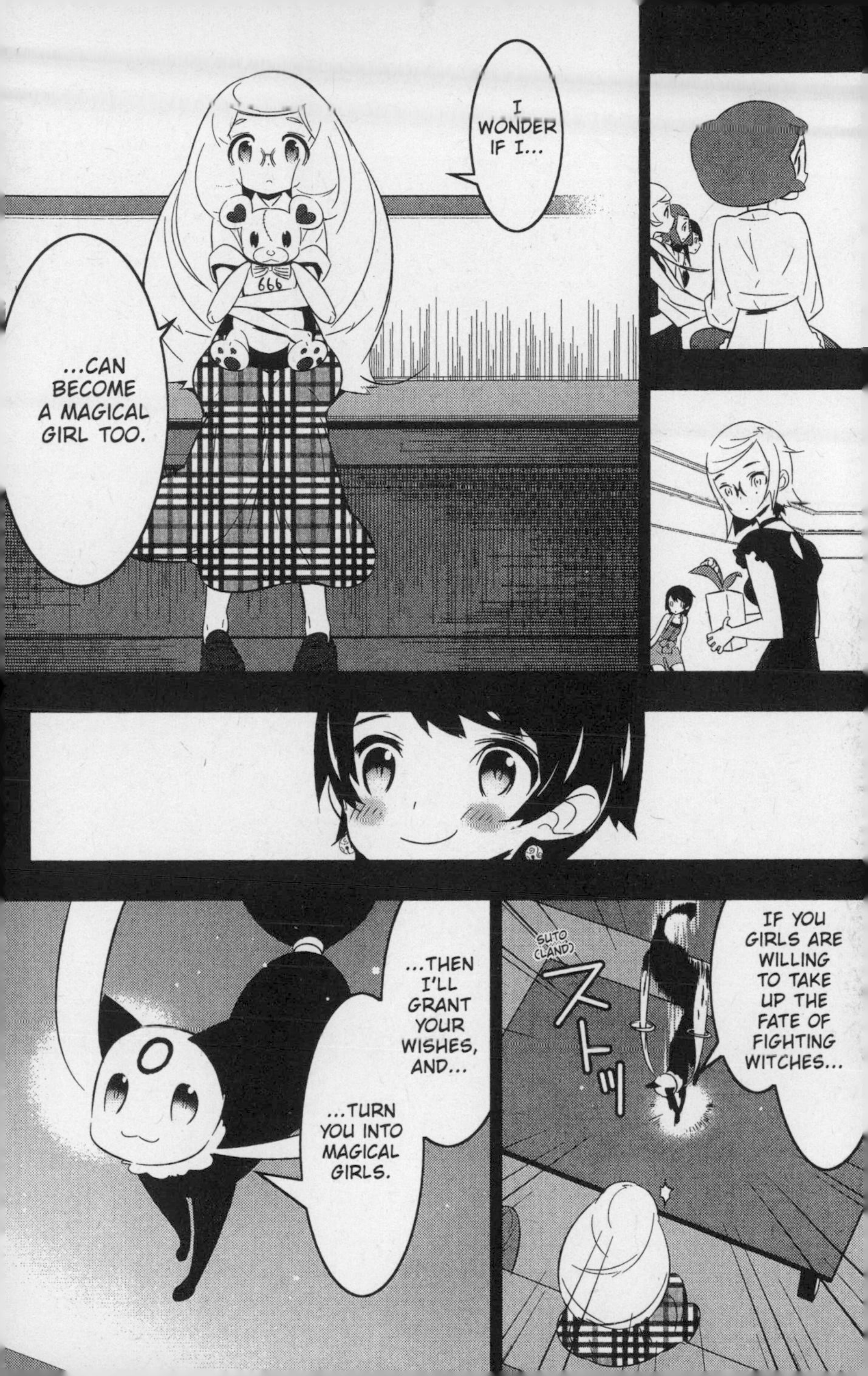
I WONDER IF I...
...CAN BECOME A MAGICAL GIRL TOO.
IF YOU GIRLS ARE WILLING TO TAKE UP THE FATE OF FIGHTING WITCHES...
SUTO (LAND)
ストッ
...THEN I'LL GRANT YOUR WISHES, AND...
...TURN YOU INTO MAGICAL GIRLS.

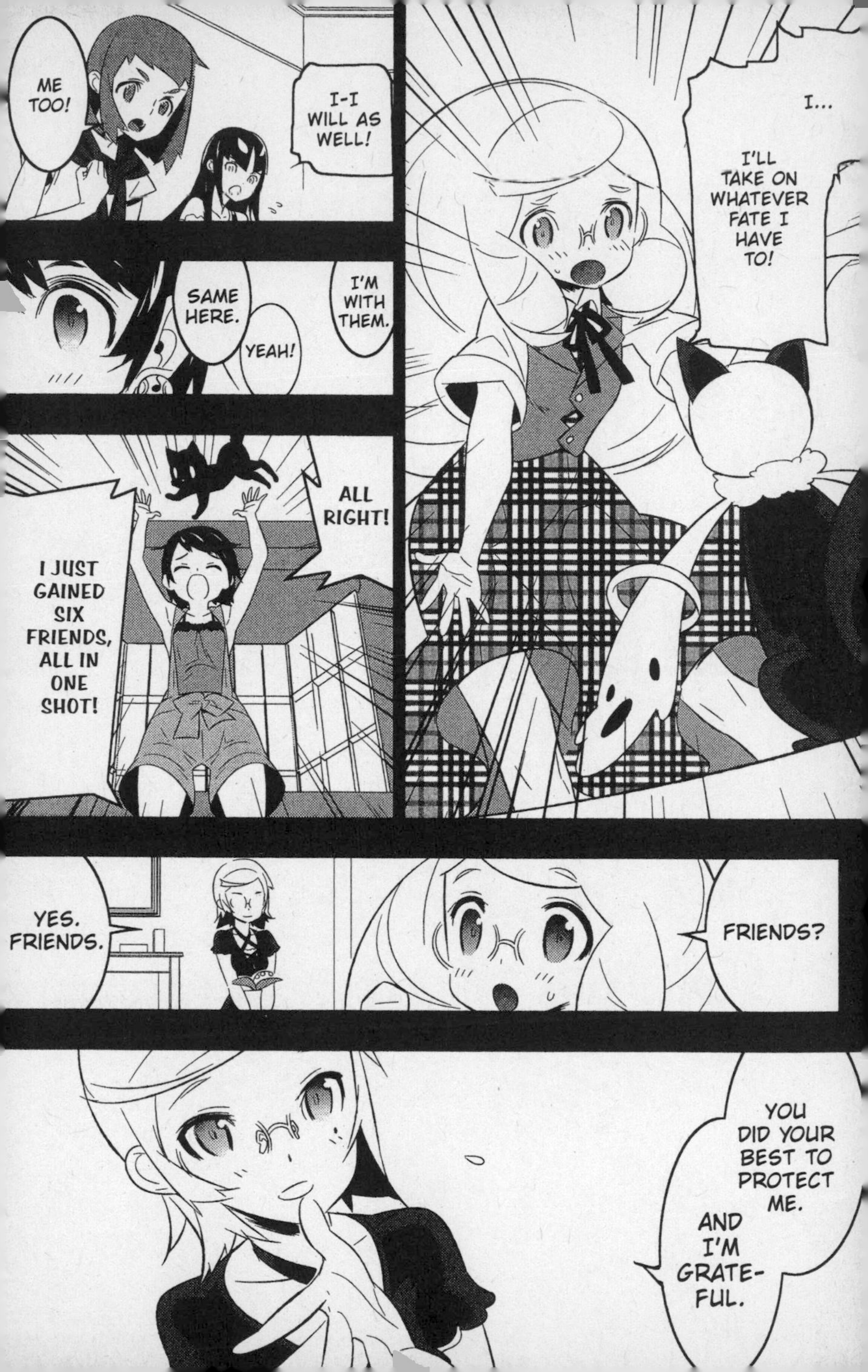
I...
I'LL TAKE ON WHATEVER FATE I HAVE TO!
I-I WILL AS WELL!
ME TOO!
I'M WITH THEM.
SAME HERE.
YEAH!
ALL RIGHT!
I JUST GAINED SIX FRIENDS, ALL IN ONE SHOT!
FRIENDS?
YES. FRIENDS.
YOU DID YOUR BEST TO PROTECT ME.
AND I'M GRATE-FUL.

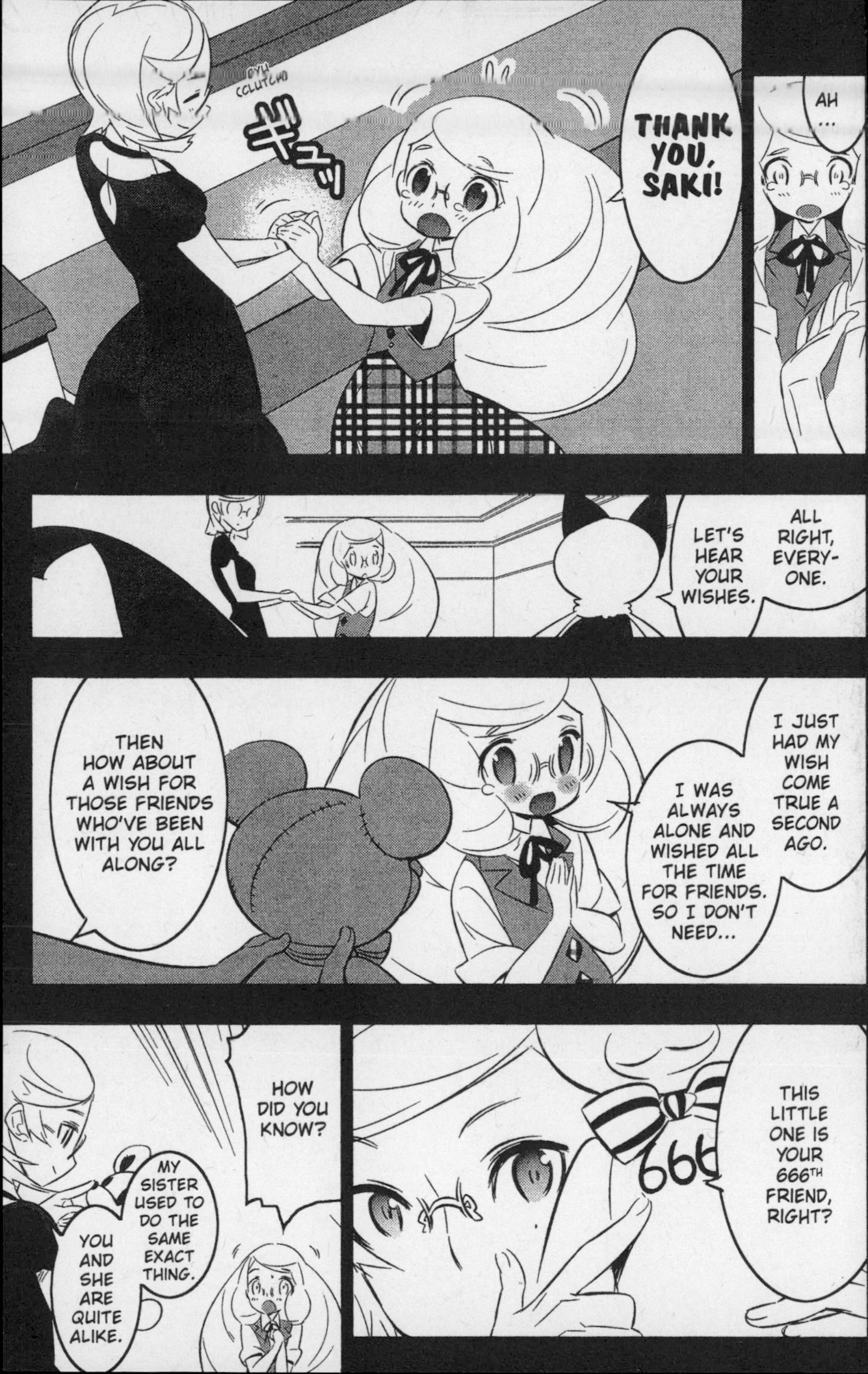
AH ...
THANK YOU, SAKI!
CLUTCH
ギュッ
ALL RIGHT, EVERY-ONE.
LET'S HEAR YOUR WISHES.
I JUST HAD MY WISH COME TRUE A SECOND AGO.
I WAS ALWAYS ALONE AND WISHED ALL THE TIME FOR FRIENDS. SO I DON'T NEED...
THEN HOW ABOUT A WISH FOR THOSE FRIENDS WHO'VE BEEN WITH YOU ALL ALONG?
666
THIS LITTLE ONE IS YOUR 666TH FRIEND, RIGHT?
HOW DID YOU KNOW?
MY SISTER USED TO DO THE SAME EXACT THING.
YOU AND SHE ARE QUITE ALIKE.

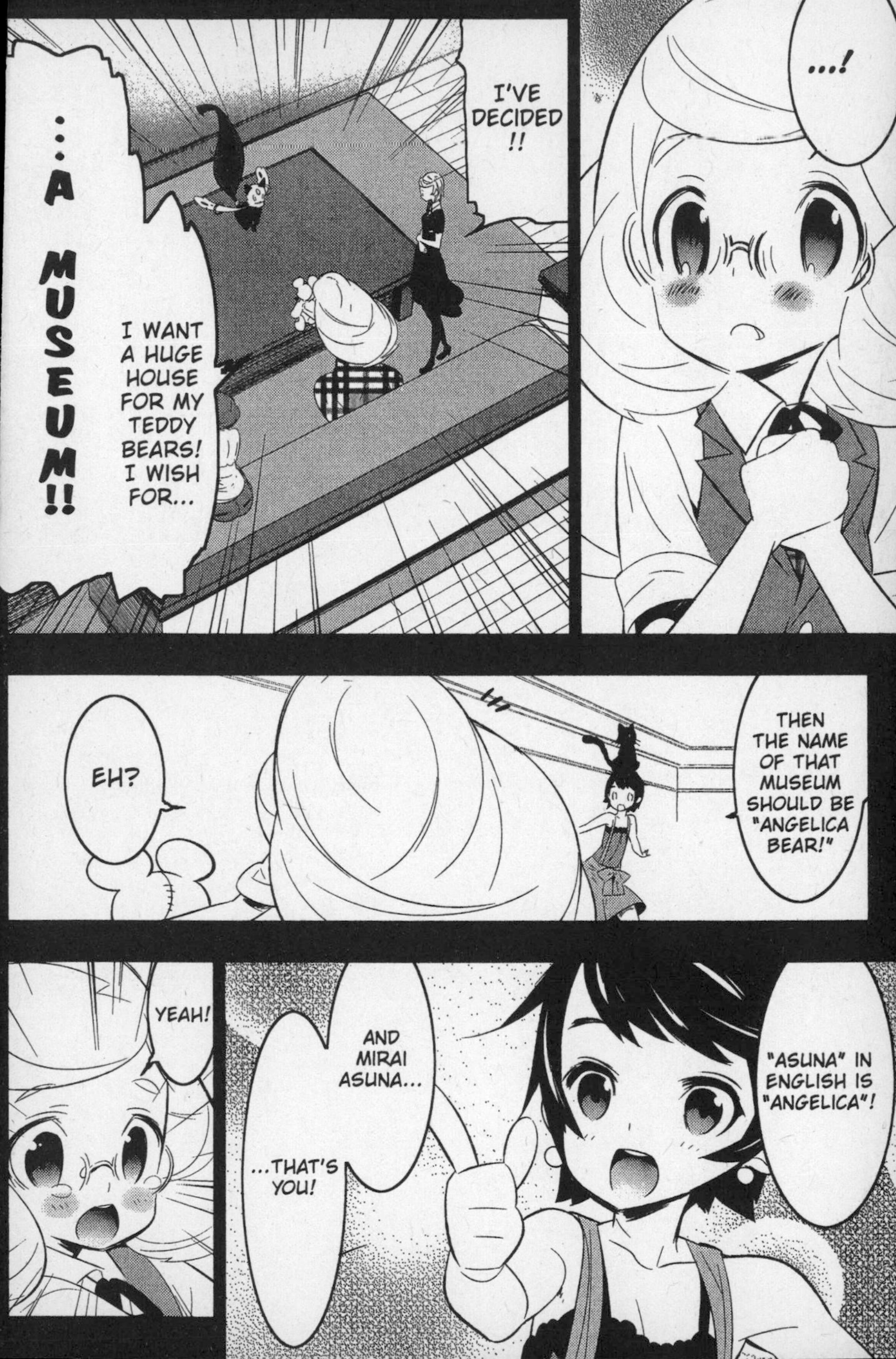
...!
I'VE DECIDED!!
I WANT A HUGE HOUSE FOR MY TEDDY BEARS! I WISH FOR...
...A MUSEUM!!
THEN THE NAME OF THAT MUSEUM SHOULD BE "ANGELICA BEAR!"
EH?
"ASUNA" IN ENGLISH IS "ANGELICA"!
AND MIRAI ASUNA...
...THAT'S YOU!
YEAH!

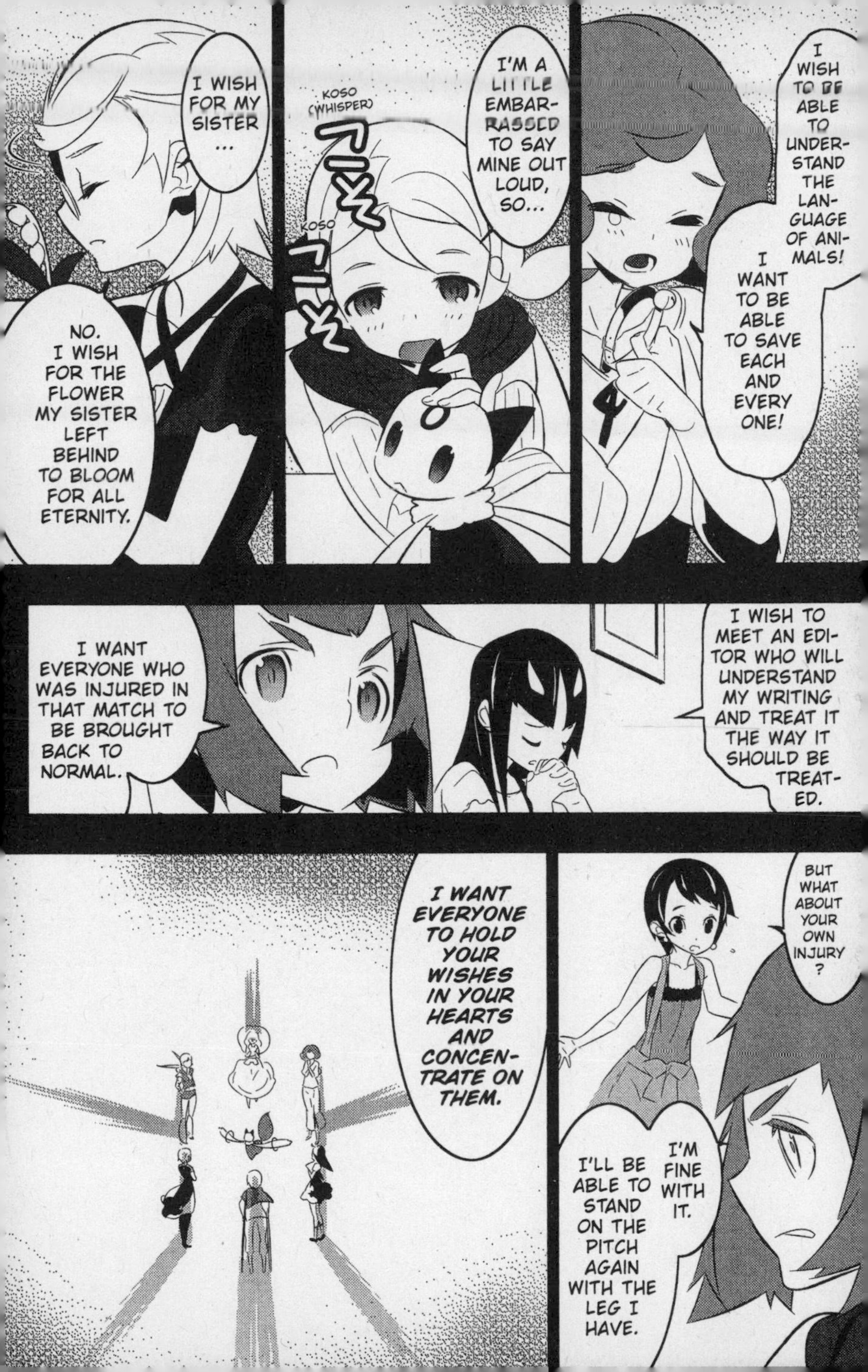
I WISH TO BE ABLE TO UNDERSTAND THE LANGUAGE OF ANIMALS!
I WANT TO BE ABLE TO SAVE EACH AND EVERY ONE!
I'M A LITTLE EMBARRASSED TO SAY MINE OUT LOUD, SO...
KOSO (WHISPER)
KOSO
I WISH FOR MY SISTER ...
NO. I WISH FOR THE FLOWER MY SISTER LEFT BEHIND TO BLOOM FOR ALL ETERNITY.
I WISH TO MEET AN EDITOR WHO WILL UNDERSTAND MY WRITING AND TREAT IT THE WAY IT SHOULD BE TREATED.
I WANT EVERYONE WHO WAS INJURED IN THAT MATCH TO BE BROUGHT BACK TO NORMAL.
BUT WHAT ABOUT YOUR OWN INJURY?
I'M FINE WITH IT.
I'LL BE ABLE TO STAND ON THE PITCH AGAIN WITH THE LEG I HAVE.
I WANT EVERYONE TO HOLD YOUR WISHES IN YOUR HEARTS AND CONCENTRATE ON THEM.

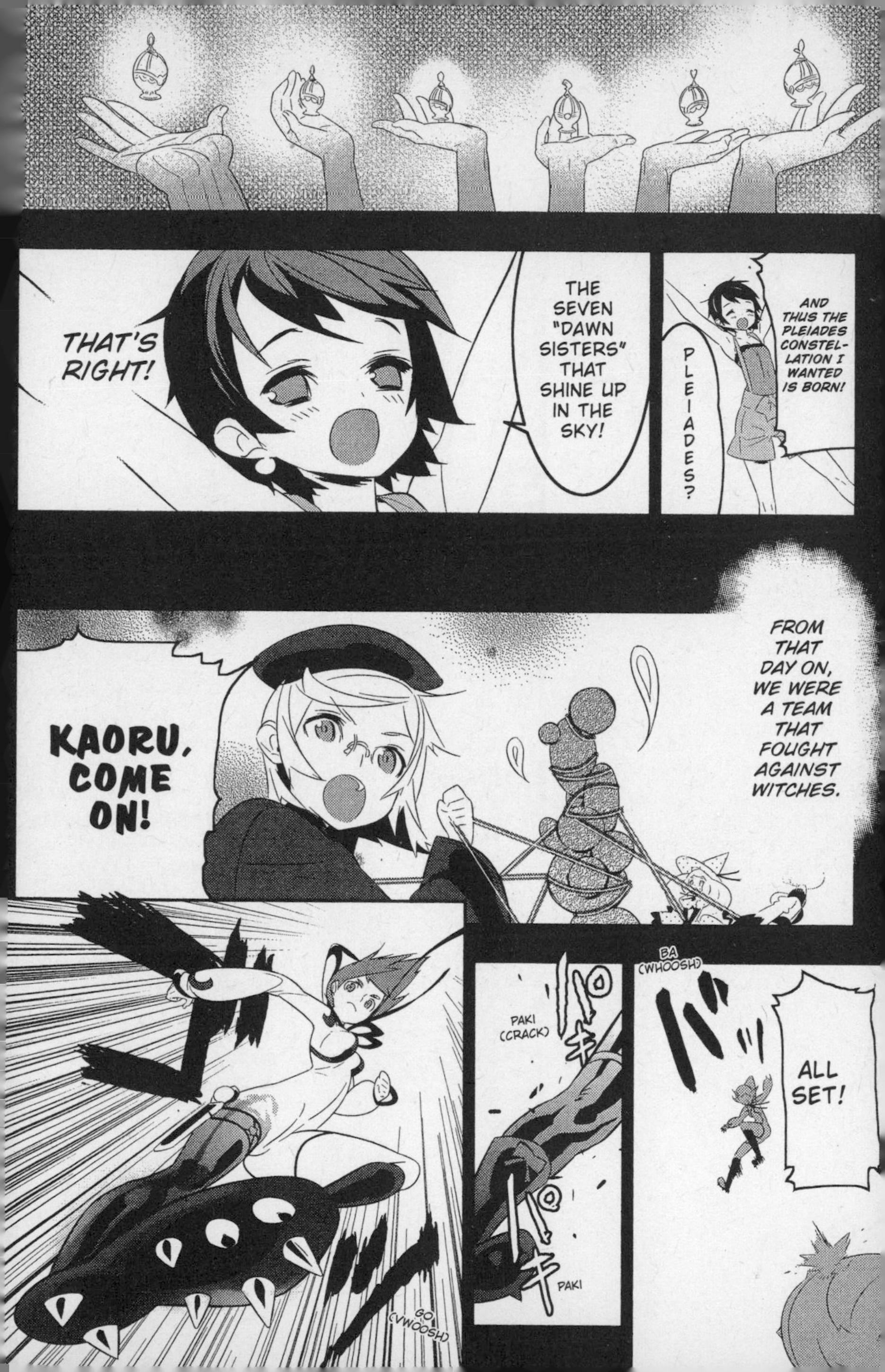
AND THUS THE PLEIADES CONSTELLATION I WANTED IS BORN!
PLEIADES?
THE SEVEN "DAWN SISTERS" THAT SHINE UP IN THE SKY!
THAT'S RIGHT!
FROM THAT DAY ON, WE WERE A TEAM THAT FOUGHT AGAINST WITCHES.
KAORU, COME ON!
BA (WHOOSH)
ALL SET!
PAKI (CRACK)
PAKI
GO (VWOOSH)

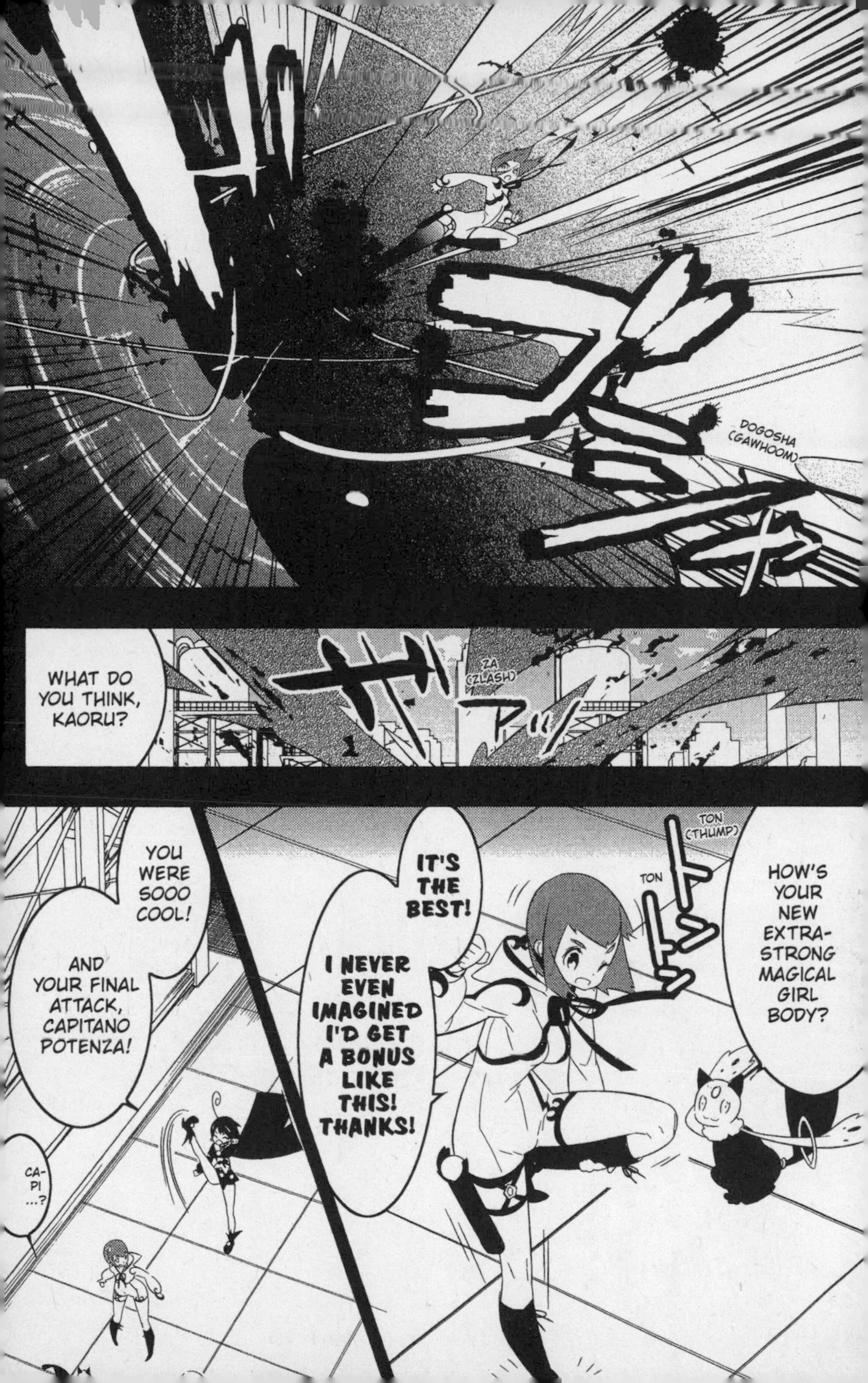
DOGOSHA (GAWHOOM)
ZA (ZLASH)
WHAT DO YOU THINK, KAORU?
TON (THUMP)
TON
HOW'S YOUR NEW EXTRA-STRONG MAGICAL GIRL BODY?
IT'S THE BEST!
I NEVER EVEN IMAGINED I'D GET A BONUS LIKE THIS! THANKS!
YOU WERE SOOO COOL!
AND YOUR FINAL ATTACK, CAPITANO POTENZA!
CA-PI ...?

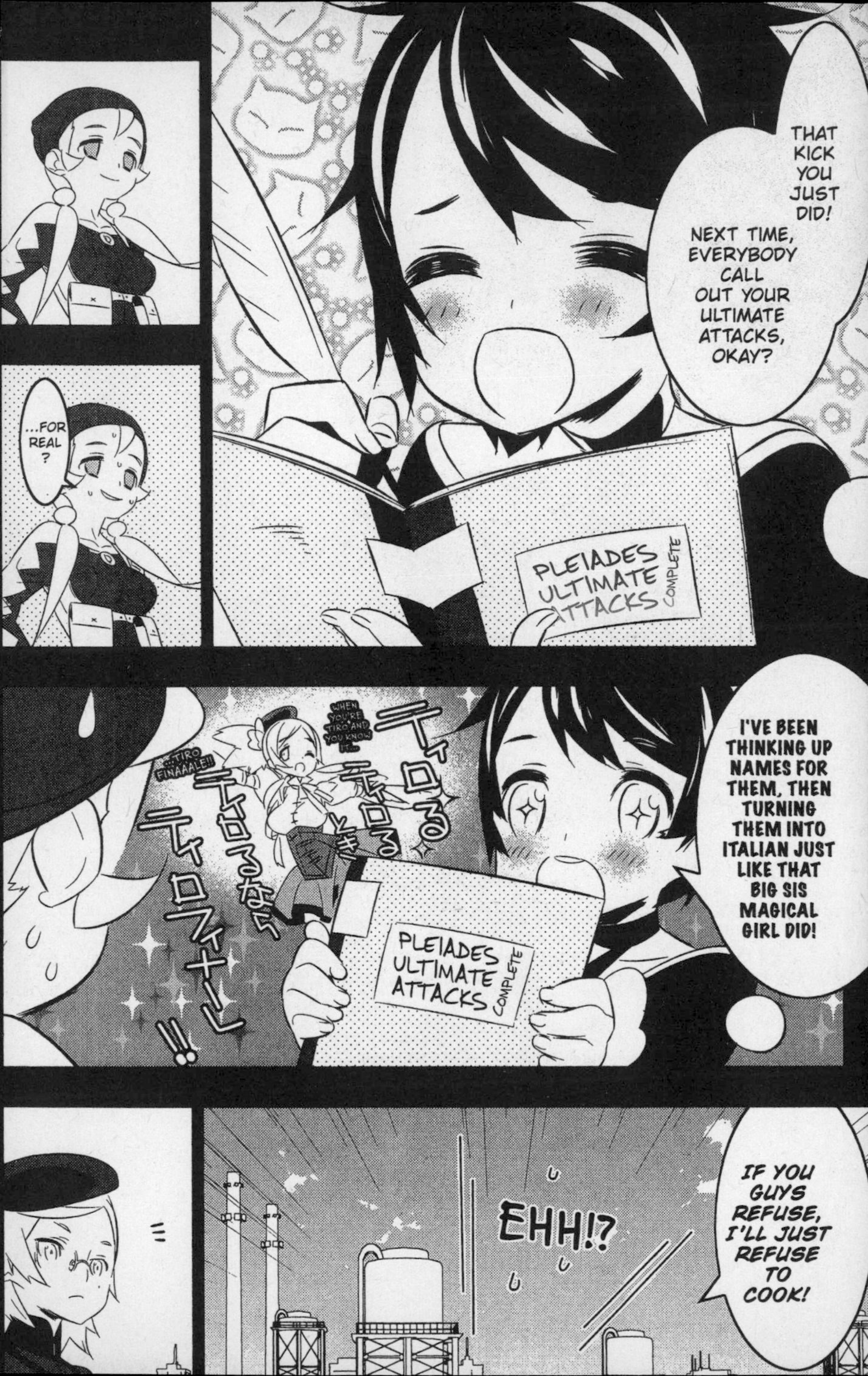
THAT KICK YOU JUST DID!
NEXT TIME, EVERYBODY CALL OUT YOUR ULTIMATE ATTACKS, OKAY?
PLEIADES ULTIMATE ATTACKS COMPLETE
...FOR REAL?
I'VE BEEN THINKING UP NAMES FOR THEM, THEN TURNING THEM INTO ITALIAN JUST LIKE THAT BIG SIS MAGICAL GIRL DID!
ティロるティロるときティロるならティロフィナーレ!!
WHEN YOU'RE TIRO AND YOU KNOW IT...
...TIRO FINAAALE!!
PLEIADES ULTIMATE ATTACKS COMPLETE
IF YOU GUYS REFUSE, I'LL JUST REFUSE TO COOK!
EHH!?

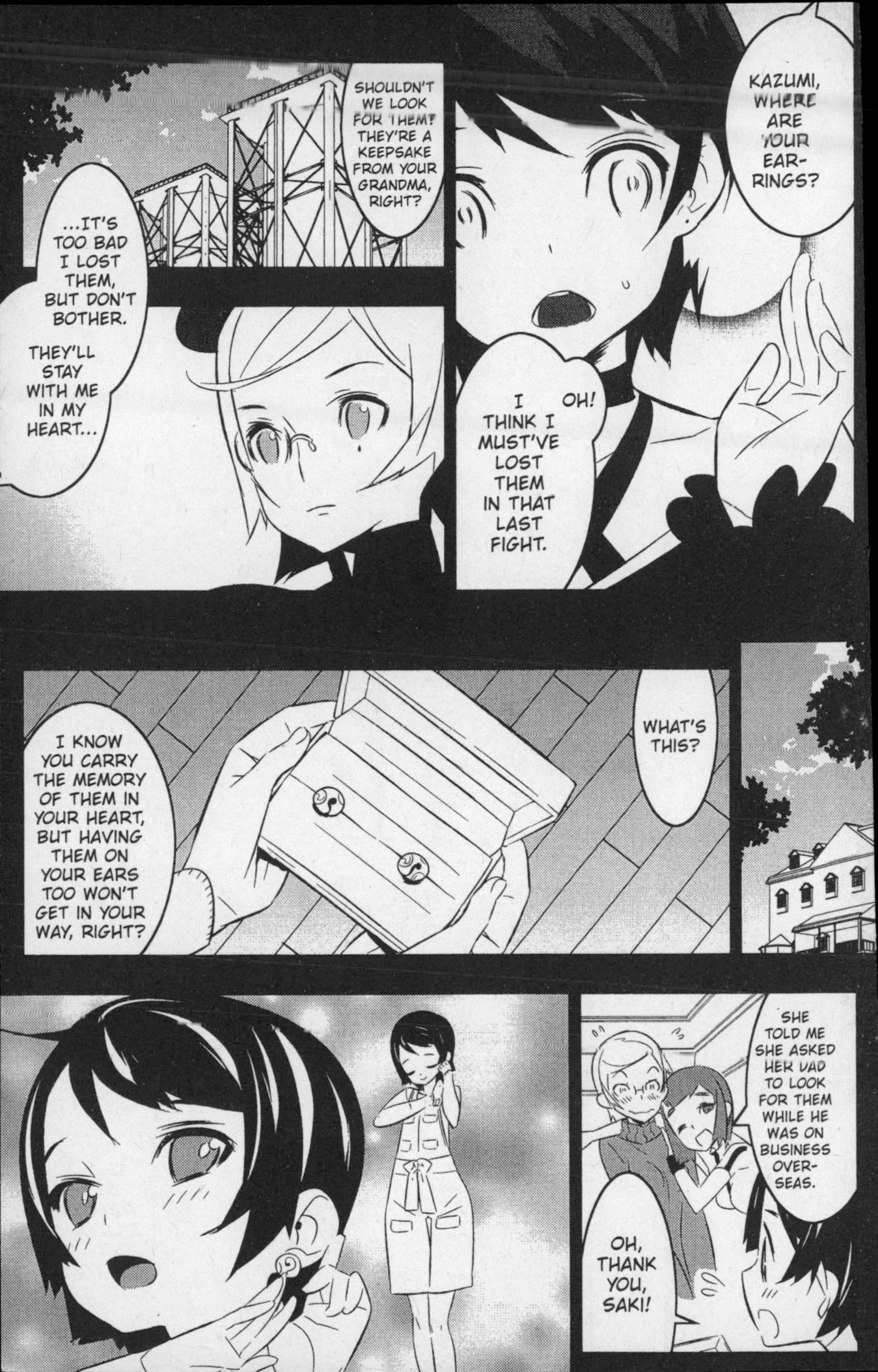
KAZUMI, WHERE ARE YOUR EAR-RINGS?
OH! I THINK I MUST'VE LOST THEM IN THAT LAST FIGHT.
SHOULDN'T WE LOOK FOR THEM? THEY'RE A KEEPSAKE FROM YOUR GRANDMA, RIGHT?
...IT'S TOO BAD I LOST THEM, BUT DON'T BOTHER.
THEY'LL STAY WITH ME IN MY HEART...
WHAT'S THIS?
I KNOW YOU CARRY THE MEMORY OF THEM IN YOUR HEART, BUT HAVING THEM ON YOUR EARS TOO WON'T GET IN YOUR WAY, RIGHT?
SHE TOLD ME SHE ASKED HER DAD TO LOOK FOR THEM WHILE HE WAS ON BUSINESS OVER-SEAS.
OH, THANK YOU, SAKI!

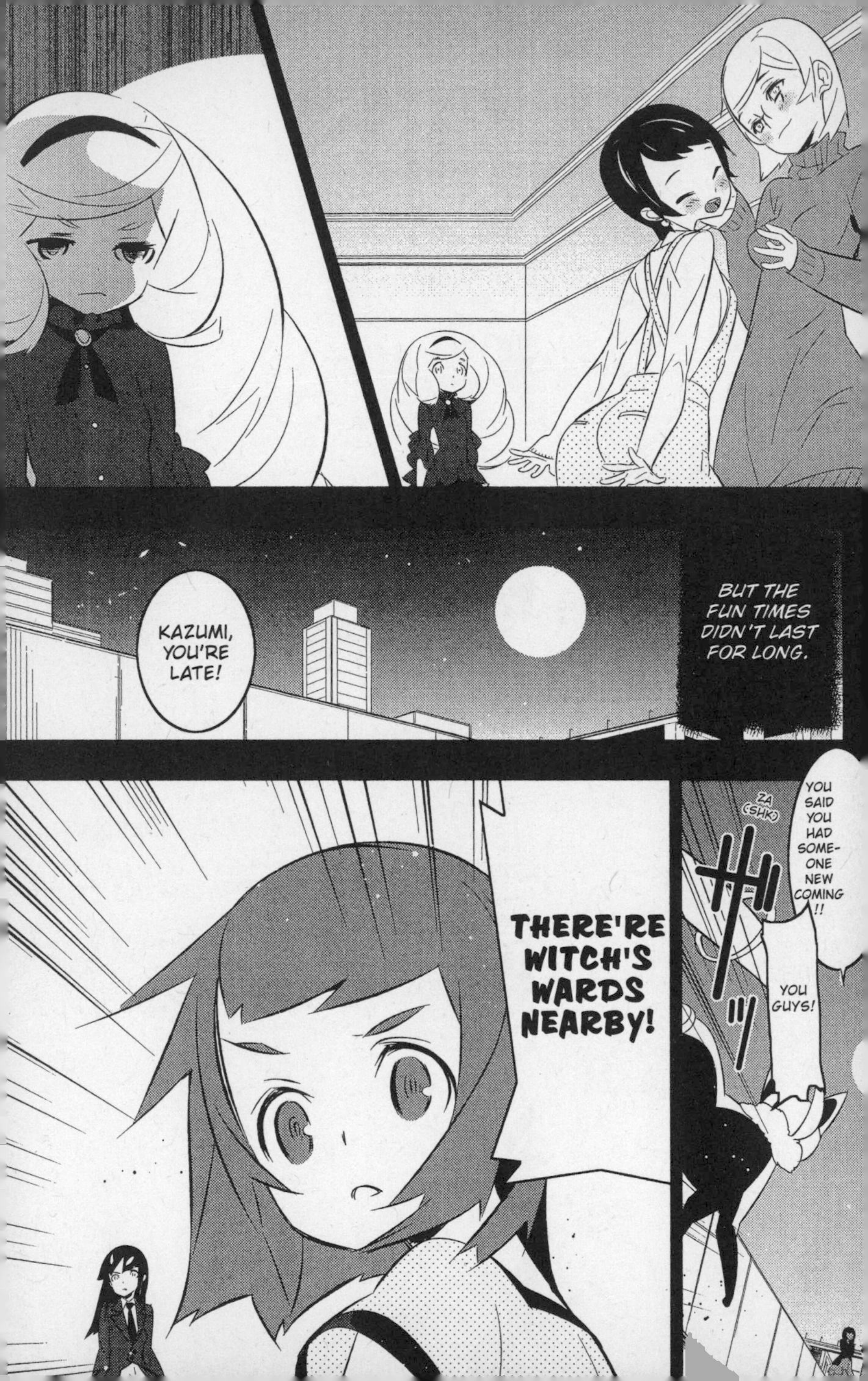
BUT THE FUN TIMES DIDN'T LAST FOR LONG.
KAZUMI, YOU'RE LATE!
YOU SAID YOU HAD SOME-ONE NEW COMING!!
ZA (SHK)
YOU GUYS!
THERE'RE WITCH'S WARDS NEARBY!

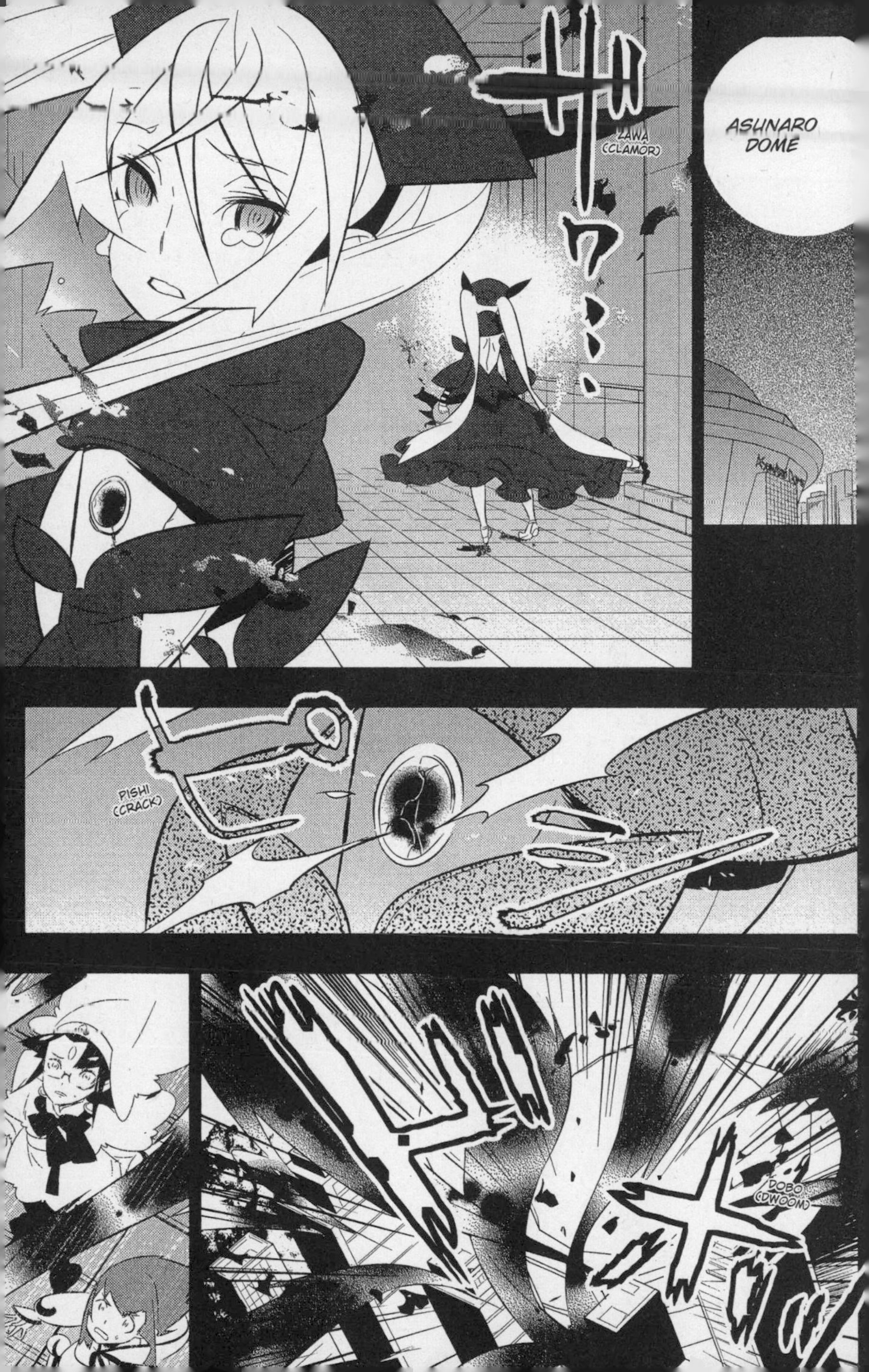
ASUNARO DOME
ZAWA (CLAMOR)
PISHI (CRACK)
DOBO (DWOOM)

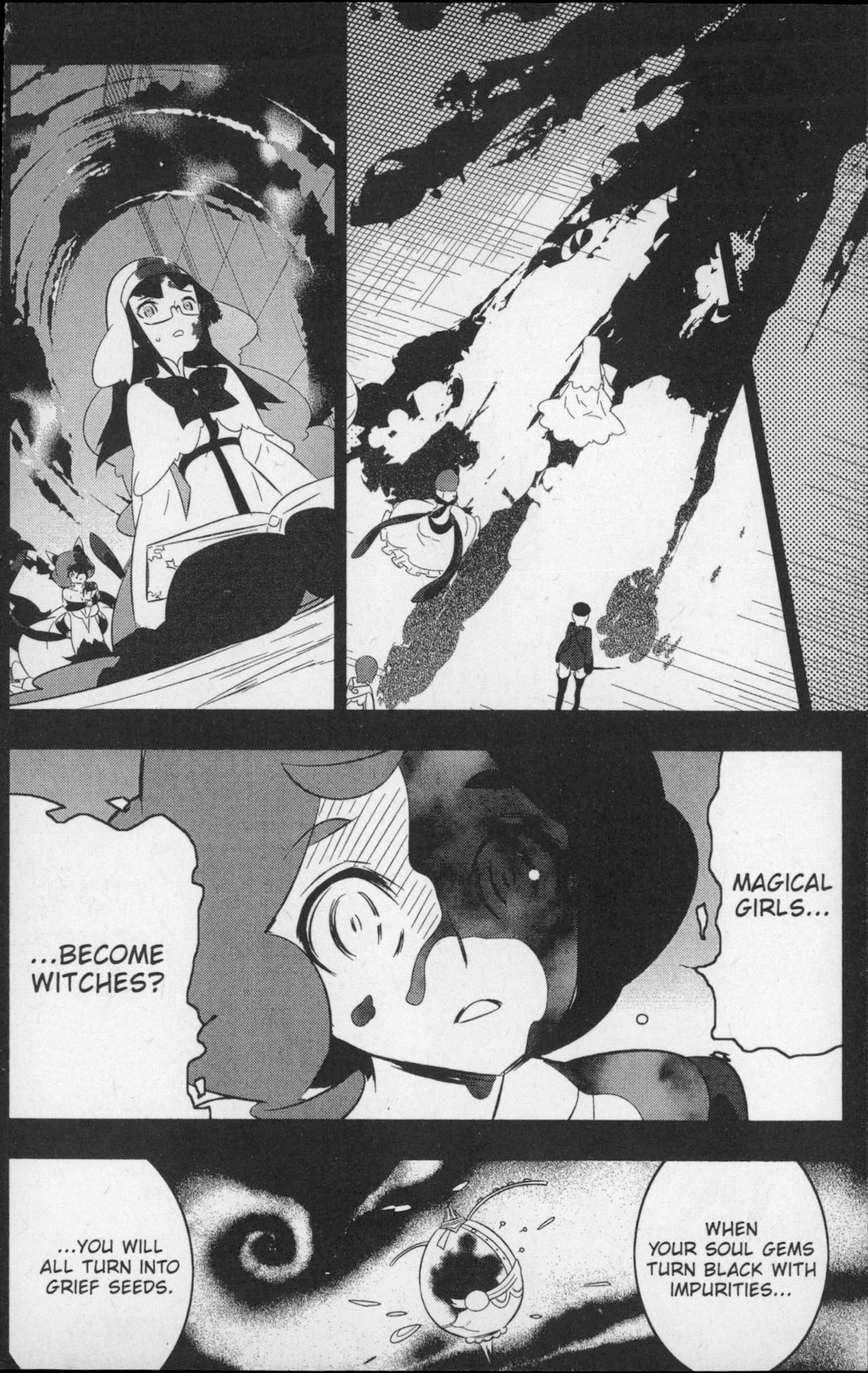
MAGICAL GIRLS...
...BECOME WITCHES?
WHEN YOUR SOUL GEMS TURN BLACK WITH IMPURITIES...
...YOU WILL ALL TURN INTO GRIEF SEEDS.

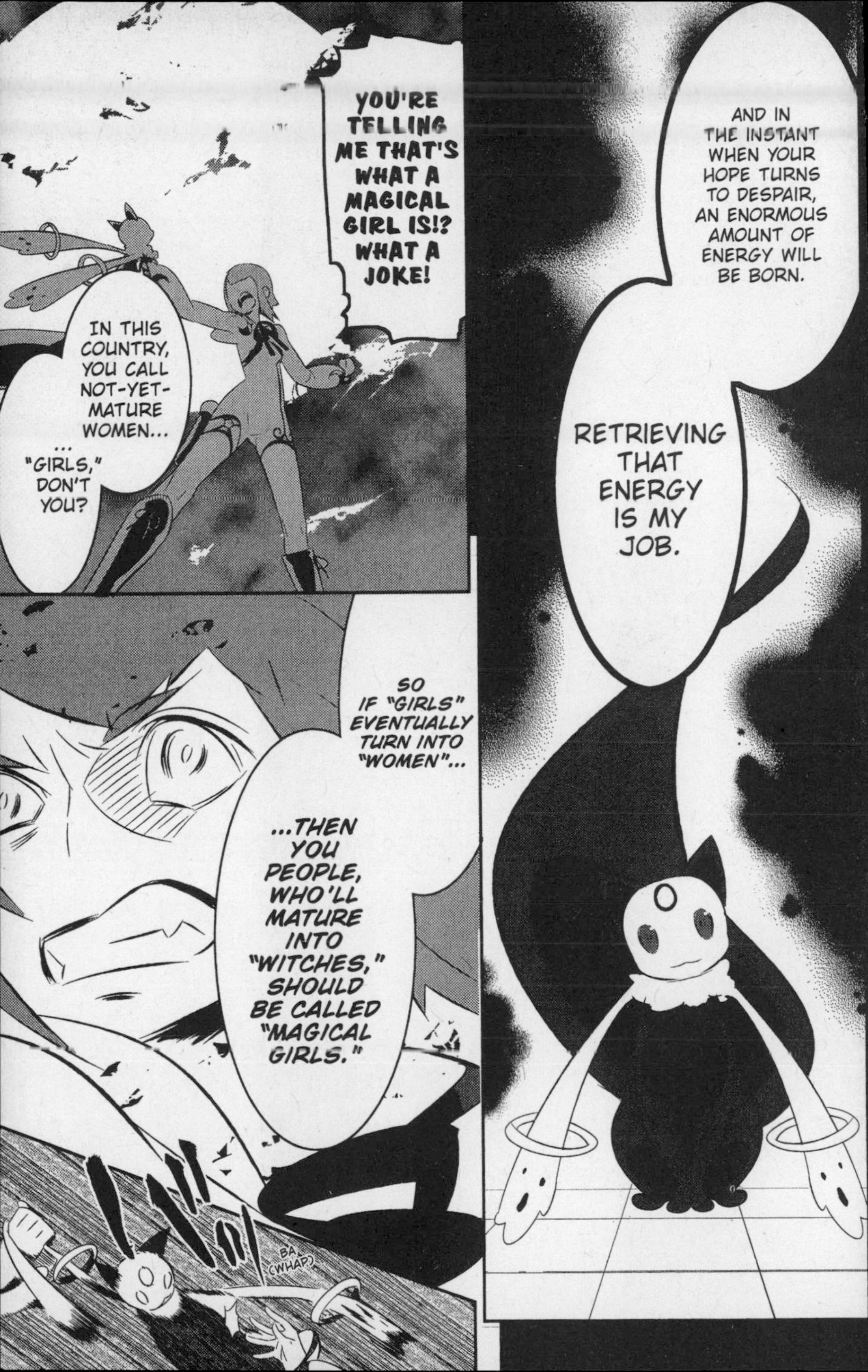
AND IN THE INSTANT WHEN YOUR HOPE TURNS TO DESPAIR, AN ENORMOUS AMOUNT OF ENERGY WILL BE BORN.
RETRIEVING THAT ENERGY IS MY JOB.
YOU'RE TELLING ME THAT'S WHAT A MAGICAL GIRL IS!? WHAT A JOKE!
IN THIS COUNTRY, YOU CALL NOT-YET-MATURE WOMEN... ... "GIRLS," DON'T YOU?
SO IF "GIRLS" EVENTUALLY TURN INTO "WOMEN"...
...THEN YOU PEOPLE, WHO'LL MATURE INTO "WITCHES," SHOULD BE CALLED "MAGICAL GIRLS."
BA (WHAP)

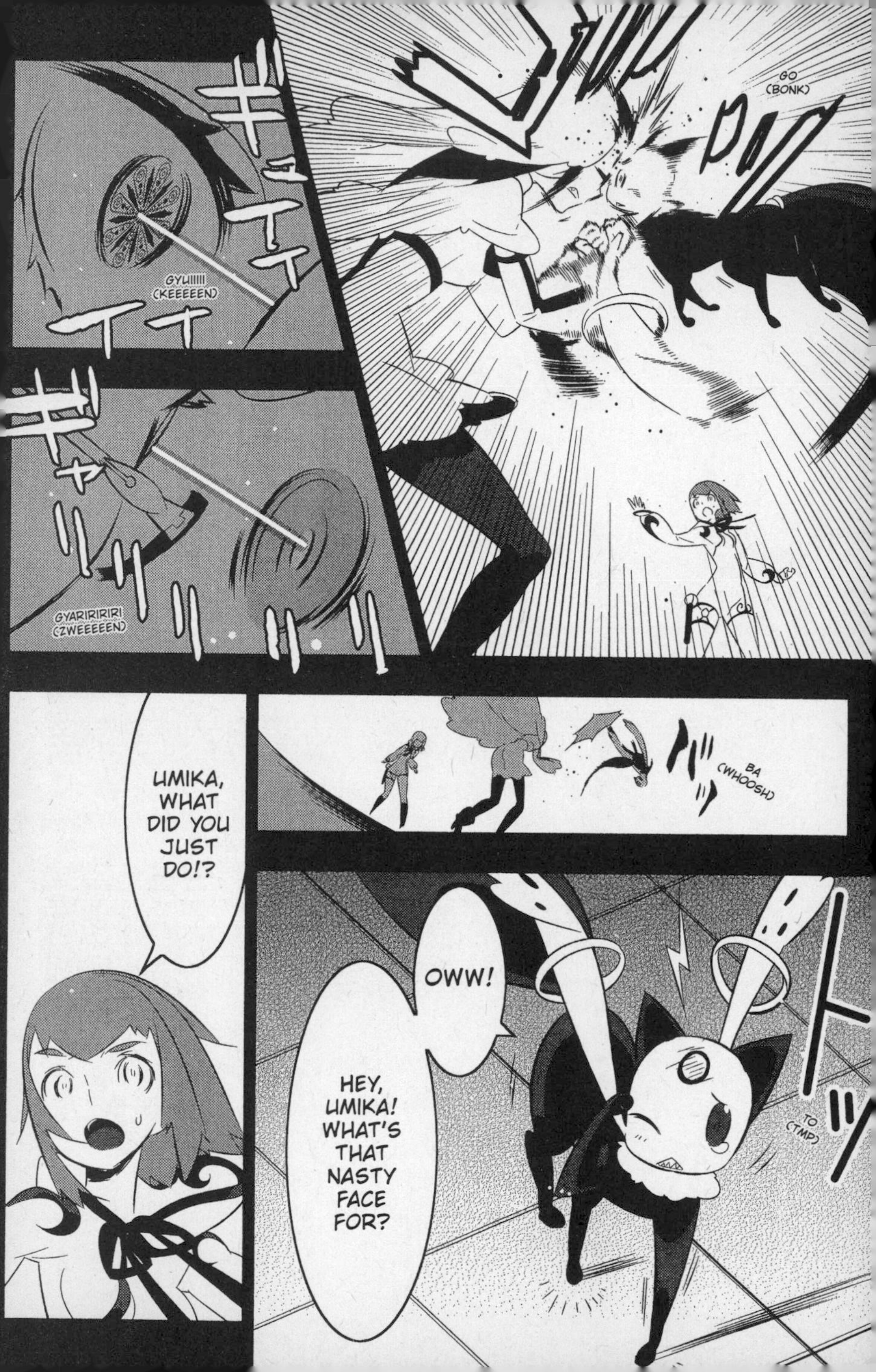
GO
(BONK)
GYUIIII
(KEEEEEN)
GYARIRIRIRI
(ZWEEEEEN)
BA
(WHOOSH)
OWW!
HEY, UMIKA! WHAT'S THAT NASTY FACE FOR?
TO
(TMP)
UMIKA, WHAT DID YOU JUST DO!?

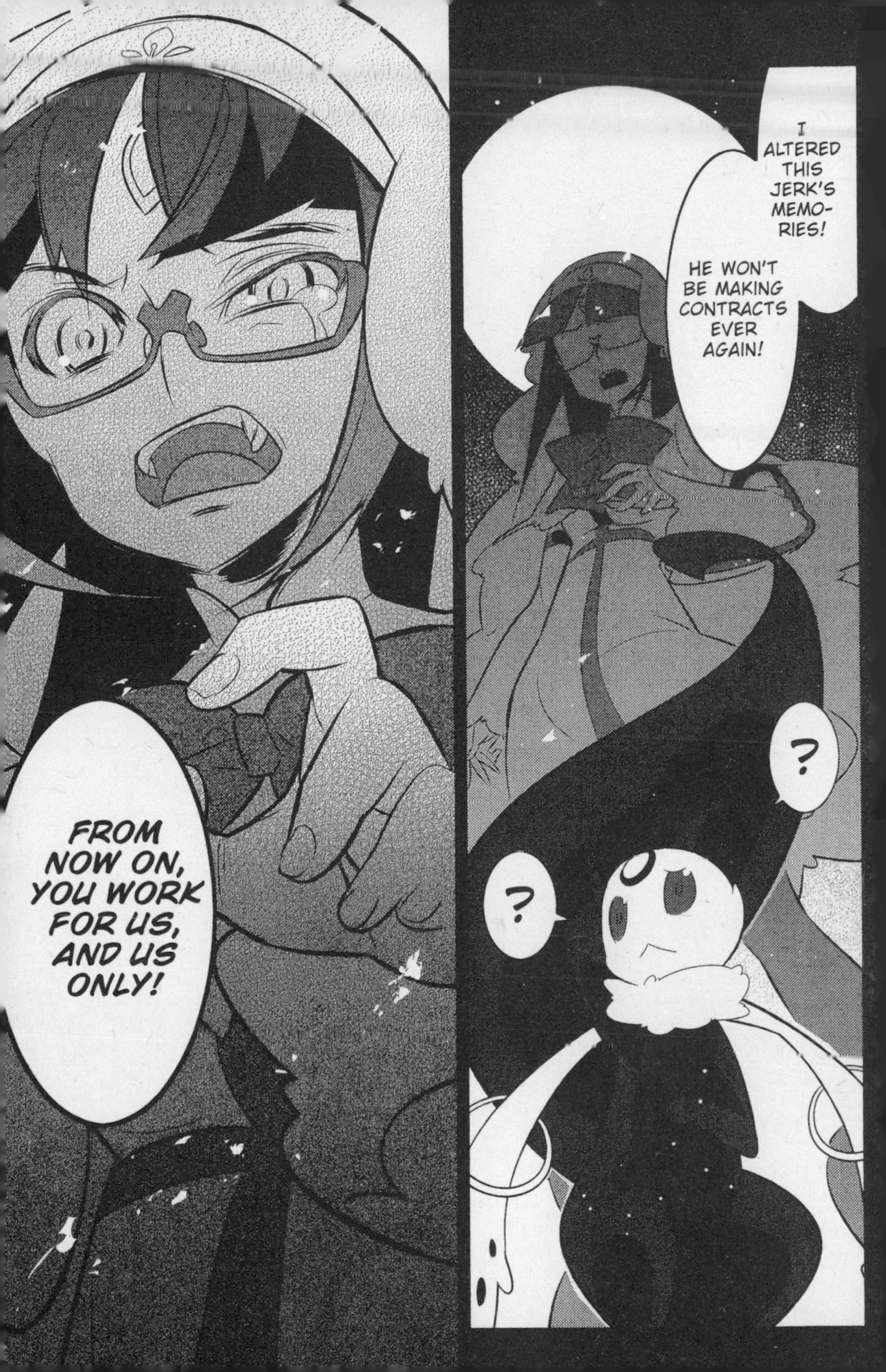
I ALTERED THIS JERK'S MEMO-RIES!
HE WON'T BE MAKING CONTRACTS EVER AGAIN!
?
?
FROM NOW ON, YOU WORK FOR US, AND US ONLY!

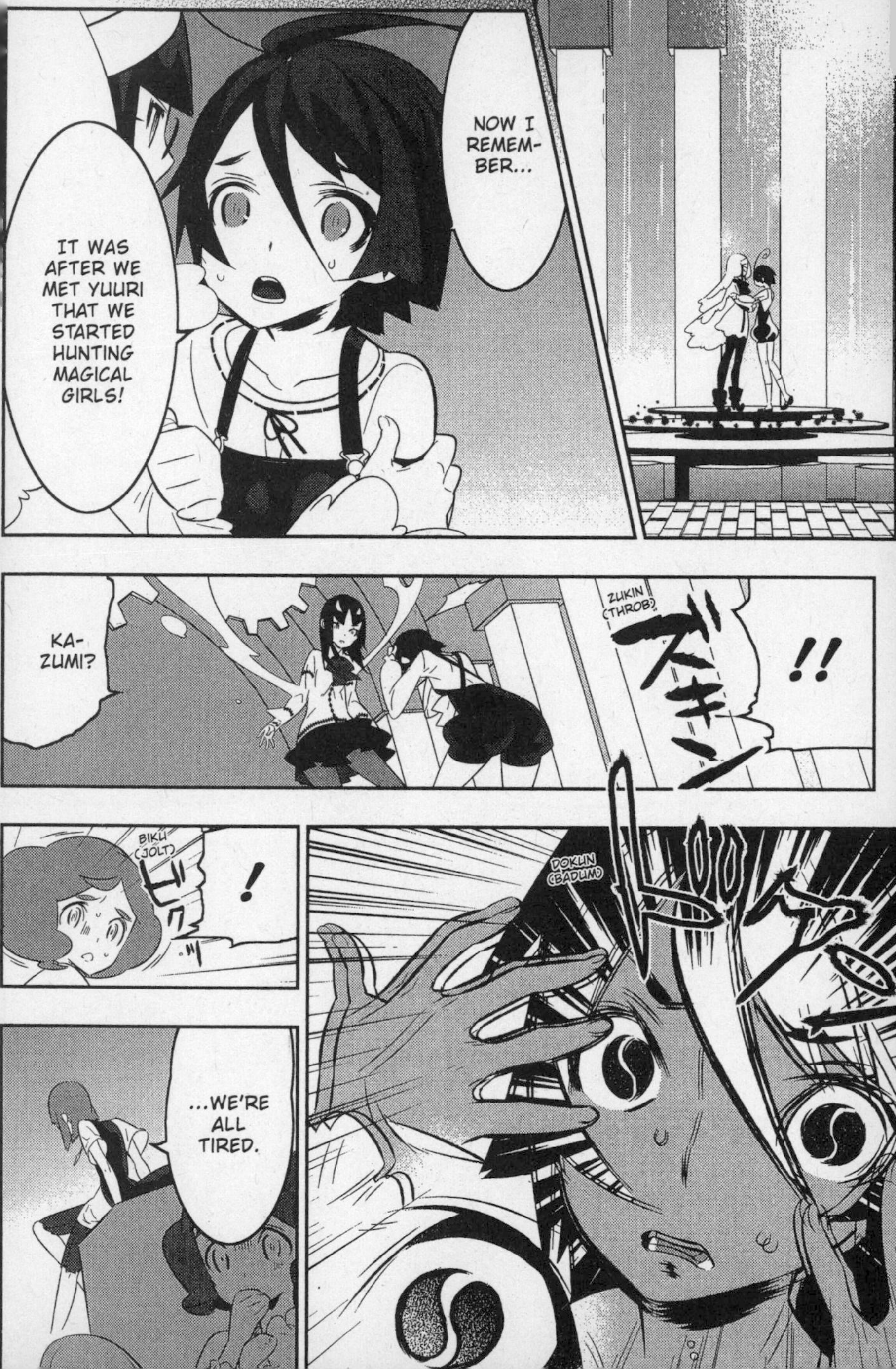
NOW I REMEMBER...
IT WAS AFTER WE MET YUURI THAT WE STARTED HUNTING MAGICAL GIRLS!
ZUKIN (THROB)
!!
KA-ZUMI?
DOKUN (BADUM)
BIKU (JOLT)
!
...WE'RE ALL TIRED.

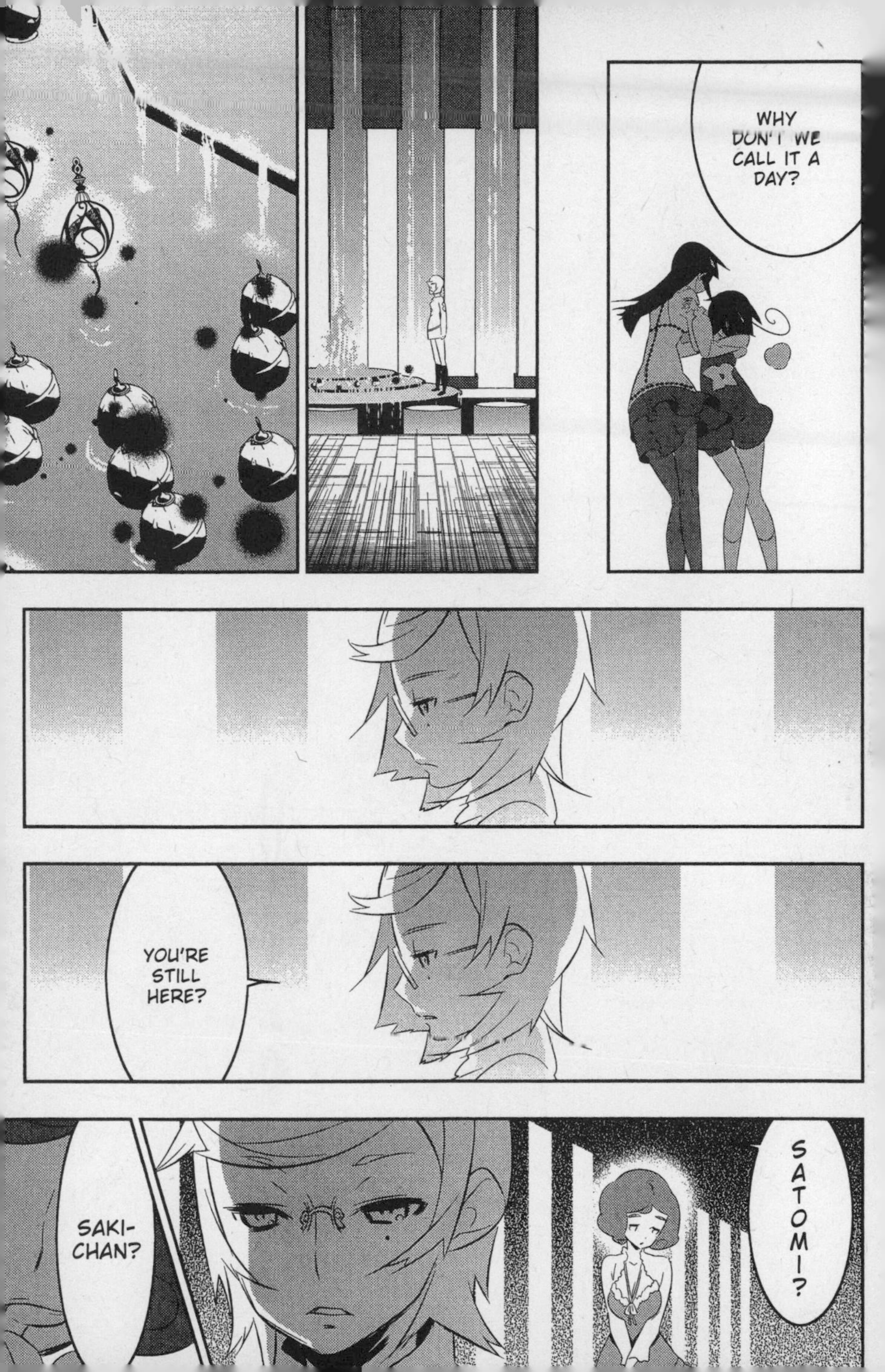
WHY DON'T WE CALL IT A DAY?
YOU'RE STILL HERE?
SATOMI-?
SAKI-CHAN?

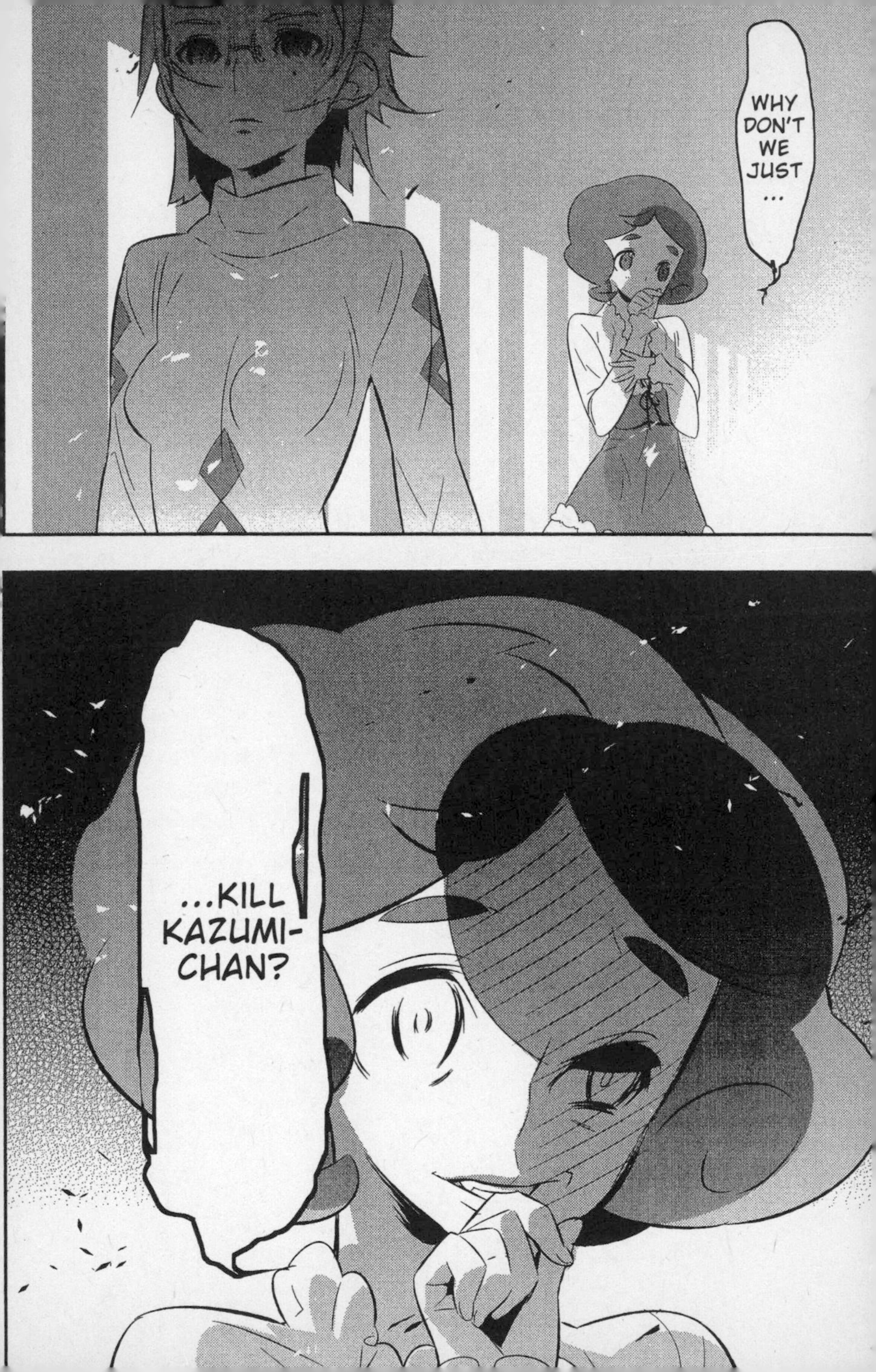
WHY DON'T WE JUST ...
...KILL KAZUMI-CHAN?

YOUNG
GRANDMA

PUELLA MAGI
KAZUMI ★ MAGICA
The innocent malice

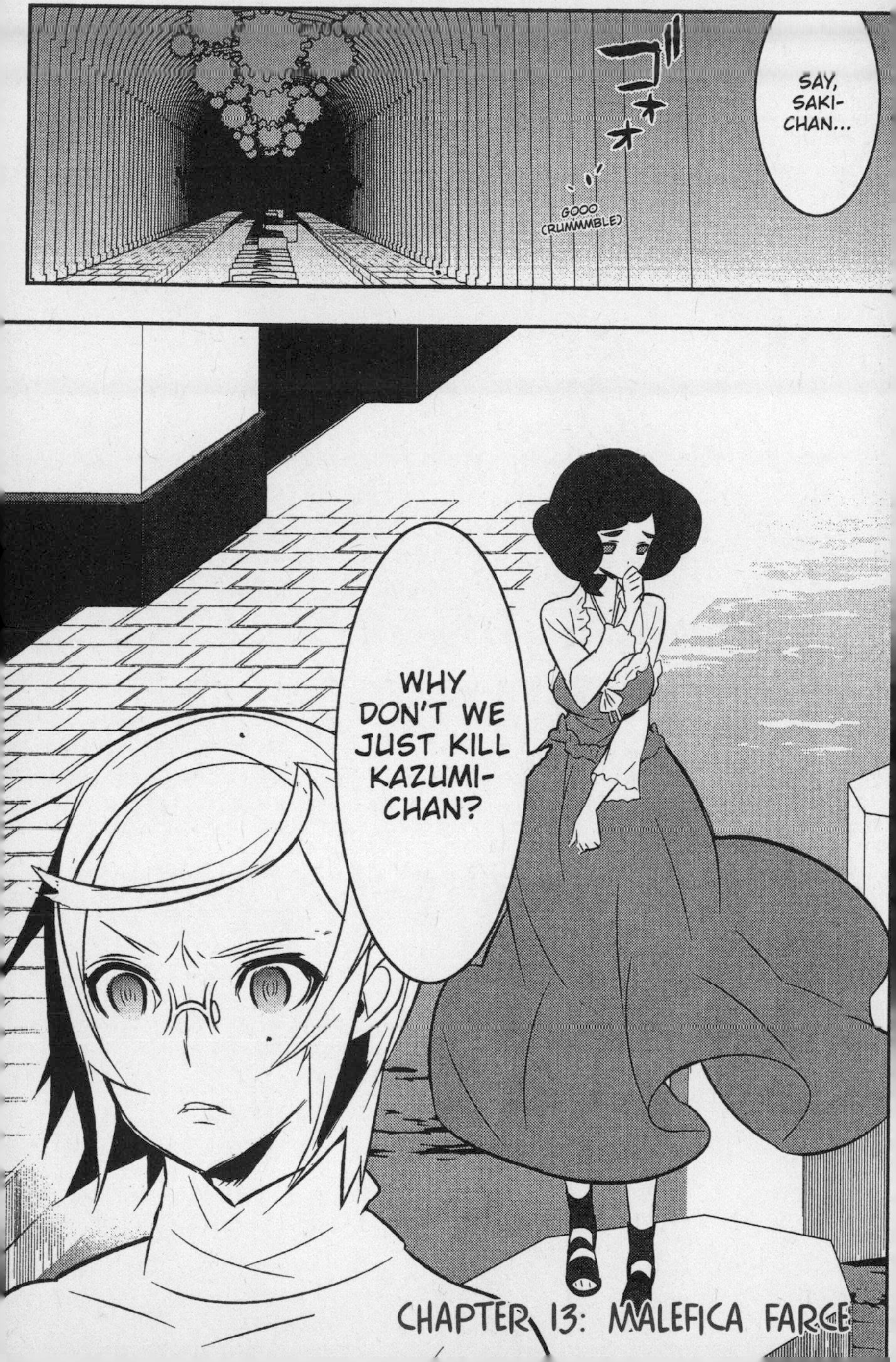
SAY, SAKI-CHAN...
ゴォォ
GOOO (RUMMMBLE)
WHY DON'T WE JUST KILL KAZUMI-CHAN?
CHAPTER 13: MALEFICA FARCE

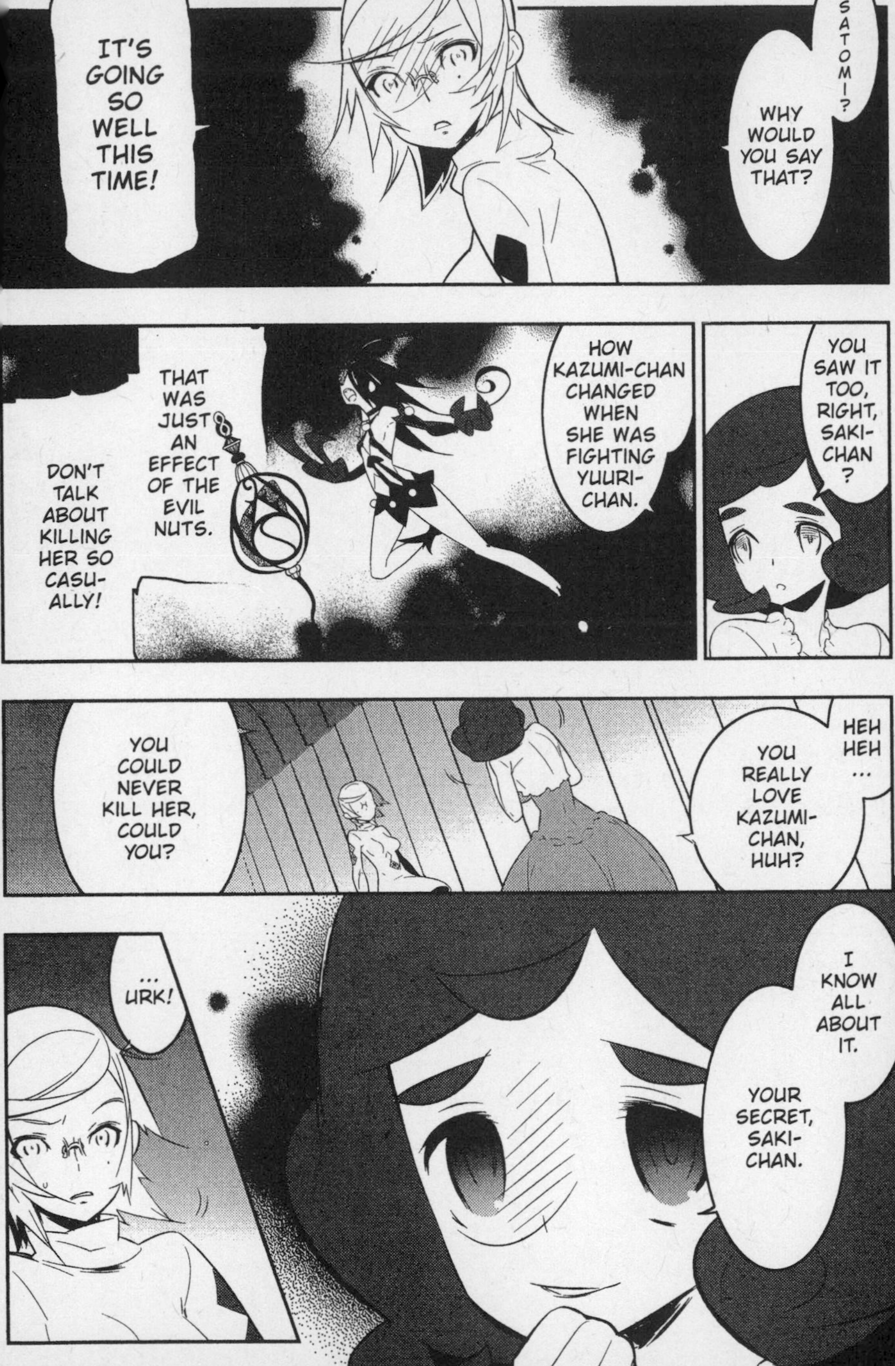
SATOMI? WHY WOULD YOU SAY THAT?
IT'S GOING SO WELL THIS TIME!
YOU SAW IT TOO, RIGHT, SAKI-CHAN?
HOW KAZUMI-CHAN CHANGED WHEN SHE WAS FIGHTING YUURI-CHAN.
THAT WAS JUST AN EFFECT OF THE EVIL NUTS.
DON'T TALK ABOUT KILLING HER SO CASUALLY!
HEH HEH...
YOU REALLY LOVE KAZUMI-CHAN, HUH?
YOU COULD NEVER KILL HER, COULD YOU?
I KNOW ALL ABOUT IT.
YOUR SECRET, SAKI-CHAN.
...URK!

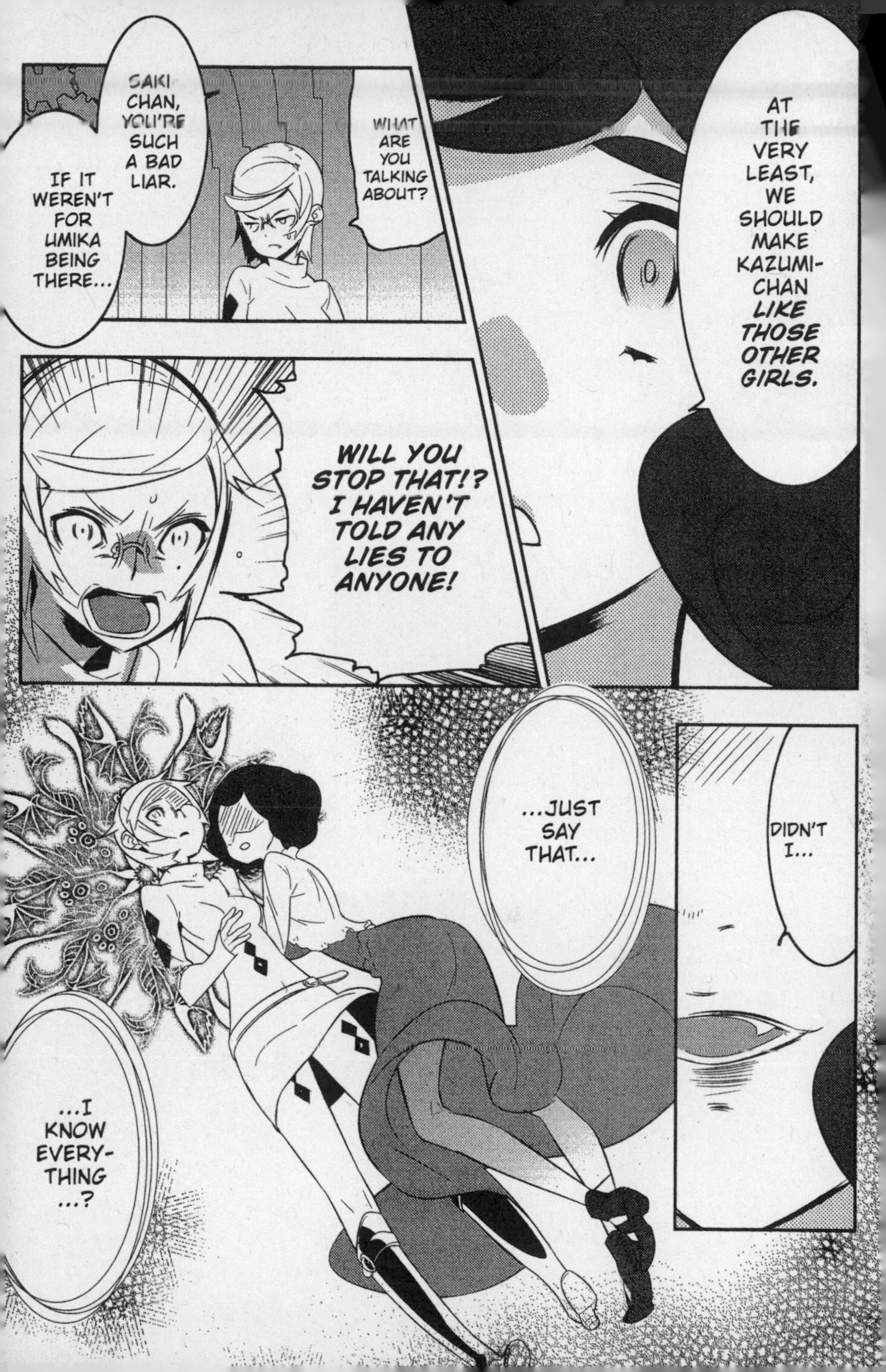
AT THE VERY LEAST, WE SHOULD MAKE KAZUMI-CHAN *LIKE THOSE OTHER GIRLS.*
WHAT ARE YOU TALKING ABOUT?
SAKI CHAN, YOU'RE SUCH A BAD LIAR.
IF IT WEREN'T FOR UMIKA BEING THERE...
WILL YOU STOP THAT!? I HAVEN'T TOLD ANY LIES TO ANYONE!
DIDN'T I...
...JUST SAY THAT...
...I KNOW EVERY-THING...?

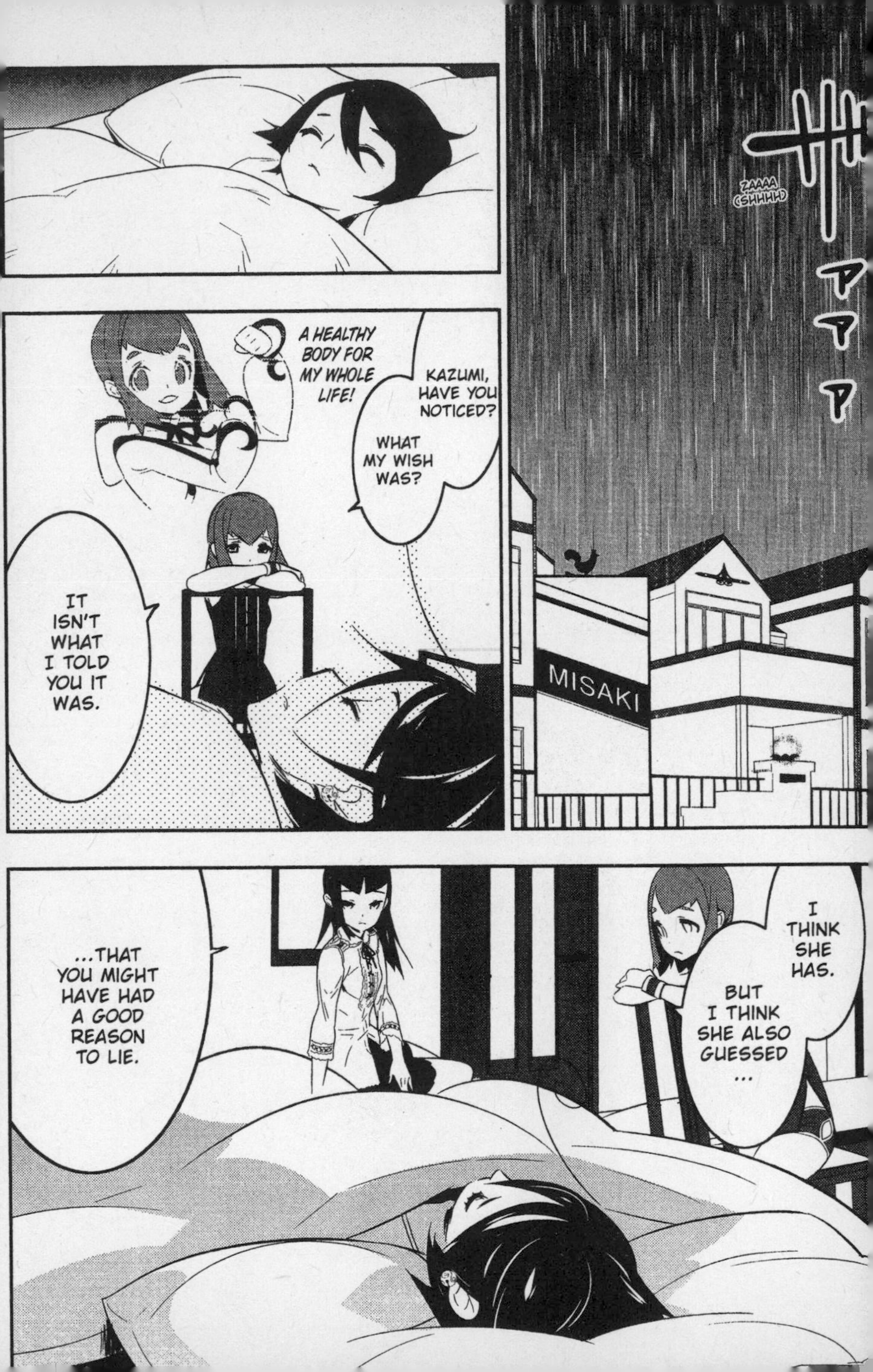
ZAAAA (SHHHH)
MISAKI
KAZUMI, HAVE YOU NOTICED?
WHAT MY WISH WAS?
A HEALTHY BODY FOR MY WHOLE LIFE!
IT ISN'T WHAT I TOLD YOU IT WAS.
I THINK SHE HAS.
BUT I THINK SHE ALSO GUESSED...
...THAT YOU MIGHT HAVE HAD A GOOD REASON TO LIE.

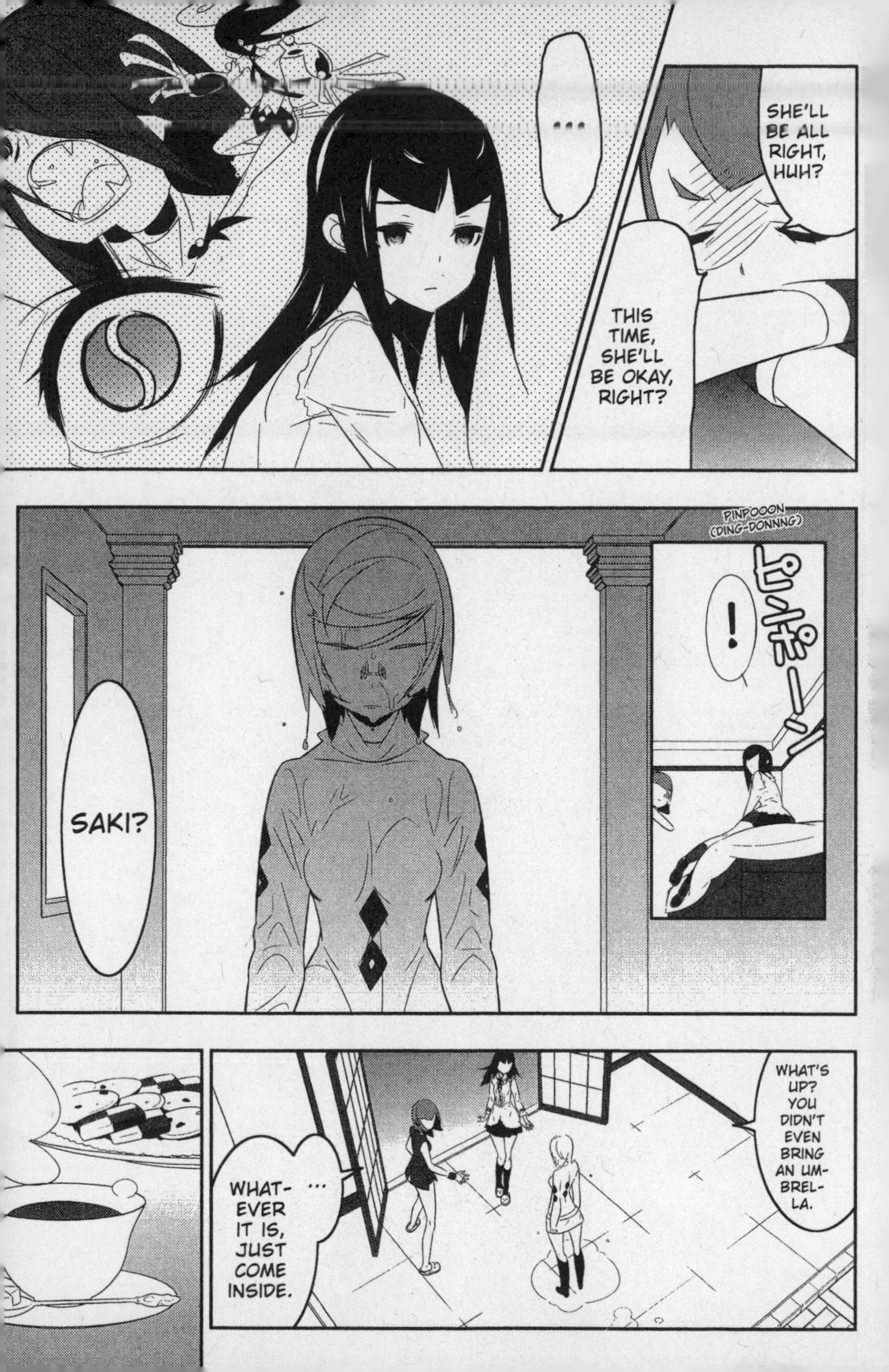
SHE'LL BE ALL RIGHT, HUH?
THIS TIME, SHE'LL BE OKAY, RIGHT?
...
PINPOOON (DING-DONNNG)
ピンポーン
!
SAKI?
WHAT'S UP? YOU DIDN'T EVEN BRING AN UM-BREL-LA.
...
WHAT-EVER IT IS, JUST COME INSIDE.

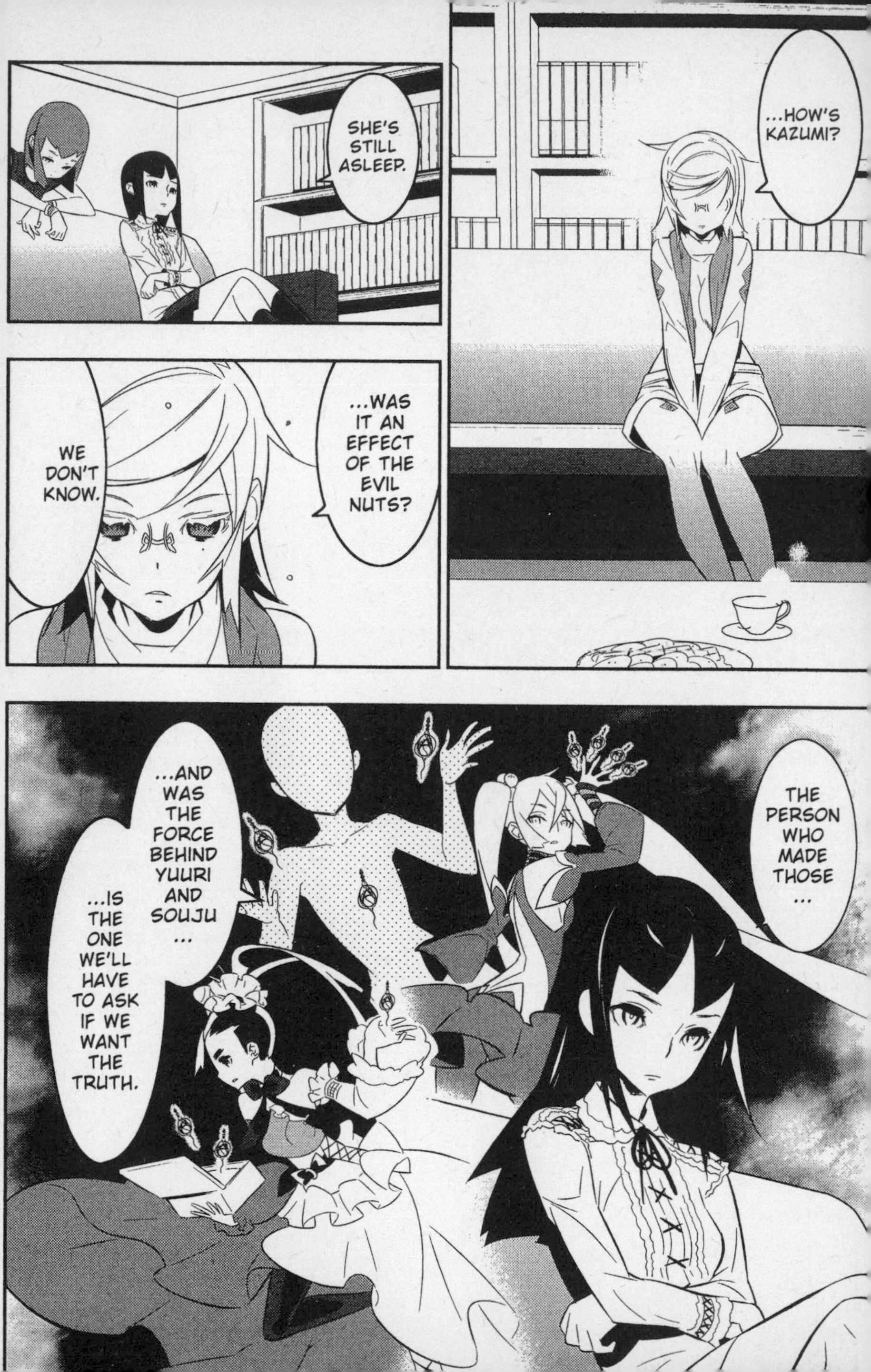
...HOW'S KAZUMI?
SHE'S STILL ASLEEP.
...WAS IT AN EFFECT OF THE EVIL NUTS?
WE DON'T KNOW.
THE PERSON WHO MADE THOSE...
...AND WAS THE FORCE BEHIND YUURI AND SOUJU...
...IS THE ONE WE'LL HAVE TO ASK IF WE WANT THE TRUTH.

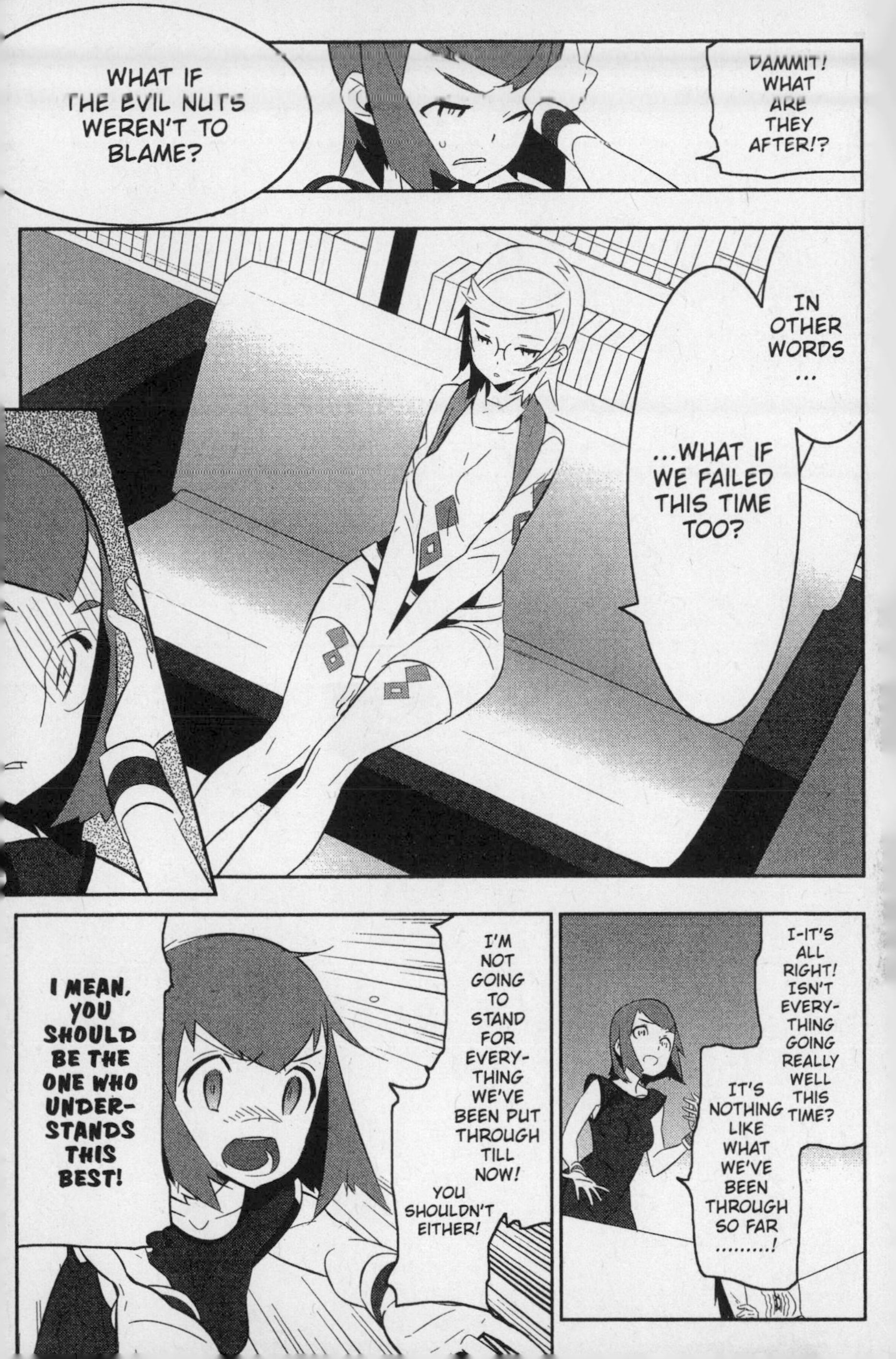
DAMMIT! WHAT ARE THEY AFTER!?
WHAT IF THE EVIL NUTS WEREN'T TO BLAME?
IN OTHER WORDS...
...WHAT IF WE FAILED THIS TIME TOO?
I-IT'S ALL RIGHT! ISN'T EVERYTHING GOING REALLY WELL THIS TIME?
IT'S NOTHING LIKE WHAT WE'VE BEEN THROUGH SO FAR..........!
I'M NOT GOING TO STAND FOR EVERYTHING WE'VE BEEN PUT THROUGH TILL NOW!
YOU SHOULDN'T EITHER!
I MEAN, YOU SHOULD BE THE ONE WHO UNDERSTANDS THIS BEST!

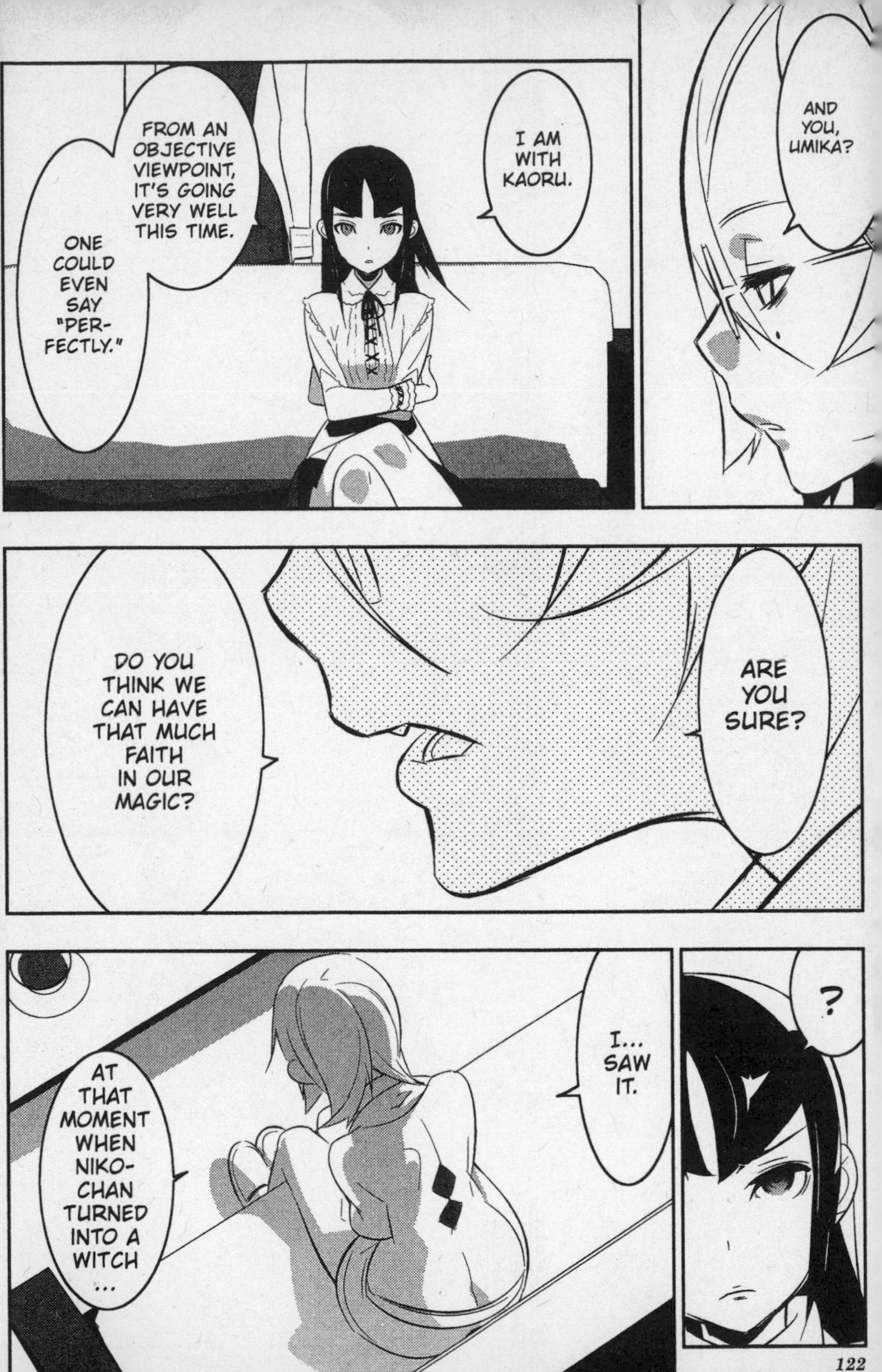
AND YOU, UMIKA?
I AM WITH KAORU.
FROM AN OBJECTIVE VIEWPOINT, IT'S GOING VERY WELL THIS TIME.
ONE COULD EVEN SAY "PER-FECTLY."
ARE YOU SURE?
DO YOU THINK WE CAN HAVE THAT MUCH FAITH IN OUR MAGIC?
?
I... SAW IT.
AT THAT MOMENT WHEN NIKO-CHAN TURNED INTO A WITCH...

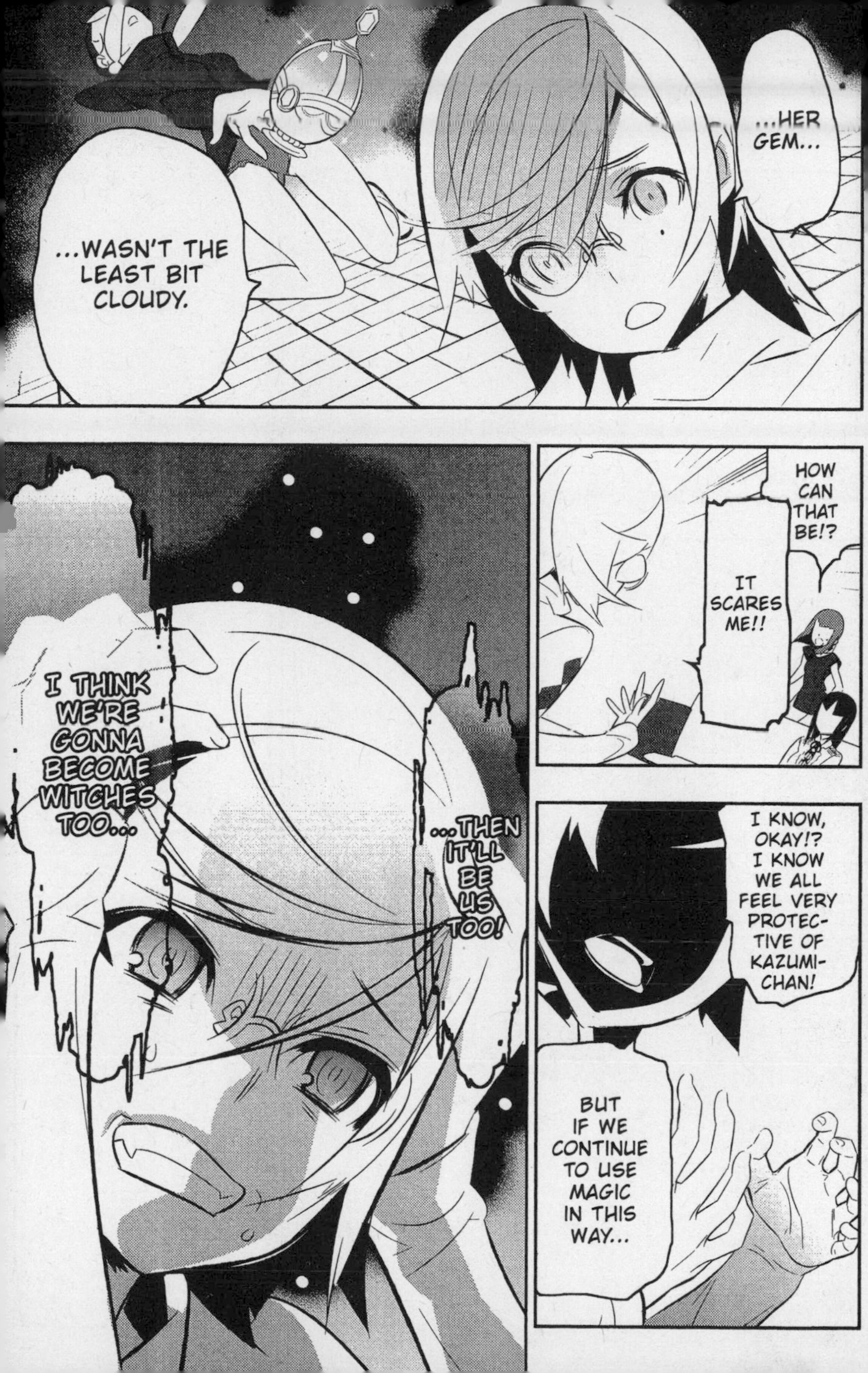
...HER GEM...
...WASN'T THE LEAST BIT CLOUDY.
HOW CAN THAT BE!?
IT SCARES ME!!
I KNOW, OKAY!? I KNOW WE ALL FEEL VERY PROTEC-TIVE OF KAZUMI-CHAN!
BUT IF WE CONTINUE TO USE MAGIC IN THIS WAY...
I THINK WE'RE GONNA BECOME WITCHES TOO...
...THEN IT'LL BE US TOO!

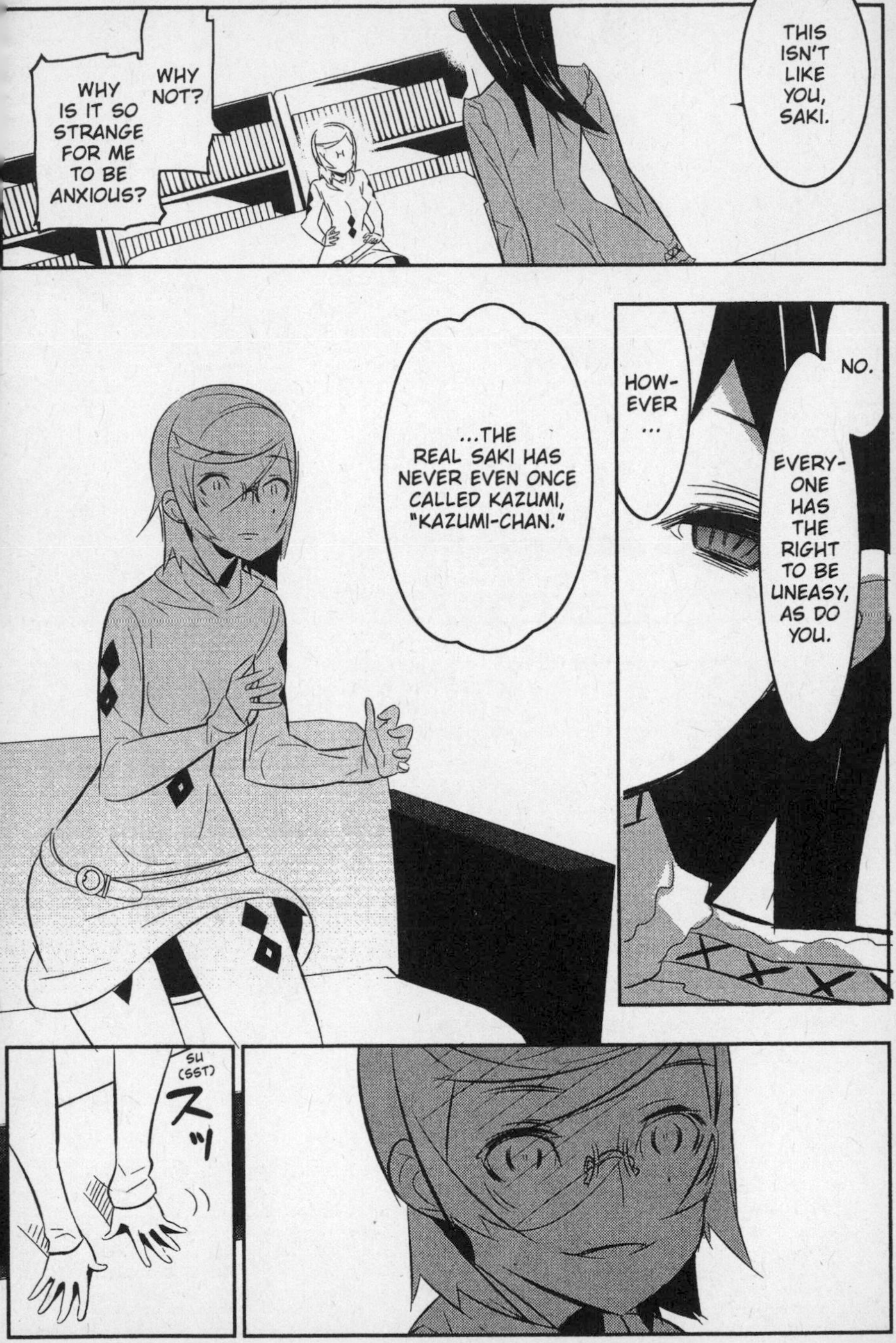
THIS ISN'T LIKE YOU, SAKI.
WHY NOT?
WHY IS IT SO STRANGE FOR ME TO BE ANXIOUS?
NO.
EVERYONE HAS THE RIGHT TO BE UNEASY, AS DO YOU.
HOWEVER...
...THE REAL SAKI HAS NEVER EVEN ONCE CALLED KAZUMI, "KAZUMI-CHAN."
SU (SST)
スッ

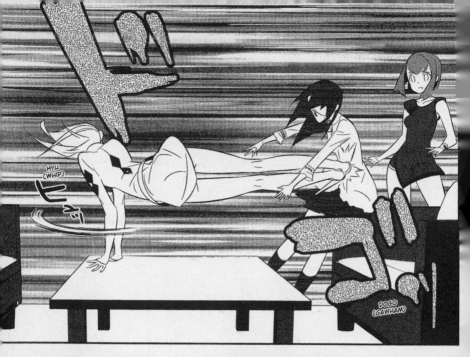

HYU
(WHIP)

DOGO
(GAWHAM)

GUH!

HFF!

UMIKA!

GASHA
(GRAASH)

SHE'S
BEING
CON-
TROLLED
!?

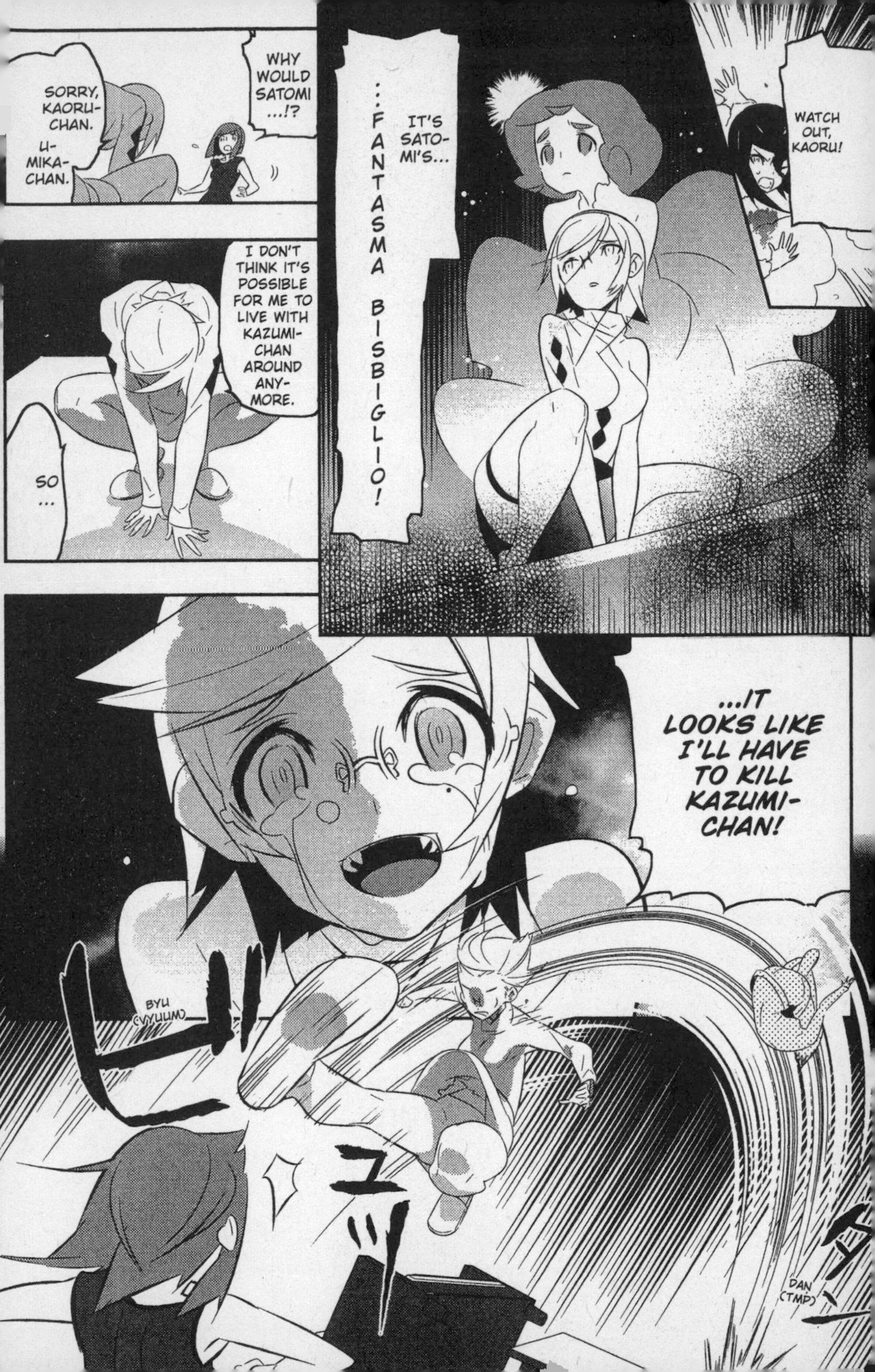

WATCH OUT, KAORU!
IT'S SATOMI'S...
...FANTASMA BISBIGLIO!
WHY WOULD SATOMI ...!?
SORRY, KAORU-CHAN.
U-MIKA-CHAN.
I DON'T THINK IT'S POSSIBLE FOR ME TO LIVE WITH KAZUMI-CHAN AROUND ANYMORE.
SO ...
...IT LOOKS LIKE I'LL HAVE TO KILL KAZUMI-CHAN!
BYU (VYUUM)
DAN (TMP)

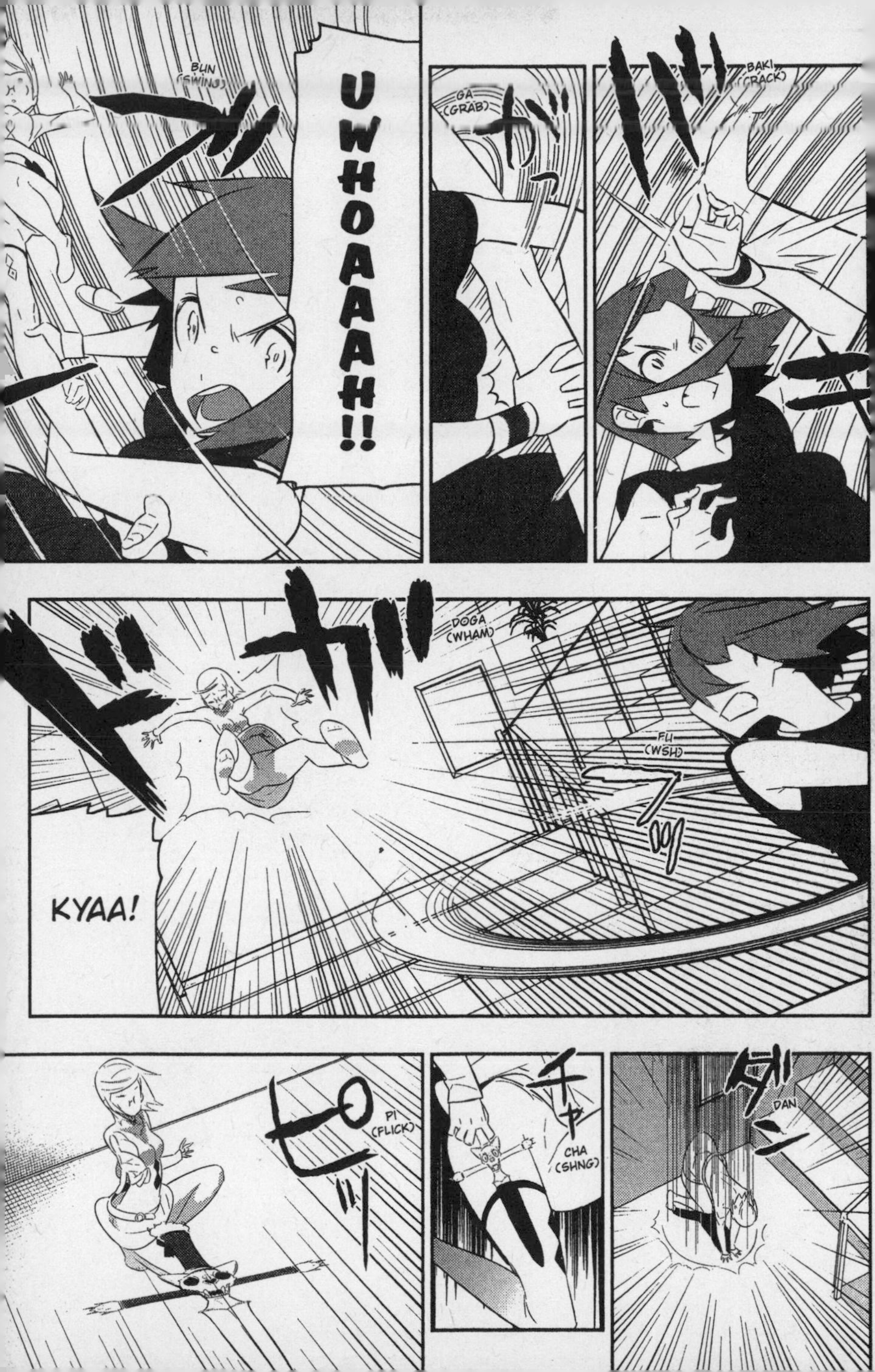
BAKI (CRACK)
GA (GRAB)
UWHOAAAAH!!
BUN (SWING)
DOGA (WHAM)
FU (WSH)
KYAA!
DAN
CHA (SHNG)
PI (FLICK)

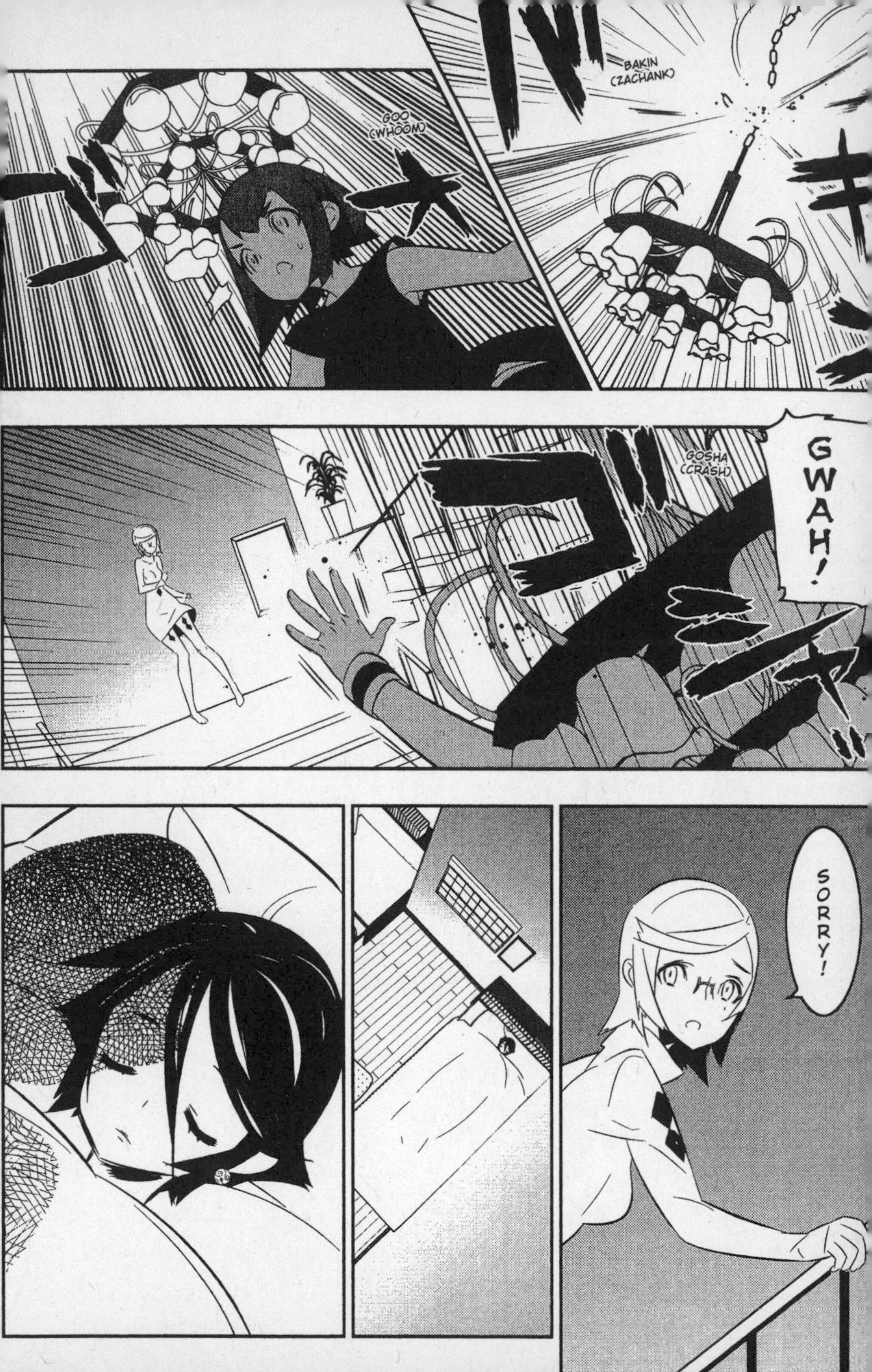
BAKIN
(ZACHANK)
GOO
(WHOOM)
GOSHA
(CRASH)
GWAH!
SORRY!

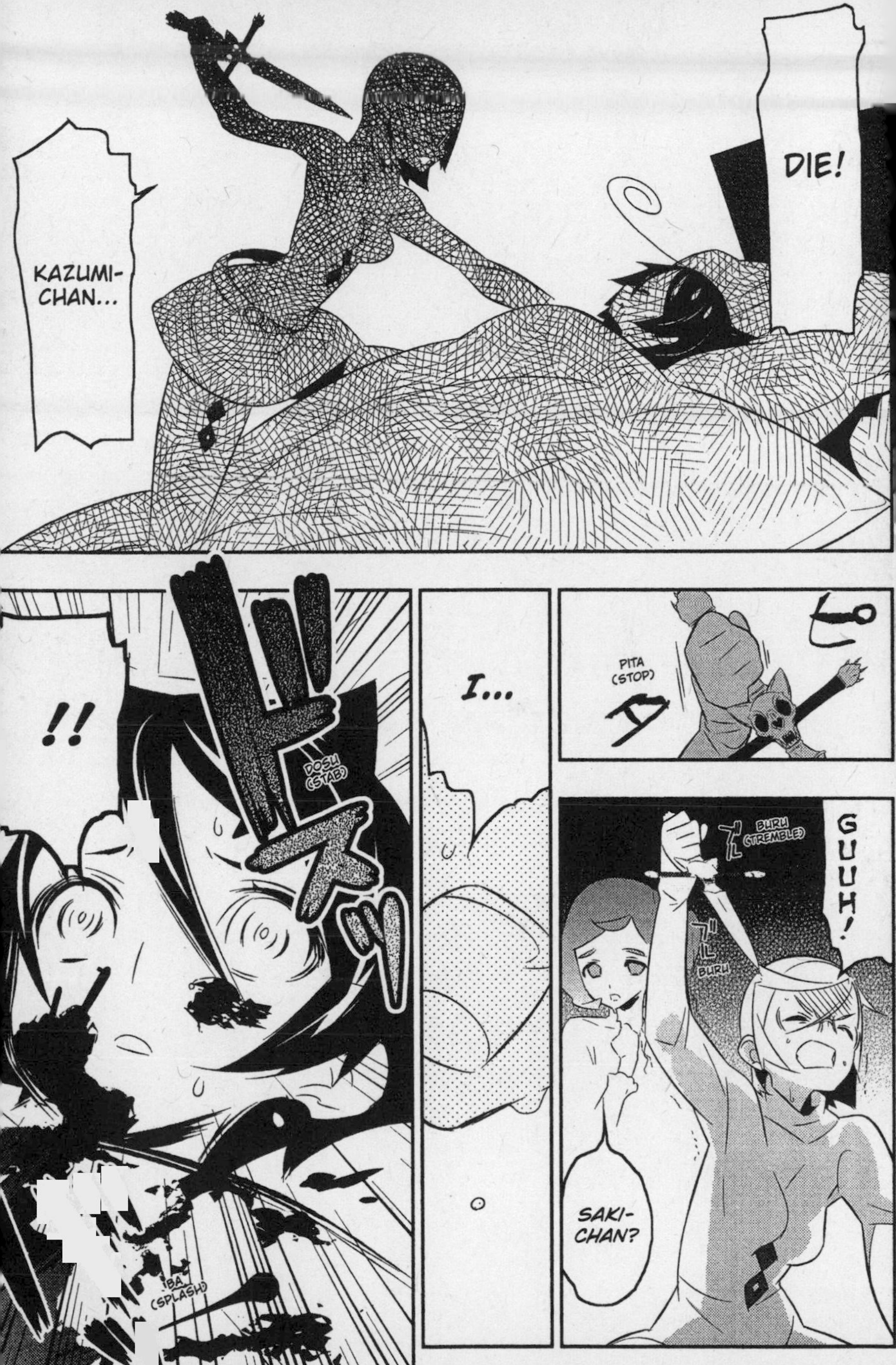
DIE!
KAZUMI-CHAN...
PITA (STOP)
GUUH!
BURU (TREMBLE)
BURU
SAKI-CHAN?
I...
!!
DOSU (STAB)
BA (SPLASH)

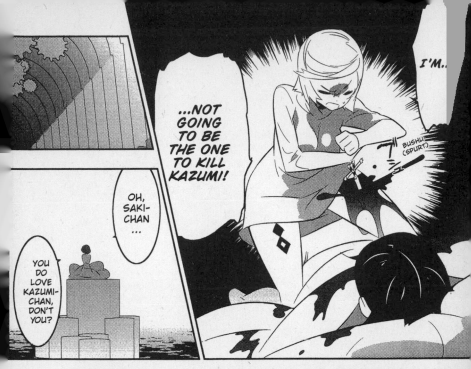

...NOT GOING TO BE THE ONE TO KILL KAZUMI!

I'M..

BUSHU (SPURT)

OH, SAKI-CHAN...

YOU DO LOVE KAZUMI-CHAN, DON'T YOU?

GAAAAH!!

!?

SO YOU GIVE ME NO CHOICE.

BRING HER HERE, SAKI-CHAN.

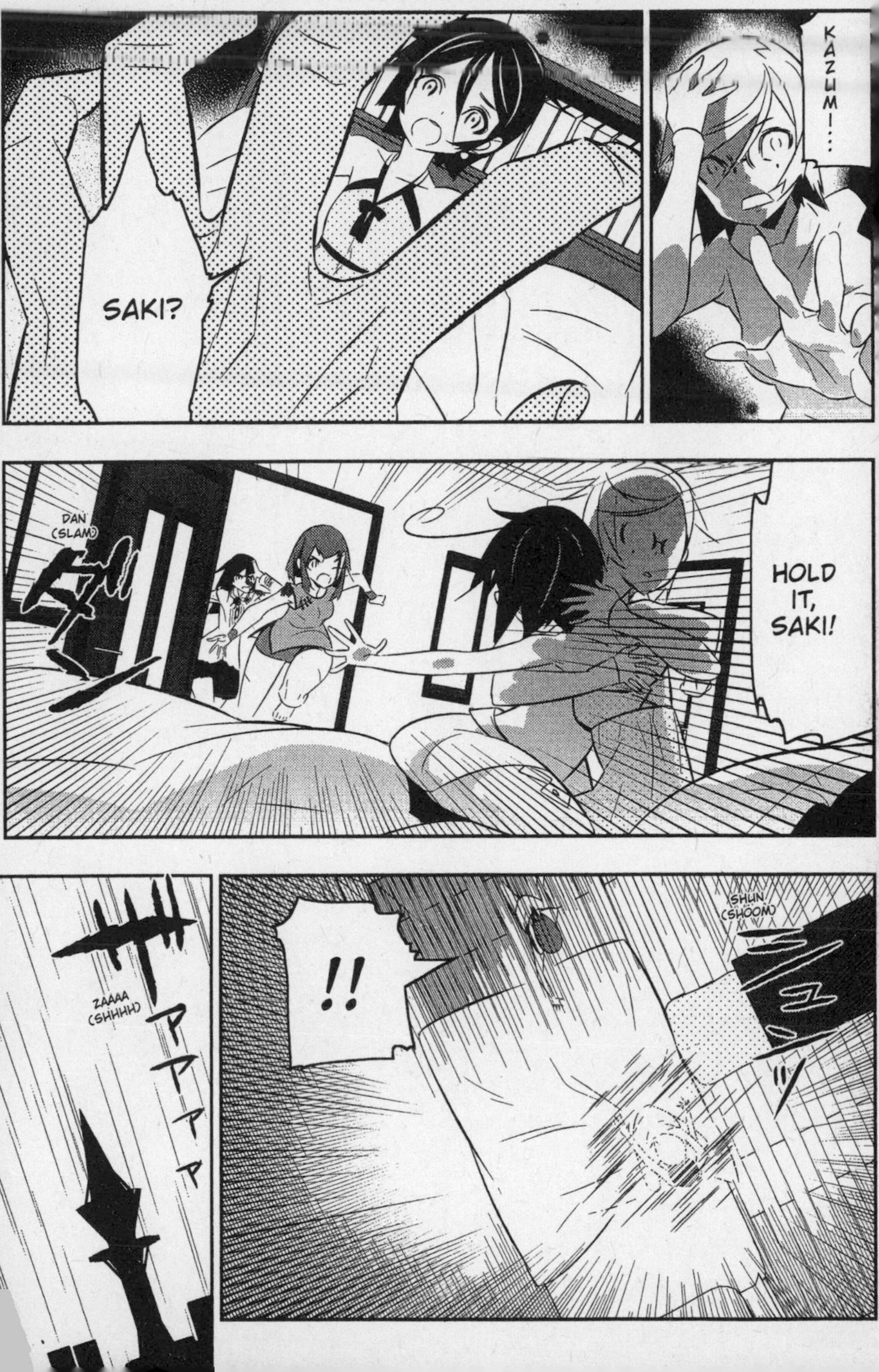
KAZUMI...
SAKI?
HOLD IT, SAKI!
DAN (SLAM)
SHUN (SHOOM)
!!
ZAAAA (SHHHH)

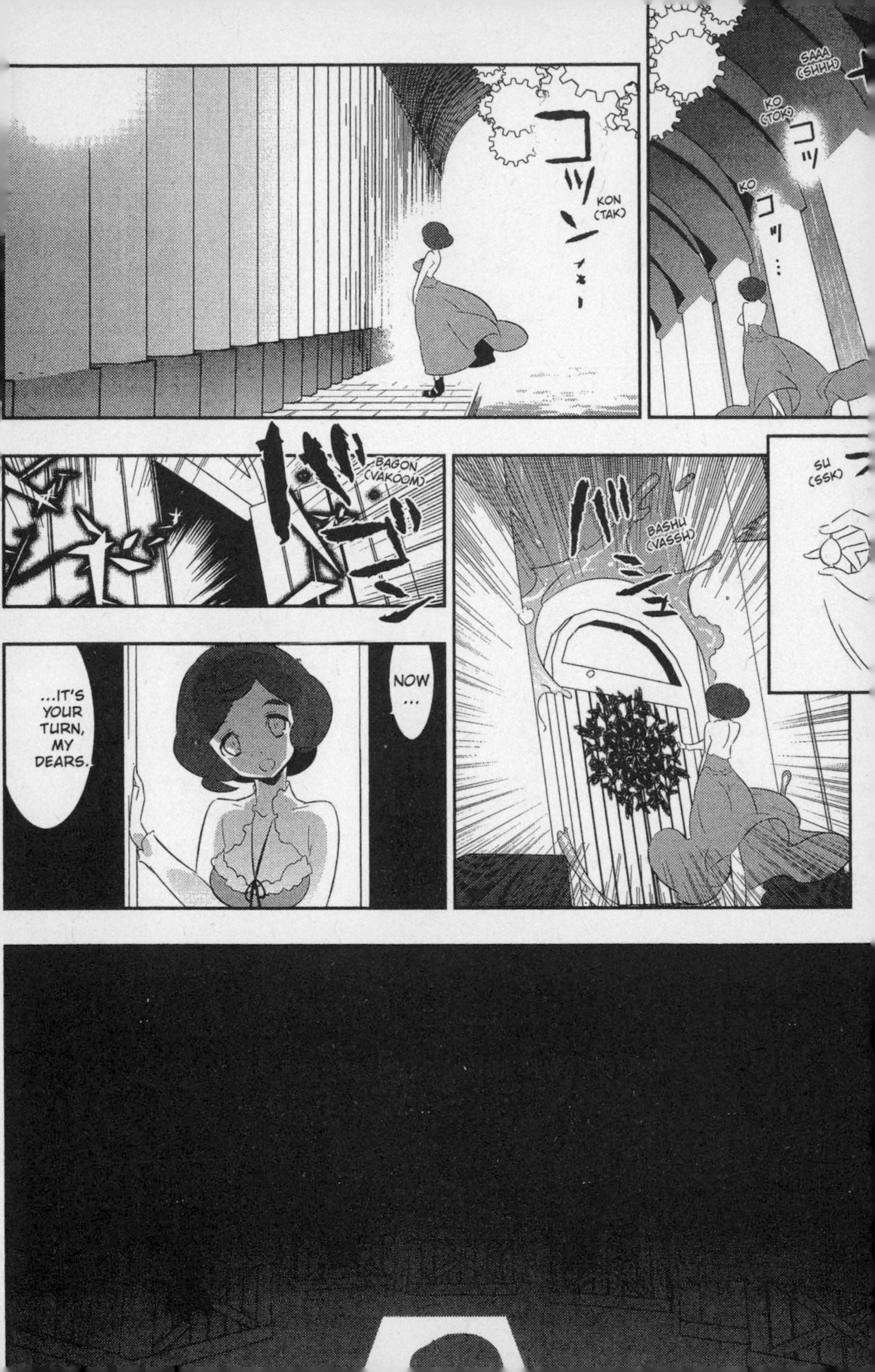
SAAA (SHHH)
KO (TOK)
KO
KON (TAK)
SU (SSK)
BASHU (VASSH)
BAGON (VAKOOM)
NOW...
...IT'S YOUR TURN, MY DEARS.

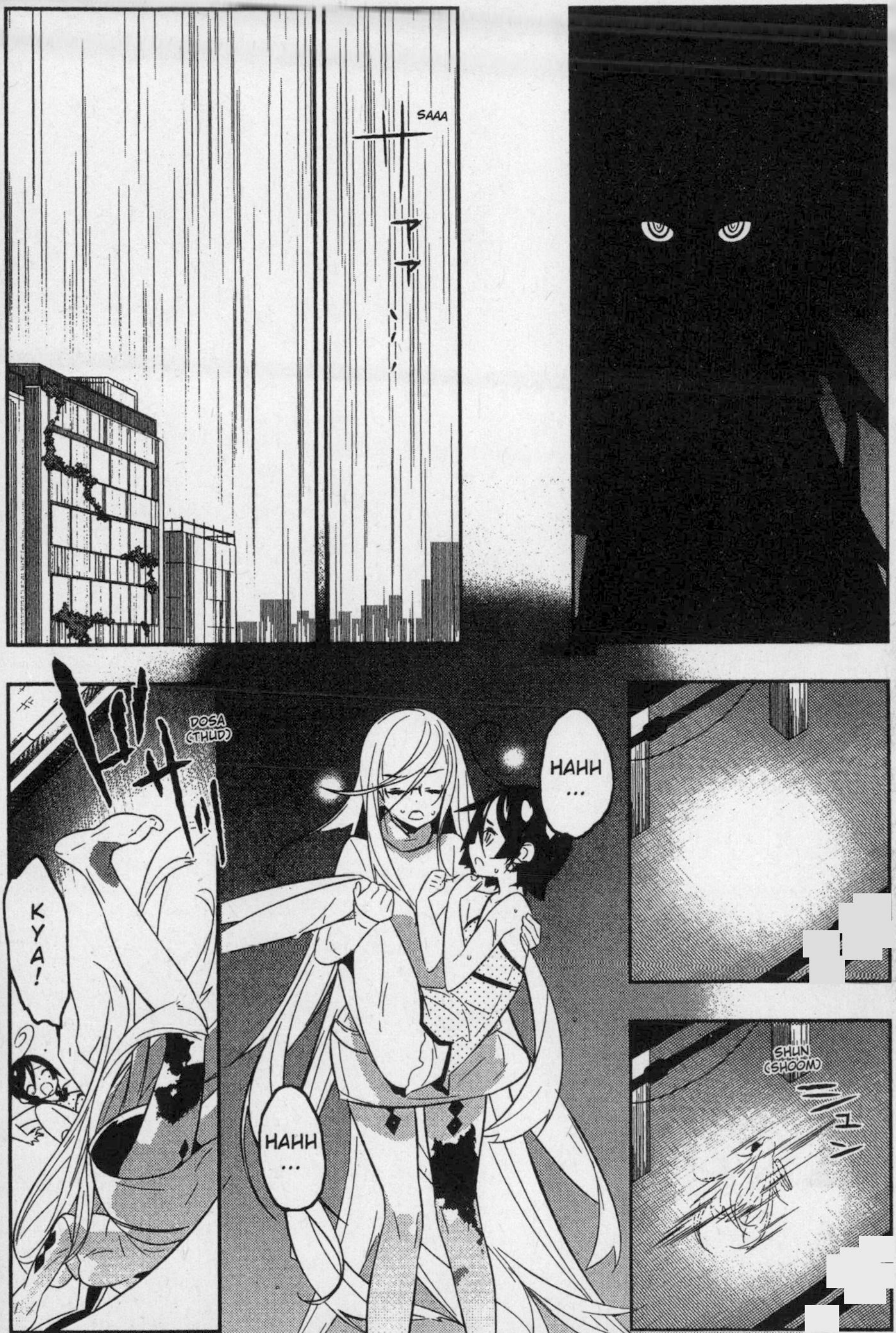
SAAA
SHUN (SHOOM)
HAHH ...
HAHH ...
DOSA (THUD)
KYA!

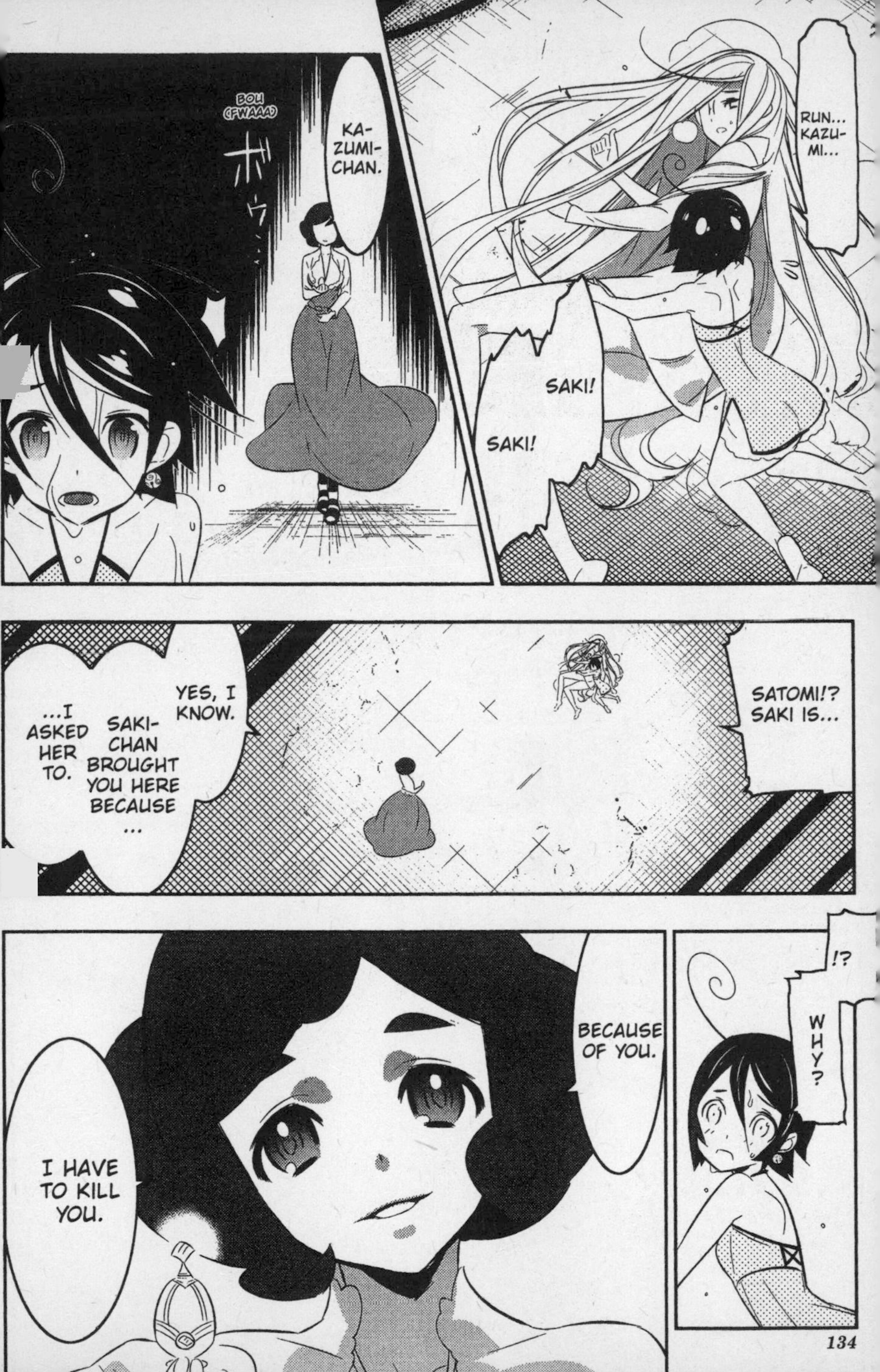
RUN... KAZUMI...
SAKI!
SAKI!
KAZUMI-CHAN.
BOU (FWAAA)
SATOMI!? SAKI IS...
YES, I KNOW.
SAKI-CHAN BROUGHT YOU HERE BECAUSE ...
...I ASKED HER TO.
!?
WHY?
BECAUSE OF YOU.
I HAVE TO KILL YOU.

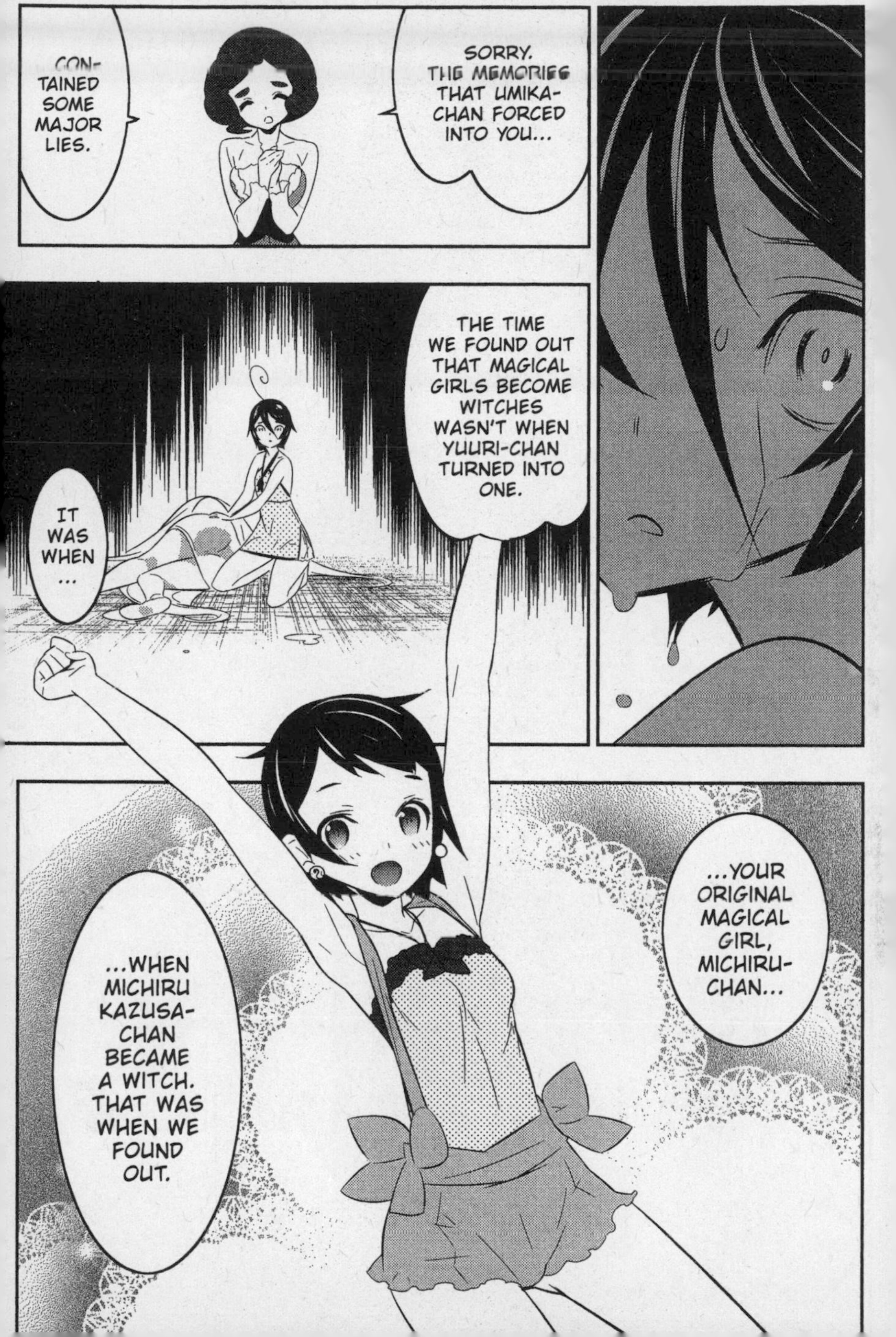
SORRY. THE MEMORIES THAT UMIKA-CHAN FORCED INTO YOU...
CON-TAINED SOME MAJOR LIES.
THE TIME WE FOUND OUT THAT MAGICAL GIRLS BECOME WITCHES WASN'T WHEN YUURI-CHAN TURNED INTO ONE.
IT WAS WHEN...
...YOUR ORIGINAL MAGICAL GIRL, MICHIRU-CHAN...
...WHEN MICHIRU KAZUSA-CHAN BECAME A WITCH. THAT WAS WHEN WE FOUND OUT.

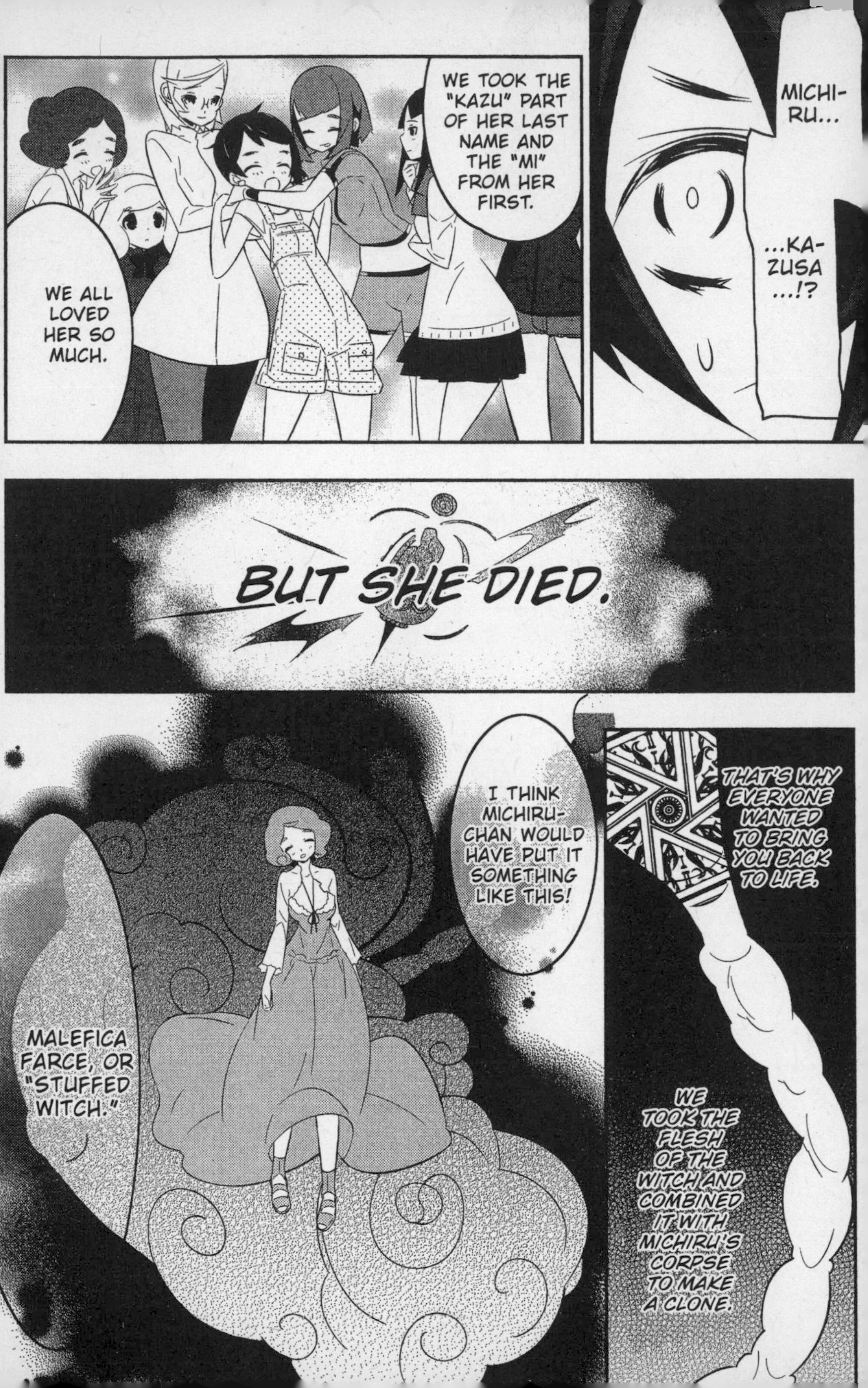
MICHI-RU...
...KA-ZUSA...!?
WE TOOK THE "KAZU" PART OF HER LAST NAME AND THE "MI" FROM HER FIRST.
WE ALL LOVED HER SO MUCH.
BUT SHE DIED.
THAT'S WHY EVERYONE WANTED TO BRING YOU BACK TO LIFE.
I THINK MICHIRU-CHAN WOULD HAVE PUT IT SOMETHING LIKE THIS!
WE TOOK THE FLESH OF THE WITCH AND COMBINED IT WITH MICHIRU'S CORPSE TO MAKE A CLONE.
MALEFICA FARCE, OR "STUFFED WITCH."

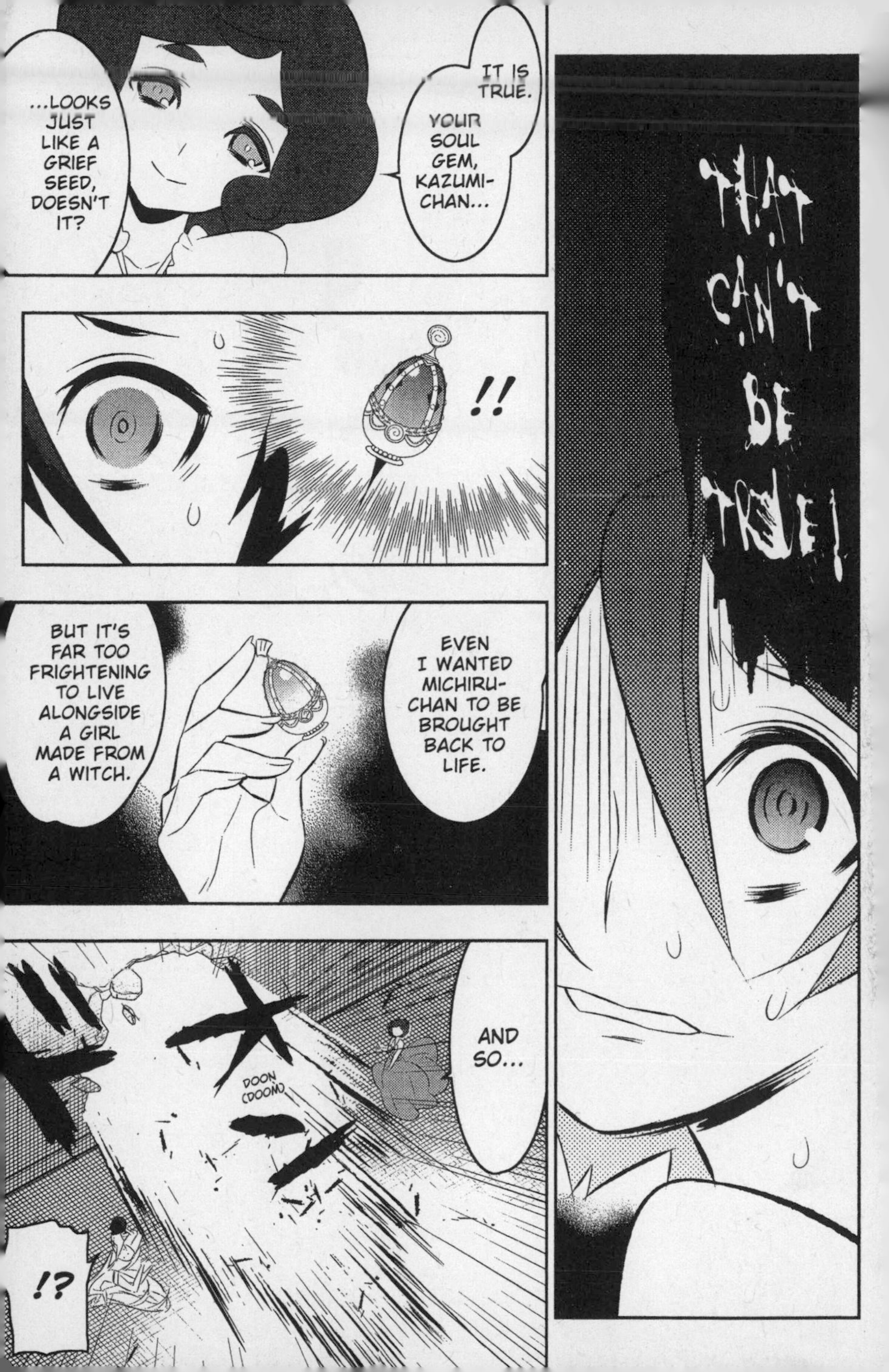
THAT CAN'T BE TRUE!
IT IS TRUE.
YOUR SOUL GEM, KAZUMI-CHAN...
...LOOKS JUST LIKE A GRIEF SEED, DOESN'T IT?
!!
EVEN I WANTED MICHIRU-CHAN TO BE BROUGHT BACK TO LIFE.
BUT IT'S FAR TOO FRIGHTENING TO LIVE ALONGSIDE A GIRL MADE FROM A WITCH.
AND SO...
DOON (DOOM)
!?

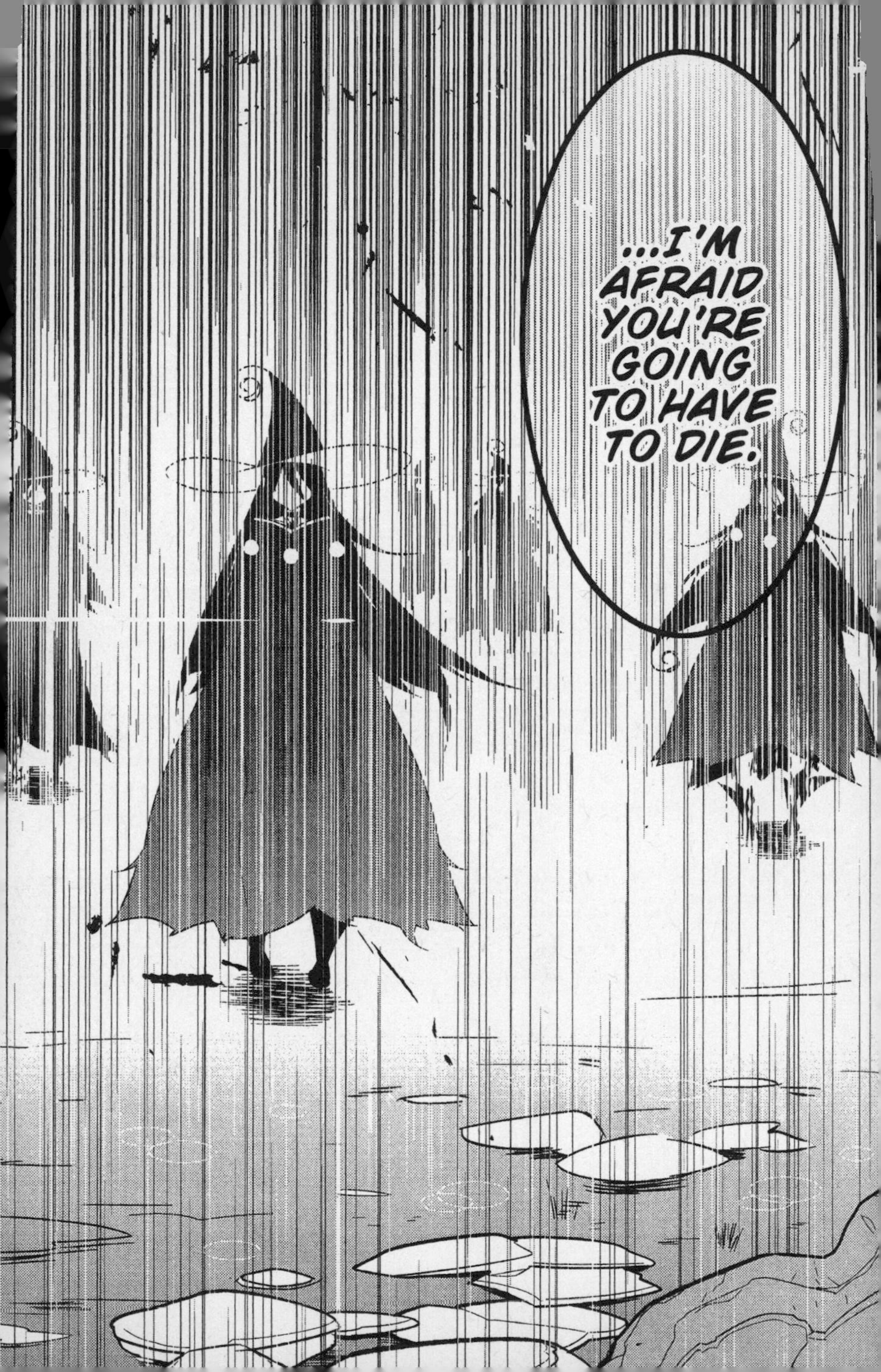
...I'M AFRAID YOU'RE GOING TO HAVE TO DIE.

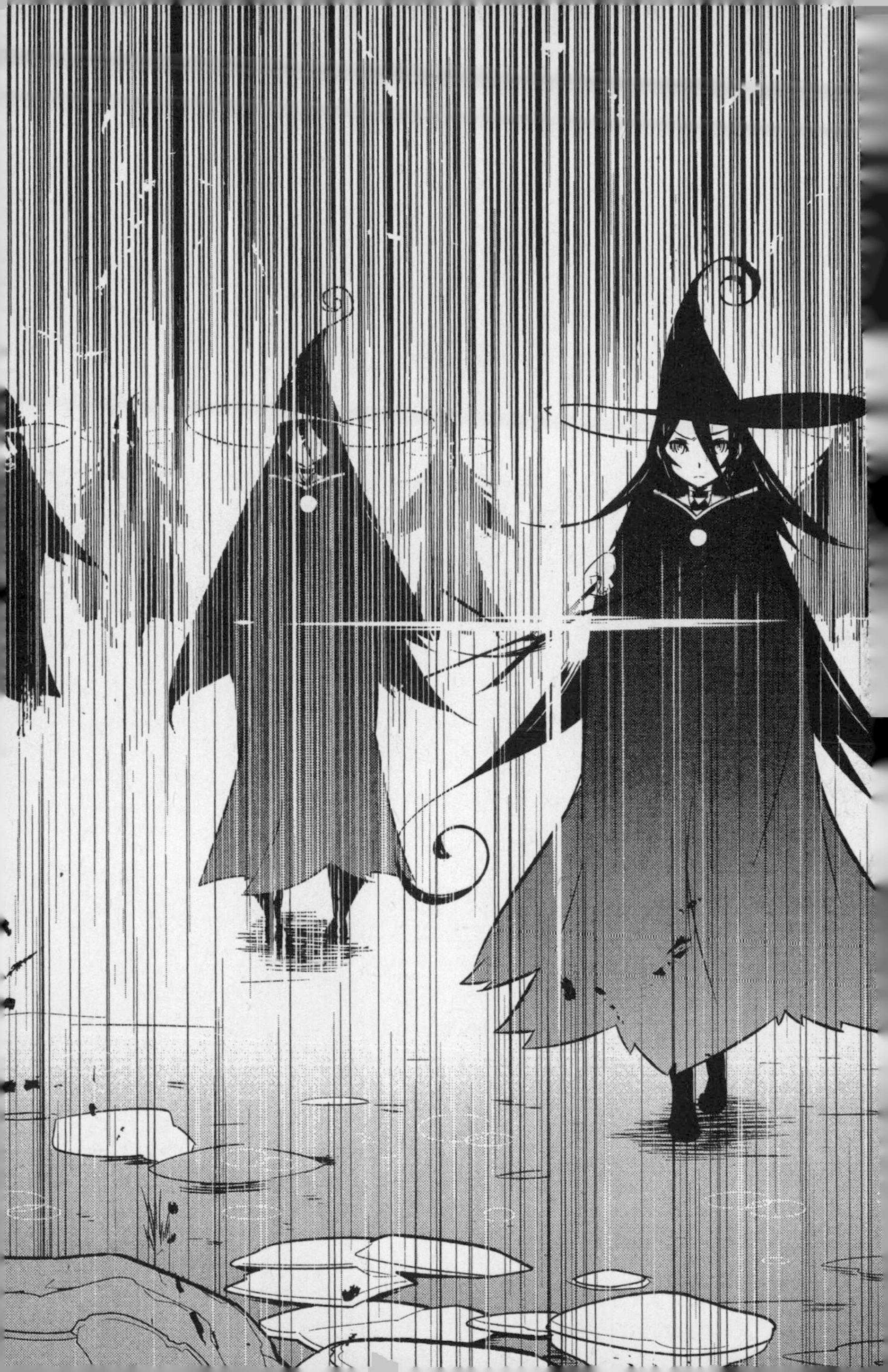

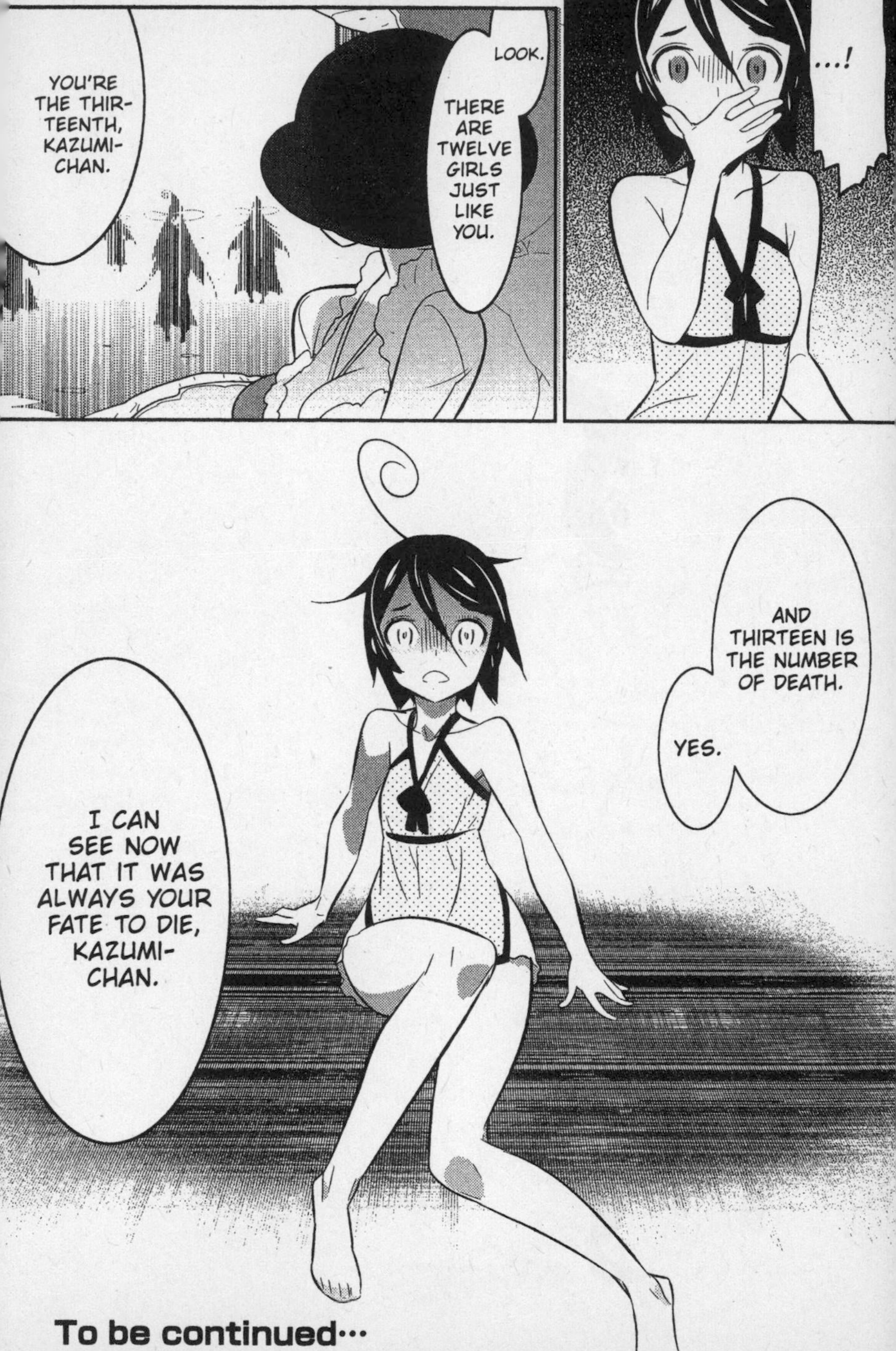
...!
LOOK.
THERE ARE TWELVE GIRLS JUST LIKE YOU.
YOU'RE THE THIRTEENTH, KAZUMI-CHAN.
AND THIRTEEN IS THE NUMBER OF DEATH.
YES.
I CAN SEE NOW THAT IT WAS ALWAYS YOUR FATE TO DIE, KAZUMI-CHAN.
To be continued…

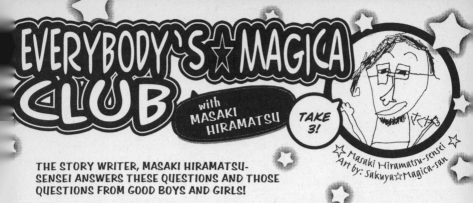

EVERYBODY'S ☆ MAGICA CLUB

with MASAKI HIRAMATSU

TAKE 3!

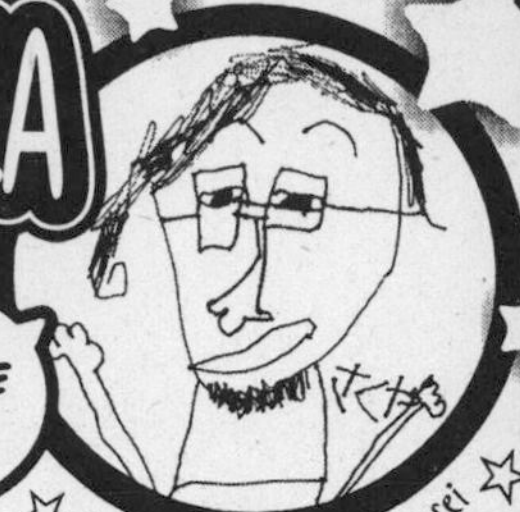

☆ Masaki Hiramatsu-sensei ☆
Art by: Sakuya☆Magica-san

THE STORY WRITER, MASAKI HIRAMATSU-SENSEI ANSWERS THESE QUESTIONS AND THOSE QUESTIONS FROM GOOD BOYS AND GIRLS!

Q1 *CIAO, HIRAMACCI! I DREW YOU YOUR FACE! COME OVER TO PLAY AGAIN, OKAY?*
(SAKUYA☆MAGICA-SAN)

HIRAMACCHI: CIAO! YO, NEPHEW, THANKS! YOU DID A GOOD JOB DRAWING IT, HUH? LET'S TELL STORIES ABOUT DRAGONS AGAIN WITH DAI AND KOUKI! AND LET'S PLAY *RIDER* AGAIN!

Q2 *CIAO, HIRAMACCHI! SO WHEN'S FEMINA MAGI PASSIONATE WOMAN MISAKO GONNA SHOW UP?*
(HIBIYA☆MAGICA-SAN)

HIRAMACCHI: CIAO, HIBIYA-SAN! THANK YOU FOR SENDING IN THIS COLUMN'S VERY FIRST ACTUAL LETTER! I WAS SO MOVED, MY TEARS CAME PLOPPING DOWN! AND SINCE WE HAVE THE GIRL RIGHT HERE WITH US, HOW ABOUT I ASK HER DIRECTLY!? MISAKO, WILL YOU CONTRACT WITH ME AND BECOME A FEMINA MAGI PASSIONATE WOMAN?

MISAKO: YOU ARE UNDER ARREST ON THE CHARGE OF SEXUAL HARASSMENT OF A PUBLIC OFFICIAL.

HIRAMACCHI: WHY!? 'COS I HAD A HEAVY NOSEBLEED WHEN I SAW YOUR QUITE-FRANKLY-EROTIC COSTUME? WELL, THE ONE WHO CALLED YOU "PASSIONATE" WAS THE EDITOR, N-SAN! I WAS AGAINST IT! I CAME OUT AND SAID THAT SINCE YOU'RE TWENTY-NINE YEARS OLD, HOW ABOUT WE SAY, 'HIGH-BORN LADY,' INSTEAD? YOU GOTTA BELIEVE ME, OFFICER!

MISAKO: WELL BEFORE THE 'PASSIONATE WOMAN' FIASCO, YOU WERE GUILTY OF THE CRIME OF LEWD STARES IN MY DIRECTION!

HIRAMACCHI: I ADMIT IT! YOU GOT ME! AND YOU CAN GO LOCK ME UP IN THE PRISON CALLED LOVE! MISAKO, MARRY ME! MARRY ME TOMORROW!

MISAKO: YOU'RE A NUISANCE! (⇒SMACK⇐⇒CRACK⇐)

HIRAMACCHI: OOAWW! AND THERE YOU GO TURNING INTO A FAKE WITCH!! BUT DON'T WORRRY, HIBIYA-SAN! IF THE WORLD TRULY WISHES FOR IT, SHE'LL TURN BACK INTO A MAGICAL PASSIONATE WOMAN! DOROMISURE EGAMIYO!

Q3 *CIAO, HIRAMACCHI! SO WHO IS THE LEADER OF THE PLEIADES CONSTELLATION?*
(SARE☆MAGICA-SAN)

HIRAMACCHI: CIAO, THE PLEIADES ARE KINDA "KNIGHTS OF THE ROUND TABLE"-LIKE, SO THERE IS NO OFFICIAL LEADER. EVERYONE CONTRIBUTES THEIR THOUGHTS AND EVERYONE FIGHTS. THAT IS THE WILL OF THE GIRLS...OR IT WAS, ANYWAY.

Q4 *CIAO, HIRAMACCHI! WHO IS STRONGER, MADOKA OR KAZUMI?*
(MIYAJI☆MAGICA-SAN)

HIRAMACCHI: CIAO, MIYAJI-SAN! ESTIMATING COMPARATIVE STRENGTHS? THAT'S A KIND OF VIOLENT QUESTION, ISN'T IT? BUT I'LL ANSWER IT ANYWAY! A FIGHT BETWEEN MADOKA AND KAZUMI! THAT WOULD HAVE TO BE THE BEST MAGICAL GIRL FIGHT IN ALL THE WORLD! HOWEVER, BARRING ALIENS CONTROLLING THEIR EVERY MOVEMENT, THE TWO OF THEM WOULD NEVER COME TO BLOWS. AFTER ALL, BOTH OF THEIR HEARTS FEEL PURE HOPE, SO THEY'D COME TO AN UNDERSTANDING BETWEEN THEMSELVES. THE TWO OF THEM WOULD COMBINE FORCES AND FIGHT FOR PEACE IN THE GALAXY FOR THE REST OF THEIR LIVES!

SO EVERYONE, KEEP ON ROOTING FOR KAZUMI IN THE NEXT VOLUME TOO! YOU JUST GOTTA READ IT!

WE FINALLY GOT SOME ACTUAL QUESTIONS SENT IN BY MAIL TO THIS COLUMN! WILL THE NEXT TIME BE THE ULTIMATE CLIMAX? IF YOUR QUESTION IS SELECTED FOR THE COLUMN, YOU'LL GET A SPECIAL PRESENT OF A SIGNED COPY OF THE BOOK THAT HIRAMACCHI SPECIALLY SKIPPED LUNCH AND WENT HUNGRY TO BUY! MANGA OR RICE? SO COME AND JOIN THE EVERYBODY'S ☆ MAGICA CLUB!

Afterword★Magica

The third volume is already here! Not only that, but it's continuing on after this too. I want to thank the originators, Magica Quartet-sama, the writer Hiramatsu-san, N-san, the editor, and all of you readers! I know it's what everybody says, but those are the only words that express my true gratitude! okay! Since I have this space, I thought I'd tell you about a feeling I'm feeling right now. "How am I going to express the excitement I feel when reading the scenario for this manga directly to the readers?" As we're putting together this collected edition from the magazine installments, I'm reminded of the emotions I felt when reading the scenario for each chapter. And I get to thinking, "I should have made this scene about ten times more exciting!" I think, "I should have done more of this or more of that!" All the time, I had this feeling that I didn't do it as well as I'd like. I want that excitement for you!

I WANT TO THANK YOU SO MUCH FOR READING!

Let's meet again in the next KAZUMI★MAGICA!

TAKASHI TENSUGI

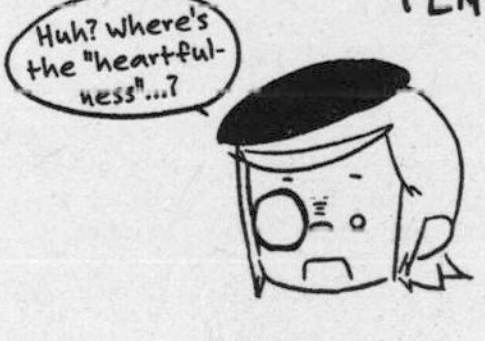
Huh? Where's the "heartfulness"...?

Poor Saki...

PUELLA MAGI
KAZUMI★MAGICA
The innocent malice

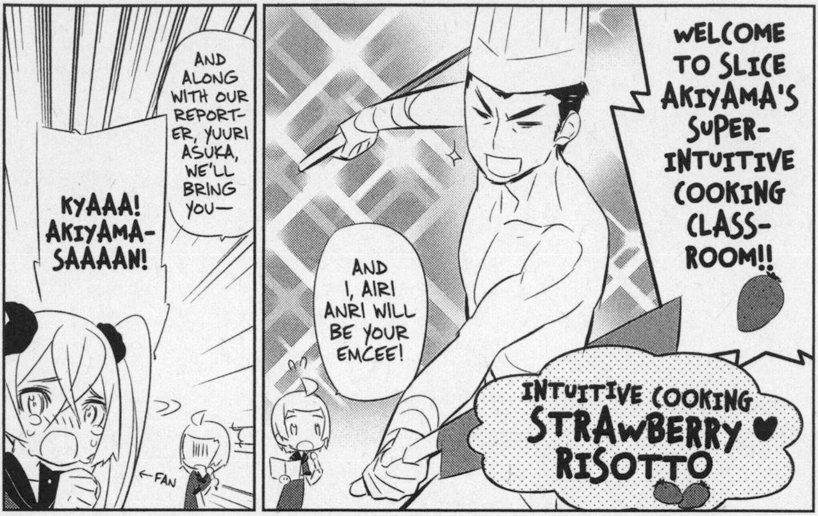

WELCOME TO SLICE AKIYAMA'S SUPER-INTUITIVE COOKING CLASSROOM!!
AND I, AIRI ANRI WILL BE YOUR EMCEE!
INTUITIVE COOKING STRAWBERRY ♥ RISOTTO
AND ALONG WITH OUR REPORTER, YUURI ASUKA, WE'LL BRING YOU—
KYAAA! AKIYAMA-SAAAAN!
←FAN

FOR ANYONE WHO DOESN'T KNOW THESE CHARACTERS, CHECK OUT VOLUMES 1 & 2 RIGHT NOW!

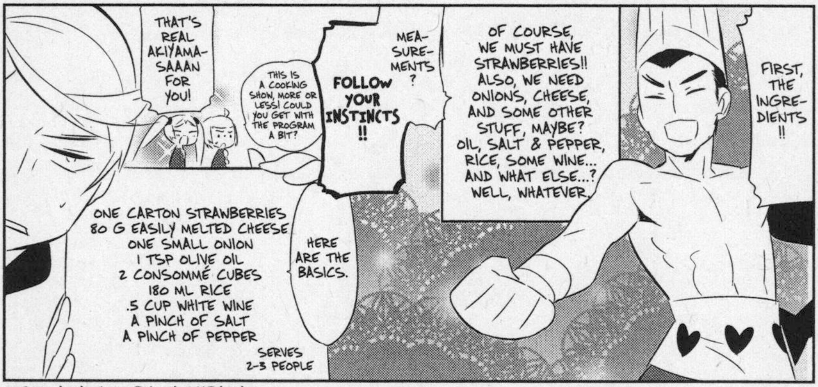

FIRST, THE INGREDIENTS!!
OF COURSE, WE MUST HAVE STRAWBERRIES!! ALSO, WE NEED ONIONS, CHEESE, AND SOME OTHER STUFF, MAYBE? OIL, SALT & PEPPER, RICE, SOME WINE... AND WHAT ELSE...? WELL, WHATEVER.
MEASUREMENTS?
FOLLOW YOUR INSTINCTS!!
THIS IS A COOKING SHOW, MORE OR LESS! COULD YOU GET WITH THE PROGRAM A BIT?
THAT'S REAL AKIYAMA-SAAAN FOR YOU!
HERE ARE THE BASICS.
ONE CARTON STRAWBERRIES
80 G EASILY MELTED CHEESE
ONE SMALL ONION
1 TSP OLIVE OIL
2 CONSOMMÉ CUBES
180 ML RICE
.5 CUP WHITE WINE
A PINCH OF SALT
A PINCH OF PEPPER
SERVES 2-3 PEOPLE

EXPLANATION BY TACHIBANA

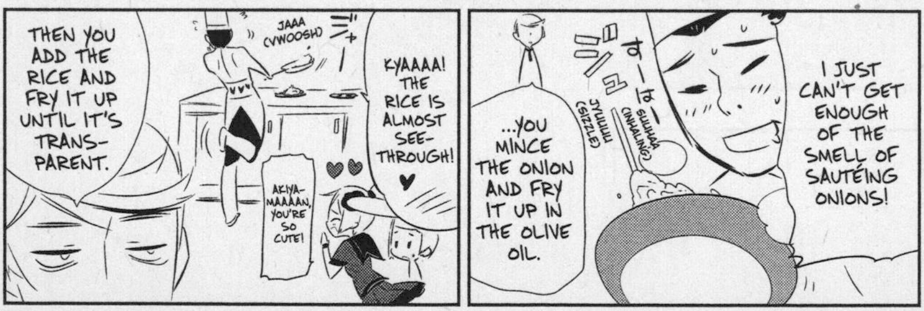

I JUST CAN'T GET ENOUGH OF THE SMELL OF SAUTÉING ONIONS!
SUHAA (INHALING)
JYUUUU (SIZZLE)
...YOU MINCE THE ONION AND FRY IT UP IN THE OLIVE OIL.
THEN YOU ADD THE RICE AND FRY IT UP UNTIL IT'S TRANSPARENT.
JAAA (VWOOSH)
KYAAAA! THE RICE IS ALMOST SEE-THROUGH! ♥
AKIYAMAAAAN, YOU'RE SO CUTE!

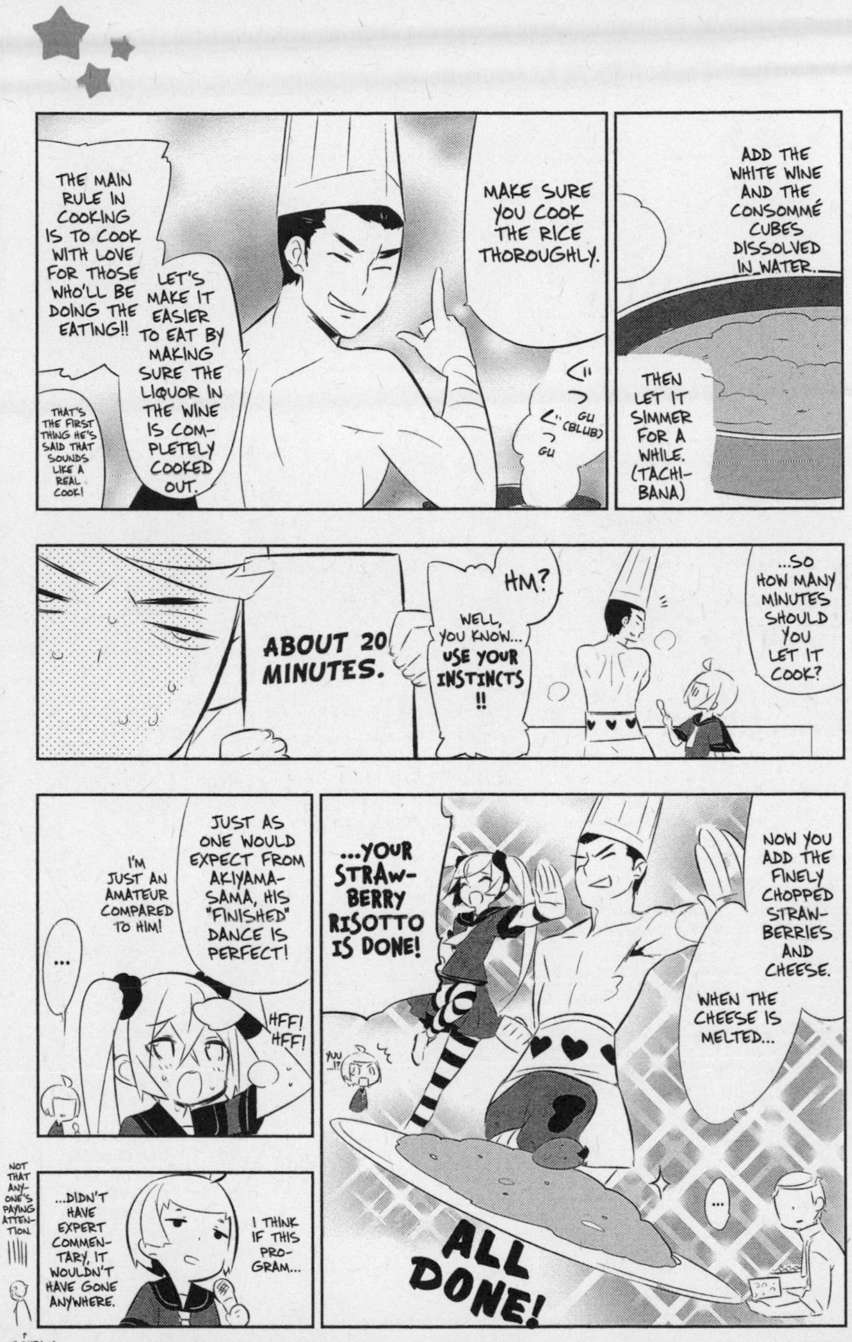
ADD THE WHITE WINE AND THE CONSOMMÉ CUBES DISSOLVED IN WATER.
THEN LET IT SIMMER FOR A WHILE. (TACHIBANA)
MAKE SURE YOU COOK THE RICE THOROUGHLY.
GU GU (BLUB)
THE MAIN RULE IN COOKING IS TO COOK WITH LOVE FOR THOSE WHO'LL BE DOING THE EATING!!
LET'S MAKE IT EASIER TO EAT BY MAKING SURE THE LIQUOR IN THE WINE IS COMPLETELY COOKED OUT.
THAT'S THE FIRST THING HE'S SAID THAT SOUNDS LIKE A REAL COOK!
...SO HOW MANY MINUTES SHOULD YOU LET IT COOK?
HM?
WELL, YOU KNOW... USE YOUR INSTINCTS!!
ABOUT 20 MINUTES.
NOW YOU ADD THE FINELY CHOPPED STRAWBERRIES AND CHEESE.
WHEN THE CHEESE IS MELTED...
...YOUR STRAWBERRY RISOTTO IS DONE!
YUU...!?
ALL DONE!
...
JUST AS ONE WOULD EXPECT FROM AKIYAMA-SAMA, HIS "FINISHED" DANCE IS PERFECT!
I'M JUST AN AMATEUR COMPARED TO HIM!
HFF! HFF!
...
I THINK IF THIS PROGRAM...
...DIDN'T HAVE EXPERT COMMENTARY, IT WOULDN'T HAVE GONE ANYWHERE.
NOT THAT ANYONE'S PAYING ATTENTION.
TACHIBANA

PUELLA MAGI
KAZUMI☆MAGICA
~The innocent malice~ ❸

MAGICA QUARTET
MASAKI HIRAMATSU
TAKASHI TENSUGI

Translation: William Flanagan • Lettering: Carl Vanstiphout

MAHO SHOJO KAZUMI ☆ MAGICA ~The innocent malice~ vol. 3
© Magica Quartet / Aniplex, Madoka Partners, MBS. All rights reserved. First published in Japan in 2012 by HOUBUNSHA CO., LTD, Tokyo. English translation rights in United States, Canada, and United Kingdom arranged with HOUBUNSHA CO., LTD. through Tuttle-Mori Agency, Inc., Tokyo.

Translation © 2013 by Hachette Book Group, Inc.

Yen Press
Hachette Book Group
237 Park Avenue, New York, NY 10017

www.HachetteBookGroup.com
www.YenPress.com

Yen Press is an imprint of Hachette Book Group, Inc. The Yen Press name and logo are trademarks of Hachette Book Group, Inc.

First Yen Press Edition: November 2013

ISBN: 978-0-316-25426-7

10 9 8 7 6 5 4 3 2 1

BVG

Printed in the United States of America